TOPOLOGIES OF POWER

Topologies of Power amounts to a radical departure in the way that power and space have been understood. It calls into question the very idea that power is simply extended across a given territory or network, and argues that power today has a new-found 'reach'. Topological shifts have subtly altered the reach of power, enabling governments, corporations and NGOs alike to register their presence through quieter, less brash forms of power than domination or overt control. In a world in which proximity and distance increasingly play across one another, topology offers an insight into how power remains continuous under transformation: the same but different in its ability to shape people's lives.

Drawing upon a range of political, economic and cultural illustrations, the book sets out a clear and accessible account of the topological workings of power in the contemporary moment. It will be invaluable for both students and academics in human geography, politics, sociology and cultural studies.

John Allen is Professor of Economic Geography in the Faculty of Arts and Social Sciences at The Open University. His publications include *Lost Geographies of Power* (2003), in addition to twelve books, both authored and edited.

CRESC
Culture, Economy and the Social
A new series from CRESC – the ESRC Centre for Research on Socio-cultural Change

The Culture, Economy and the Social series is committed to innovative contemporary, comparative and historical work on the relations between social, cultural and economic change. It publishes empirically-based research that is theoretically informed, that critically examines the ways in which social, cultural and economic change is framed and made visible, and that is attentive to perspectives that tend to be ignored or side-lined by grand theorising or epochal accounts of social change. The series addresses the diverse manifestations of contemporary capitalism, and considers the various ways in which the 'social', 'the cultural' and 'the economic' are apprehended as tangible sites of value and practice. It is explicitly comparative, publishing books that work across disciplinary perspectives, cross-culturally, or across different historical periods.

The series is actively engaged in the analysis of the different theoretical traditions that have contributed to the development of the 'cultural turn' with a view to clarifying where these approaches converge and where they diverge on a particular issue. It is equally concerned to explore the new critical agendas emerging from current critiques of the cultural turn: those associated with the descriptive turn for example. Our commitment to interdisciplinarity thus aims at enriching theoretical and methodological discussion, building awareness of the common ground that has emerged in the past decade, and thinking through what is at stake in those approaches that resist integration to a common analytical model.

Series titles include:

The Media and Social Theory
Edited by David Hesmondhalgh and
Jason Toynbee

Culture, Class, Distinction
Tony Bennett, Mike Savage,
Elizabeth Bortolaia Silva, Alan Warde,
Modesto Gayo-Cal and David Wright

Material Powers
Edited by Tony Bennett and Patrick Joyce

The Social after Gabriel Tarde
Debates and assessments
Edited by Matei Candea

Cultural Analysis and
Bourdieu's Legacy
Edited by Elizabeth Silva and Alan Ward

Milk, Modernity and the Making
of the Human
Richie Nimmo

Creative Labour
Media work in three cultural industries
Edited by David Hesmondhalgh and
Sarah Baker

Migrating Music
Edited by Jason Toynbee and
Byron Dueck

Sport and the Transformation of
Modern Europe
States, media and markets 1950–2010
Edited by Alan Tomlinson,
Christopher Young and Richard Holt

Inventive Methods
The happening of the social
Edited by Celia Lury and Nina Wakeford

Understanding Sport
A socio-cultural analysis
By John Horne, Alan Tomlinson,
Garry Whannel and Kath Woodward

Shanghai Expo
An international forum on the future
of cities
Edited by Tim Winter

Diasporas and Diplomacy
Cosmopolitan contact zones at the
BBC World Service (1932–2012)
Edited by Marie Gillespie and
Alban Webb

Making Culture, Changing Society
Tony Bennett

Interdisciplinarity
Reconfigurations of the social and
natural sciences
Edited by Andrew Barry and
Georgina Born

TOPOLOGIES OF POWER

Beyond territory and networks

John Allen

Routledge
Taylor & Francis Group
LONDON AND NEW YORK

Centre for Research on
Socio-Cultural Change

E·S·R·C
ECONOMIC
& SOCIAL
RESEARCH
COUNCIL

First published 2016
by Routledge
2 Park Square, Milton Park, Abingdon, Oxon OX14 4RN

and by Routledge
711 Third Avenue, New York, NY 10017

Routledge is an imprint of the Taylor & Francis Group, an informa business

British Library Cataloguing in Publication Data
A catalogue record for this book is available from the British Library

Library of Congress Cataloging in Publication Data
Allen, John, 1951- author.
  Topologies of power / by John Allen.
    pages cm
  1. Human geography. 2. Power (Social sciences) 3. Political geography. I. Title.
    GF50.A4533 2016
    304.2–dc23
                    2015030588

ISBN: 978-0-415-52133-8 (hbk)
ISBN: 978-0-415-52134-5 (pbk)
ISBN: 978-0-203-10192-6 (ebk)

Typeset in Bembo
by Taylor & Francis Books
Printed by Ashford Colour Press Ltd, Gosport, Hants

CONTENTS

FIGURES

ACKNOWLEDGEMENT

I have been trying to make up my mind about topology and its exploratory promise for some time now, and have been nudged and provoked in equal measure by helpful colleagues in that respect, among them Allan Cochrane, Mathew Coleman, Nick Bingham, Liza Griffin, Steve Hinchliffe, Engin Isin, Michael Pryke, Steve Pile, Jenny Robinson, Ola Soderstrom and Linn Axellson. I have benefitted enormously from conversations with them and, in a number of instances, from their direct comments on draft chapters, for which I am truly grateful. Kevin Hetherington read and commented on the whole text and improved it considerably.

Chapter titles, book titles even, sometimes just jump out at you, and the 'changing same of power' did just that. I owe the reference not to mathematical topology, but to the writings of Paul Gilroy, who in turn drew upon Leroi Jones, the Black Arts Movement writer who first coined the 'changing same' in the 1960s to capture the continuity that persists in changing cultural forms. Needless to say, I have twisted it for my own ends.

On a more practical note, I am indebted to Jan Smith and Radha Ray at The Open University for their help in preparing the text for publication, especially to Jan, who I have worked with for the best part of two decades and owe far more than she is aware. Thanks are also due to Gerhard Boomgaarden, Emily Briggs and Alyson Claffey at Routledge for their encouragement and support.

Finally, I owe it to my two grown-up sons, Jack and Adam, for the pleasure of just being themselves and, as always, keeping me in touch with what matters.

John Allen

1

INTRODUCTION

The changing same of power

There are many different ways in which people experience a brush with power. Of late, though, the defined times and distances that mark such encounters have loosened somewhat. The routine ability of governments to reach directly into our lives, the striking capacity of financial corporations to make their presence felt across the globe, and the ease with which non-governmental organizations (NGOs) fold in distant harms to provoke our compassion and pity, all speak to a world in which physical distance is no longer a good indication of either separation or proximity. Such actions speak to contexts in which proximity and distance play across one another, where the spatial habits of a lifetime can easily be drawn into question. On a number of fronts, what we appear to be witnessing is not just another redefining of territory, of scale or of networks, but a willingness to think about spatial and temporal change in an altogether different way: most notably, through the lens of topology.

While the use of topological terms has often been selective, frequently eclectic, something nonetheless is happening to the way that we think about space and time – as stretched or folded, compressed even – that seems to chime with how the world is progressively experienced. Often, however, the use of such familiar words in unfamiliar contexts – the 'stretching' of political borders inside out or the 'folding' of the global into the local – has served to confuse rather than enlighten. That confusion, whilst real, nonetheless masks a fallible attempt to capture something new, or rather spatial shifts less well understood, within a makeshift, often borrowed vocabulary. To my mind, a topological sensibility prompts us to think again about such shifts, together with notions of scale and territory, networks and connections, but above all about power and its habitual geometry, in ways that make a difference.

Topology is not a new way of thinking about social matters, nor has the world turned topological overnight, but shifts in the mix of times and spaces embedded in the here and now of much social interaction have subtly altered many of the ways in which contemporary power works. The measured times and distances of the modern era no longer quite capture the felt experience of being on the receiving end of a so-called 'distant' corporate or financial power, or the intensive reach that states can have over the lives of migrants far removed from territorial borders. As I see it, quieter registers of power have come to the fore, often holding together formations that can be used to influence and shape the will of others without the 'brash' constraining edges of power. As power is commonly associated with constraint and control, the impersonal touch of authority, it can take us by surprise when it is exercised in more subtle, less overt ways. Manipulation that conceals intent, inducements too great not to want, enticement and seduction even, are among the quieter registers of power that have found a place, not least for their ability to turn a situation to particular advantage without recourse to more strident forms of power such as domination and coercion. In its topological frame, power is still power, it is just *reproduced differently*: the same, but different.

The 'changing same' of power represents one side of the topological equation where a relationship of power is often reproduced through different registers. The ability to get others to do things that they would otherwise not have done is reproduced, yet often changes as the relationship is folded or stretched through time to enable powerful actors to interact directly or indirectly with others elsewhere. Power remains, as topologists of all persuasions would say, continuous under transformation; it is transformed through a process of spatial distortion, yet continuous in its presence, heightened or otherwise. This folding, stretching or distorting of a relationship of power through time represents the other side of the topological equation, and, for me, it is what gives power its new found 'reach'. Much of this book is given over to exploring how the *topological reach* of actors enables them to make their presence felt in more or less powerful ways that transcend a landscape of fixed distances and well defined proximities.

What does it mean to talk about 'topological reach' as opposed to reach in general? Conventionally, reach is thought about as an extensive arrangement: when something like power is extended outwards over mappable distances, it is common to expect that the greater the distance over which it is extended, the greater its reach. With greater reach, however, it is also supposed that control and influence will likely diminish in line with its extension over greater numbers across ever-expanding distances. The extensiveness of power and its intensity are usually assumed to be conversely related; increase one and the other diminishes or lessens. No such assumption holds, however, when topology enters the frame. Reach, when grasped topologically, is more about *presence* than distance; it is *intensive* rather than extensive, a *relational* arrangement where power *composes* the spaces of which it is a part by stretching, folding or distorting relationships to place certain outcomes within or beyond reach.

Expressed in so few words, the topological glossary is curiously different in many respects, a jolt to our settled topographic imaginations, but not so far removed perhaps from daily encounters in which presence and absence are reconfigured so that the space between 'here' and 'there' is measured less by miles and kilometres and more by the social relationships, exchanges and interactions involved. For my part, topology poses a challenge to the more clear-cut topographies common to the spatial arrangements of territorial and networked power, although it neither displaces nor replaces either. Topological understandings merely bring us into line with many shifting practices of power routinely exercised by ostensibly 'over-stretched' NGOs and campaign activists, 'overbearing' government authorities, and economic corporations that have supposedly 'over-reached' themselves, not to mention 'overlapping' supranational institutions and 'extra-territorial' political bodies. Prosaic as many of these descriptions may be, they have yet to catch up with how such spatial and temporal practices are increasingly experienced. It is, to all intents and purposes, as if our vocabulary is out of synch with our practice and lived experience.

The vocabulary of topology that I wish to work with in this book, and the difference it makes to an understanding of power in its diverse registers, is principally a relational one. Reach, on this understanding, is a form of relational distance, not a spatial metric; it is something that has to be leveraged by the stretching or folding of relationships if a powerful presence of one kind or another is to be secured. Without such leverage, power may take a relational form, but it is neither continuous nor transformed in any topological sense. I take topology to be about relationships that are reproduced differently through a process of equivalence, where equivalence refers to what remains related despite having been folded or stretched every which way. It is the processes of spatial distortion and how they have effectively enabled relationships of power to change, yet remain the same, that I am after.

Already, though, with the use of such terms as 'equivalence', I have strayed deeper into the spirited language of mathematical topology, where indeed the notion of relationships as 'continuous under transformation' is also drawn. Any borrowed vocabulary comes with risks attached, among them the issues of fidelity and how appropriate the terms of one domain of study are to a redescription of another. Nonetheless, I do believe that the standpoint of topology provides us with an opportunity to bring an understanding of the spatial shifts in the architecture of power into line.

Borrowed terms

Short of inventing new terms to capture how things are increasingly experienced, we often have little choice but to borrow them from another likely domain. In talking about spatial shifts, the recasting of proximity, presence and distance in a more composed, relational fashion, the *non-metric* nature of topology is an obvious candidate for such borrowings. As a mode of thinking, topology evolved as an independent branch of mathematics, more or less as a curiosity-driven response to the perceived rigidities of geometric shapes and surfaces that take their cue from the clear-cut co-ordinates of Cartesian space (Barr, 1964; Sklar, 1974). Its appeal for those who have tried to get to grips with the transformations in the spacing and timing of deceptively continuous social arrangements lay with its more relaxed, qualitative approach to the shapes and patterns of everyday life.

The anthropologist Edmund Leach, back in the 1960s, described topology as a 'geometry of elastic rubber sheeting' precisely because the shape and size of things or the distance between them is held to be less significant than what holds them together; that is, the ways in which they are connected, the nature of their relatedness, so to speak (Leach, 1961). For Leach, it was the possibility of kinship patterns reproducing themselves in similar ways across different societies that caught his attention. In this, one can perhaps also see the initial attraction of topology for Bruno Latour and other actor–network theorists, where object invariance, what holds networks together, is of paramount importance (Latour, 1987, 2005; see also Law, 1999). More recently, Celia Lury with others (2012) and Rob Shields (2013) have all been drawn to the similarities between topology's equivalences and the way contemporary cultural life is subject to continuous change in seemingly enduring relationships. Each, in their own way, has been tempted by the resemblances between a world of topological invariants and the constancy of social relationships that nonetheless change through space and time, and has borrowed accordingly.

Interestingly, abstract proofs of one kind or another and the algebraic properties of many of the shapes and figures explored in topology do not play a part in such borrowings, largely I suspect because they have been bundled together with the mathematical stuff so obviously tied to geometry and its measurable shapes. In the immeasurable of topology, the freedom to distort one shape into another more or less at will, so long as the figures remain related in the same way, foregrounds their shape-shifting properties, not their metrics. The angles and distances between things that bind shapes to numbers in geometry is conspicuously absent from the topological transformation of its favourite surfaces, be they flat planes, two-sided cylinders or cut-out strips of one kind or another. That does not mean to say that abstractions of mathematical formulae are strikingly absent from such figures, merely that algebraic notation and inferential proofs show up more readily on geometric rather than topological shapes (see Blackett, 1962).

Ian Hacking, in his book *Why is There a Philosophy of Mathematics At All?* (2014), puts this down to the fact that arithmetic and geometry are pretty much, in his words, the 'same stuff', where number and calculation are intertwined with geometry. Geometry, because of its association with measurement from the earliest of times, he points out, has turned up all over the place in physics, for example, despite its overarching concerns with spatial configurations and shapes of different kinds. With topology, the 'same stuff' would appear to be a world of continuous relationships under transformation which fill out space and time, so to speak. The qualities of shapes and figures rather than their quantitative dimensions perhaps then explain, in part, why topology has crept up on the social sciences of late, less, of course, its more abstract mathematical properties. Whether such selective, rather than wholesale, borrowings are the result of a real or imposed similarity is one of life's great see-saw debates for which I have no reassuring answers. With this, I tend to side with Hacking's observation about the export of one body of mathematical practice to another domain:

> It is not so clear whether we are discovering that the second domain has the same structure as the first domain, or whether we are sculpting the second domain so that it comes out shaped like the first. Probably both sorts of things happen.
>
> *(Hacking, 2014, 175)*

Indeed, probably they do, and not for the first time in the case of the export of topological thinking to the social sciences (see Adams, 1998; DeLanda, 2006; Deleuze, 1988; Harvey, 1969; Rosen, 2006). It is not my intention here, however, to review the range of borrowings from the different fields of topology, past and present (see Martin and Secor, 2013; Paasi, 2011), but rather to set out what I take to be the 'stuff' core to both domains, the social and the topological. In doing so, I will probably fall prey to a little sculpting of my own, although I hope I can go some way to overcome that by drawing attention to instances where the sculpting of the social sciences to look like its topological counterpart misses the mark somewhat. In that respect, I am suggesting that there should be a certain fidelity to terms borrowed.

Fidelity implies a degree of faithfulness, in this case to the broad legacy of topological thinking, and a nod in the direction of its semantic character. That does not mean to say that the vocabulary of topology should be comprehensively appropriated, only that what is borrowed for its exploratory promise should admit some resemblance to its evident characteristics. Bearing that in mind, it seems to me that the 'stuff' common to social sciences and the domain of topology is principally of two kinds.

One, as indicated, lies with their shared concern for relationships that remain continuous under transformation; that is, relationships that remain the same whatever shape a figure is distorted into. The 'sameness', in this instance, is a form of equivalence between the two figures, before and after they have been twisted and turned one into the other. But, and this is the crucial point, through the process of distortion that very 'sameness' is reproduced differently: where the surfaces of a figure were previously, say, flat, they are now distended; where its edges beforehand were straight, they are now curved. The figure has *changed* shape, yet it remains related to the original figure in the *same* way. In much the same vein, for instance, it is possible to comprehend the recent distortion of political borders, where they have been 'pushed' outwards and 'pulled' inwards, as a process that has borne witness to the state reproducing its powers of exclusion and inclusion differently. The sovereign borders of North America and Europe, for example, may have changed shape through the creation of deterrent 'buffer zones', but there is an equivalence between past and present shapes that seems to preserve the intensity of border relationships, only this time by establishing their power and authority differently.

That, however, can only really come about because of a second characteristic shared by the two domains; namely, that the relationships under continuous transformation *compose* the very spaces of which they are a part. When, for instance, the iconic figures of the Möbius strip, the Klein bottle and the Trefoil knot are puzzled over by topologists, it is not the measurable properties of their surface area or the distance between one figure and its distorted counterpart that is of interest, but rather the *relations* between them. Once the idea takes hold that relationships can be transformed through space and time as they are stretched, folded or distorted in some way, attention is drawn to the fact that it is the actual process of spatial distortion that enables such continuous relationships to be reproduced differently. On such an understanding, to return to the example of contemporary political borders, it could be argued that it is precisely their distorted character that has enabled states to maintain a heightened presence at and away from the border proper. Asylum seekers on the 'inside' may be removed as if already part of the 'outside', whilst those held in detention 'offshore' may be denied access to the rights they would have if present on the 'inside'. When grasped topologically, the sovereign power to exclude and include remains continuous yet is transformed in terms of intensity.

Or at least that is the exploratory promise that I think topology can hold for an understanding of the concertina-like pushing and pulling of state borders taking place in parts of the world today. The kind of spatial redescription involved borrows from a manifestly topological vocabulary, one that a mathematically minded topologist would recognize, but does so in a selective way that may prompt us to think again about political borders and what is happening to them. The appropriation of topology is not strictly literal, in that topological terms are not lifted wholesale from one domain to another, but recontextualized to make sense of political and social shifts, rather than merely abstract, figurative shifts. The notion of spatial distortion, for example, so central to topological transformations, when used in the context of political and social change, may serve to disrupt a familiar sense of what is near and what is far by virtue of its borrowed roots, where rigid proximities and distances are customarily relaxed. As such, even the idea that power may be simply extended over a given territory is called into question and its intensive qualities brought into the reckoning for their potential insight.

Whether I have just sculpted political and social change to look like its topological counterpart, or the two worlds really are close to the 'same stuff', is probably, as Hacking suggests, down to a bit of both. What it is not is an attempt either to invoke a nice line in topological metaphor or to invent supposedly new ones that have little or no fidelity to topological thinking as such. The former may refer to something like time as 'folded' or space as 'plaited', 'knotted' even, but simply to invoke such metaphors is more or less an empty gesture. Such metaphors may have a certain evocative charm, but their appeal is simply that unless, as Richard Rorty (1989, 1991), a North American pragmatist broadly in the John Dewey tradition, has stressed, they can be shown to work for certain purposes and not others. A deckchair does not fold in the way that a political border does, nor does space stretch and twist like a rope. Invocation is not the same as explication. Likewise, topology is not simply an excuse for drawing together multiplicities of things from here and there and calling the resultant outcome complex or heterogeneous, as Stephen Collier (2009) is wont to do. His concern, interestingly, is with what replaces Foucault's shift away from the distributed geometries of institutional power towards the more topological arrangements that biopolitics implies, but you could be forgiven for thinking otherwise. There is little that is borrowed from topology as such and nothing really that can shift a conversation around space, time and relatedness in the way that topological equivalence can.

Richard Rorty had much to say about borrowed languages and shifting conversations. For him, all that anyone can really do is 'redescribe lots and lots of things in new ways' (1989, 9) to tempt others to adopt descriptions that make previous ones appear limited. The kind of spatial redescriptions drawn from topology that I have spoken about above though, for Rorty, would not form part of some aimless exchange, but rather spring directly out of a given purpose. In proposing, as I have, that 'reach' be conceived as intensive not extensive and 'distorted' relationships as composing the spaces of which they are a part, not simply lines drawn on a map, my intention in using familiar words in less familiar ways is precisely to help shift a conversation around proximity, distance and power that shows little sign of breaking with the habits of spatial geometry.

It is not, I should stress, that such habits are simply wrong, but that they limit what it is possible to say about power's shifting geographies in the present day. In order to change that conversation, this book tries to show why a topological redescription *works better* at grasping how the authority and presence of many a powerful body has been actively reproduced by their ability to interact directly and indirectly with others elsewhere. That there is no master copy to power, that its presence is felt and reproduced differently as it is stretched or folded through time, suggests to me that the kind of relationships that preoccupy both topology and power may well be much the 'same stuff'. Borrowed vocabularies, as noted earlier, come with risks attached and most likely overlooked baggage. In that respect, I am not sure how far Hacking would be with me on this one, but I wager he would make space for topology and its relationality as a possible candidate, without, that is, falling into the trap of 'topologizing' the whole world.

Making space for topology

In a previous book, *Lost Geographies of Power* (Allen, 2003a), I was grappling with the language of what it meant for power to be exercised at-a-distance or close at hand, and puzzling over the difference that a topological account of space and spatiality could make. In the second decade of the twenty-first century, I think we are perhaps less in awe of the latest wave of globalization than we once were, and more curious about its particularities so as to be able to think through how power relationships actually compose the distances enacted and place certain possibilities within reach or indeed beyond reach. This book, I hope, is a contribution towards that end. It is divided into two parts, the first of which sets out how a topology of power can take us beyond territory and networks.

As will be apparent from the following chapter, I am not suggesting that territorial and networked understandings of power have become moribund or stuck in their ways. In fact, quite the contrary; if anything, a more relaxed spatial vocabulary has sprung up around notions of scale, boundaries, and the ties and connections that link sites to one another, challenging some of our well worn spatial habits and geometrical assumptions. Yet for all the advances made, rarely in my view do such understandings fully break with them. It is as if an extensive landscape of power that is already 'out there', with its flattened surfaces and mappable distances, acts as a limit to grasping where power's reach is exercised intensively not just extensively, where a topological not a topographical spatiality holds sway.

Much can be made of the contrast between topology and topography, indeed sometimes too much. It is easy to slide into an oppositional understanding of the contrast, where topology is defined against all that is topographical. In such matters, I tend to side with Hannah Arendt (1958, 1961, 1970), who drew distinctions between things on the basis of how experience had shifted their meaning. Distinctions are not the same as dualisms; the specification of what something is requires one to know what it is not, but that does not necessitate that whatever contrasts are drawn the result is a diametrically opposed set of characteristics. Distinction is about differentiation, not dichotomization. Topology and topography share a concern with surfaces and sides, boundaries and connections, but they part company when the metrics of size, distance and length enter the picture. Once the surfaces and sides of a spatial figure are subject to distortion of one kind or another, topology's interests are with the continuous but transformed relationships that survive the process of distortion, not the volume and scale of the surfaces or the extended length of the boundaries.

Arendt drew distinctions between, for example, power and violence, and compassion and pity, distinctions that will be picked up in the following chapters, and tracked their shifts in use and meaning as contexts shifted. Her experiential essentialism is not to everyone's taste, nor the unacknowledged ambiguity of many of her distinctions, although the practice of making distinctions is not disavowed (Benhabib, 1996; Habermas, 1977; Young-Bruehl, 2006). The difficulty perhaps lies with the fact that our experiences often exceed our descriptions of them, with the latter playing a game of 'catch-up', where the significance of how things are or have become is not altogether clear (Eagleton, 2005; Jay, 2005). The topographical and the topological can play across one another like that, where the nature of their co-existence remains unclear, as are the shifts that have taken place between the two spatialities. It is not, as noted, that the world has suddenly become topological, but rather that our experiences of what is near and what is far, what is past and what is present, even how it is possible for others elsewhere to be more or less present in the here and now of daily life, has been shifting for a while, for some at least.

Stephen Kern's *The Culture of Time and Space 1880–1918* (1983) is an interesting case in point. In that work, he showed how, at the start of the twentieth century, the sense of the present was thickened temporally to include tracts of the past and portentions of the future, as well as expanded spatially by the shared experience of simultaneity created by the new transportation and communication technologies. Both sets of dynamics provided an insight into the forces that shaped spatial as well as temporal experience for a largely European audience in that period. Experiences, though, as noted, do not come with their spatial and temporal implications attached. They require interpretation, and for Kern the topological formed no part of the description. In retrospect, much of what Kern described could have fallen under the lexicon of topological distortion and transformation, but its significance was not drawn. The intensity of the new distorted experiences of space and time, particularly in the dramatic transformations of the sense of distance involved, was duly recorded, but the shift in experience prompted no curiosity as to their topological resemblance.

Nowadays, a number of unrelated shifts have acted as a spur for topological reflection, coming as they do from a variety of directions and standpoints. The work of Latour, already mentioned, as well as others such as John Law and Annemarie Mol, who have pushed beyond the initial assumptions of actor–network theory, are considered in Chapter 2 for their use of topology as a spatial and temporal analytic, where the topographical plays across it in manifold ways. Other areas where the conversation has taken a more topological slant include the changing experience of the urban, where cities are grasped as relational sites of interaction shaped by distant proximities (Amin, 2007; Amin and Thrift, 2002; see also Secor, 2013; Soderström, 2014) or through a more distanciated urban politics and policy making (McCann and Ward, 2011; Robinson, 2011a, 2011b). Likewise, in the realm of political borders, where control over the movement and circulation of people now stretches from within states to well beyond their outer territorial edges, the blurring of the distinction between the 'internal' and 'external' spaces of a political community has provoked much topological speculation (Bigo, 2000, 2001; Mezzadra and Neilson, 2012; Parker and Vaughan-Williams, 2009).

Despite the obvious differences between such settings, there appears to be something of a shared recognition among such commentators that the twisted and distorted shapes of topology, rather than their flattened topographical counterparts, seem to work better at grasping the mix of spaces and times progressively experienced in much urban, social and political interaction, provoking, in turn, questions way beyond those posed by Kern. In today's more spatially ambiguous world, it seems important to demonstrate the limits of topographical thinking, especially in relation to more familiar approaches that take territory or networks as their starting point. Each of those spatial frames has its place in understanding the contemporary social landscape, but when the questions asked turn on issues of presence and proximity, which bear no relation to physical distance, or continuous change brought about by others elsewhere exercising a disconcerting reach, it is to topology's spatialities and equivalences that one should, I think, look for answers.

Continuity and change, sameness and difference, presence and proximity, do not of course require a topological referent to convey meaning. But when they do form part of the topological lexicon, their meaning shifts to one where a continuous presence is reproduced differently: where an equivalence is established between here and there that enables the same relationship to be reproduced, but in a different spatial arrangement, and perhaps register. In Chapters 3 and 4, it is through such a topological lens that I try to spell out how power as a continuous *relationship* is transformed through a *process* of distorted reach. The distinction between topological processes and relationships is a critical one and I treat them, as indicated earlier, as two sides of the topological equation: although possible to analyse separately, they are part and parcel of the same topological 'stuff'. My reason for separating and then combining the two sides is straightforward, however, in that it allows me to set out one of the central arguments of the book.

In short, that argument, as indicated earlier, is that topological processes have subtly altered many of the ways in which power relationships are exercised today, enabling quieter, more impalpable registers of power to be exercised alongside, and sometimes in place of, more blunt forms of control and constraint. That there are ways other than domination or coercion to get people to do things they would otherwise not have done is, I would have thought, uncontroversial. People have long been induced into situations that work against their interests, or manipulated into such arrangements by deception and dissimulation. The difference today, as I see it, is that powerful actors – financial institutions, corporate multinationals, state agencies and government bodies among them – have a greater ability to reach into the lives of others through a wider variety of means. Crucially, that ability to draw others within close reach or place them out of reach opens up many more possibilities for less strident registers of power to be exercised.

Although the intent concealed through an act of manipulation or the pull of inducement may appear somewhat flimsy alongside the imposition of authority or the blanket force of domination, their modest nature is, in fact, a strength. The ability to leverage such means from afar, without recourse to more overt means of control and constraint, or in tandem with them, has the potential to mask the instrumental nature of any arrangement. Dissimulation among bankers and brokers, for example, involves a form of pretence, yet it is a pretence that relies not on the disguise of investment motives, but rather on not revealing all that lies behind them. The 'power to' broker a deal that may appear to benefit all parties can, in such circumstances, turn into the kind of power that is held over others, skewing rewards in the favour of some but not all. Where professional authority and a dominant role may raise doubts over impartiality and disinterestedness, manipulation and dissimulation can close off avenues and limit choices by more wily means. In many respects, such areas can be more, not less, insidious than power that is conspicuous and in your face.

My point is not that power has somehow gone 'soft', in the sense made meaningful by Joseph Nye (2002, 2004, 2011), although the recognition that 'hard', coercive or constraining means do not meet all contemporary situations and challenges is to be welcomed. Nye's account of 'soft power', which works through shaping the preferences of others to get them to want what you want, is a stylish description of indirect influence and co-option, but the instrumental mobilization of bias involved is something that appears not to have crossed his mind. Marshalling the wants and preferences of others in a quiet fashion through incitement and manipulation, for instance, is far from a benign or soft practice, and one exercised with a controlling purpose in mind. The fact that the motives behind such acts, even those behind, say, artful persuasion and seduction, may be deliberately obscured makes them all the more duplicitous. If such acts were simply niche ploys, then one may rightly wonder what all the fuss is about, but the greater topological reach afforded to such instrumental means makes their significance abundantly clear.

The greater leverage of reach enabled by the folding and stretching of space through time highlights the diverse modes of power through which actors and institutions bring their influence to bear, reacting to forces present by seeking what works best for given purposes and adapting their means accordingly. A practical, improvised element is key to understanding how power is played out in such situations. We have Charles Tilly (2002, 2008) to thank for drawing attention to the significance of improvisation in the mediated arrangements of power, where, should authority pass unrecognized or persuasion fall on deaf ears, other forms of leverage may be drawn upon to make a presence felt. Quieter registers of power are likely to be part of such an adaptable mix, if only because of their enhanced reach, alongside or instead of more constraining means that best suit the demands of a given or changing situation.

The implication of this pragmatic viewpoint is one that runs throughout the book, where more weight is given to how actors *use* their resources, technological, financial or otherwise, to produce the tenuous effect that is power, and less to their organizational or institutional size and shape. That power may be practised in many ways, not one, is perhaps well understood by pragmatists who recognize that its exercise is a provisional achievement: something that is reproduced differently to sustain a continuous presence. This more provisional sense of power takes us closer to why, today, it matters how reach is distorted by institutions and organizations to establish a powerful presence of one kind or another.

Distorted reach

In the second part of the book, this topological proposition is put to the test, drawing upon examples from finance and investment banking, NGOs and social movements, and states and border controls, to show how power works by placing certain possibilities within or beyond reach. Reach, as I have stressed, when understood topologically, is more about presence than distance, something that can be folded in or stretched out by powerful actors to make their presence felt. In doing so, the relationship between near and far is distorted in ways that draw some things closer whilst pushing others further away. An analogy that springs to mind is that of telescopic reach, where if you turn a telescope one way, things that are far off are drawn closer, and if you turn it the other way, things near to you look surprisingly far away. We should resist the temptation to read too much into such an analogy, but it does help to reimagine the kind of distorted spatiality that topology can evoke when proximity and distance play across one another. In the worlds of finance, NGO politics and deformed state borders, such distorted reach lies behind the ability of institutions and social groups to establish their presence either directly or indirectly through space and time.

Presence can be an alarmingly unfocused term, with its predominantly spatial and temporal connotations of simply 'being there', 'present' or 'on hand', so to speak. In topological reasoning, however, you can have a presence without actually being present, or indeed be present yet have a presence elsewhere. For want of a better way of putting it, you can have a relational presence yet be physically distant or, conversely, be physically present yet relationally distant. This is what I mean by proximity and distance playing across one another. For any type of relational presence to be established, however, reach has to be distorted in one way or another.

In disembedded money markets, for instance, as set out in Chapter 5, dispersed groups of often diverse investors may be drawn within reach of the big financial centres such as those of London and New York through a form of simultaneous co-presence, where they are folded in directly through real-time technologies. There is nothing exceptional about such practices, other than the fact that a shared presence gives the arrangement a sense of 'nowness' that belies the physical distances involved. A more indirect presence may be achieved by financial actors stretching to reach interested parties by weaving them into a succession of enrolling practices. In contrast to folded financial arrangements, neither space nor time is shared in any co-present fashion, although both direct and indirect means of leverage may be drawn upon to serve the same ends. It is largely through such processes of distorted reach, it seems to me, that bankers, brokers and other financial intermediaries have in recent times been able to reproduce their 'power to' skew rewards in their favour. Not, I might add, because of any systemic bias, but because such processes have enabled dissimulation and financial manipulation to quietly take hold.

A similar set of distorted processes, I would venture, lies behind the ability of NGOs and social movements to bring different registers of power into play to get governments and corporations to do what they would not otherwise have done. In order to put pressure on such bodies, NGOs have first to mobilize and enrol 'publics' to legitimize their claims-making, whether for environmental, labour or trade justice, or something more rights-based. This, as outlined in Chapter 6, has largely been achieved by such organizations and groups drawing distant harms and hardships within reach of people far removed from them, either by folding in demands for responsibility to be taken for events elsewhere, or by stretching the indirect ties of responsibility to harmful practices in a different part of the globe. In the former, distant harms are lifted out and re-embedded among those persuaded to care through the directness of the claims, whereas the latter involves an indirect tie-up to a hardship whose political presence is registered at arm's length. There is no co-presence established, only a detached or absent presence mediated through those present elsewhere. By either means, social movements are often able to 'punch above their weight', so to speak, and reproduce their 'power to' make a difference.

In the case of political borders, the subject matter of Chapter 7, the processes of distorted reach, as touched upon earlier, have arguably made it possible for states to fold and stretch their borders in ways that reproduce their powers of exclusion and inclusion. Political borders, most notably those of Europe, North America and Australia, have been 'offshored' and outsourced as well as drawn into the interior, transforming the ability of governments to regulate the movement and circulation of people. Yet, for all that, states have been able to more or less maintain a continuous powerful presence at and away from their territorial borders, to exclude and include through an adaptable mix of quiet and constraining practices. The ability to lift out and fold in enforcement practices to establish a more detached presence is one direct means adopted, whereas a more mediated, indirect, 'offshore' presence has involved states stretching such practices beyond their outer territorial limits, reaching into other states, both neighbouring and distant.

What can be drawn within reach, however, can also be placed beyond reach by powerful bodies and institutions displacing their presence. Financial activities conducted by banks, investment managers and the like can be lifted out from one jurisdictional domain and embedded in another 'offshore' to avoid regulatory oversight; economic corporations can evade demands to take responsibility for distant harms by distancing themselves relationally in a more convoluted fashion; and states can displace demands for entry from asylum seekers and irregular migrants by the use of detention and confinement, multiplying the possibilities for delay and disruption, as well as denying access to the public realm of rights and legal protections. In all such instances, the distances folded or stretched are relational, where the distortion of reach makes the close at hand topologically distant and further removed.

In the three chapters that comprise the second half of the book, the empirical exemplification is not intended to be exhaustive of all things to do with finance, social movements and political borders, respectively, but rather discriminating in terms of its focus on how power works through its quieter equivalences. In Chapter 5, it is the changing same of financial advantage that is the focus of attention; that is, how financial actors have been able to reproduce a reward structure that benefits them disproportionately by the establishment of a topological fiction that equates onshore and offshore figures of finance. In Chapter 6, the focus switches to how NGOs and social movements reproduce their 'power to' make a difference by mobilizing and leveraging dispersed 'publics' around political claims by equating distant harms with the benefits enjoyed by others far removed from them. And finally, in Chapter 7, through the distorted nature of political borders, the focus is upon the continuity of border relationships under transformation as states reproduce their 'power to' exclude and include through a variety of different registers. In each of these fields, it is the topological equivalences that enable power to change yet nonetheless remain the same.

PART I
Topological twists

2

POWER THAT COMES WITH THE TERRITORY

An easy geometry

It seems hard to break with a vocabulary that has proven useful in helping to find our way around the territory of power, but that is precisely what has been happening of late. The sense that power and leverage may be extended outwards from a capable centre or simply tracked through their defined connections remains intuitive, yet a lingering doubt often persists that the exercise itself may not be quite so seamless. Likewise, the idea that it is possible to pinpoint the location of power in certain bodies and to map the contours of their authority and influence over a given territory seems reasonable enough, as does the view that such decision-making powers are bounded by scale, but after a moment's reflection neither sounds entirely straightforward. The capabilities of any number of corporate multinationals are open to such qualms, as indeed are the powers of the state or those of a private governing authority. Few nowadays, it would appear, actually believe that such leverage is not without its complications and setbacks, or that the boundaries of authority drawn are anything less than porous. We have moved on, it seems, in our understanding of how power works.

If power comes with the territory, then it also comes with the recognition that there is now a more supple vocabulary with which we can describe such territorial distortions. The rigid boundaries of territory and scale are routinely relaxed to accommodate shifting political relationships, with authority rescaled upwards and downwards, even sideways if need be. Networks are stretched to meet a more porous world of flows and connections, and what cannot be enclosed in this pliant landscape is often relabelled as extraterritorial. A time-honoured vocabulary with which the centres of power can be broadly fixed, the extension of their authority mapped and the boundaries of their influence drawn, has been loosened to allow for the possibility that governments or other powerful entities may extend or stretch their control in ways that appear to defy such conventional mappings. Whether or not they do actually defy everyday topographies of power, however, is less obvious.

Richard Rorty (1989) put his finger on the problem. Often, he pointed out, the terms that we use to capture new developments, new departures, are couched in the very same vocabulary that has shown itself to be too rigid or restrictive. Rather than a break with the conventions of scale and topography, then, the redescriptions of power and authority as *extra*-territorial or *re*-scaled merely represent an alternative mapping, not an actual break with topography and its familiar metrics of measured distances and flat surfaces. Even the sense in which the power of transnational institutions may be 'stretched' or made more effective at-a-distance through the 'compression' of space by time can be understood in terms of lines of connection etched on a flat surface across measurable spans of the globe. Such novel redescriptions barely disturb what appears to be a familiar topography of power, even if they point beyond it. It is, for some reason, as if such familiarity makes it all the more difficult to think about space and time differently, so that the insights gained by a more relaxed vocabulary are rarely followed through or exploited for their implicit *topological* sensibilities.

In this chapter, I want to show how the more refined territorial accounts of power elaborated by Neil Brenner, Bob Jessop and, more recently, Stuart Elden disrupt conventional 'top-down', 'centre-out' descriptions of power, as do networked approaches to power, but neither seems fully able to break with the habit of a spatial geometry that leaves power as something that is extended over space, rather than something that composes it. Indeed, even those accounts that point beyond a simple topography of power – such as the imaginative vocabulary of Bruno Latour (2005), with its stress upon mediated powers of association, or Saskia Sassen's (2006) overlapping geographies of power and authority – seem unable to break with a sense of power that has geometry at its core. And even where networked versions do appear to effect such a break, the result is not always as promising as may first appear.

But before we consider some of these more subtle attempts to capture power's shifting geographies, it is important, first, to be aware of the taken-for-granted geometry that has had such a lasting hold, and why topography seems to remain the default option.

Boxing-in power

The idea that power radiates out from a given centre, or that the spatial organization of a rule-making authority may be portrayed as a process whereby power is impelled outwards from a capable centre, is not so questionable when we consider the hold that 'top-down' or 'centre-out' vocabularies of power have in both common and academic parlance. Richard Peet, for example, outlines his *Geography of Power* thus:

> Clusters of power-generating institutions, I propose make up a power centre. In advanced modernity governance policies and practices are conceived by experts in institutions concentrated in only a few power centres, global cities

that exercise power in world space. Each power centre can be thought, in and of itself, as a place in the sense of a cluster of interconnected institutions, or what might be called an institutional complex … Power centres composed of complexes of institutions can also be mapped by looking at power relations or as power transmitted across space.

(Peet, 2007, 21–22)

That 'centre-out' hold is perhaps more habitual than anything else, and arguably owes much to the legacy of three-dimensional 'Euclidean' geometry in which circles may be drawn so long as they have an identifiable centre and a radius, in which parallel lines never meet, and in which distances are plotted in straight lines from one point to the next (see Sack, 1980). The spatial geometry itself is somewhat of a caricature, given that Euclidean and Cartesian geometries have blurred in the modern geographic imagination (Elden, 2013), leaving us with a familiar sense of bounded, flat spaces, with identifiable centres, in which events and things can be located, or extended over distances that can be calculated and their reach pinpointed.

In this topographic landscape, institutional power possesses a certain spatial integrity, so that it is straightforward to talk about an identifiable organizational 'centre', be it the political executive of the state, the HQ of a business corporation, or an entire 'global city' such as New York. Likewise it is possible to speak about the edges of their jurisdiction or managerial control which, in this landscape, are akin to the outer ring of a circle that serves to delimit authority or at least point to its furthest reaches. In the more thoughtful accounts of the strategic role that global cities perform in 'running' the global economy, the focus is less upon corporate HQs as such and more upon the concentration in one location of the right kinds of people, skills and expertise which produce a capability for global control; that is, an integrated complex of specialist services able to do the work of globalization (see Sassen, 1991, 1995, 2000). Nonetheless, the effectiveness of such a concentration in powerful cities still rests heavily on the assumption that their success depends upon their ability to extend their authority and influence outwards over much of the economic landscape.

This 'centre-out' view of power also underpins traditional accounts of bureaucratic authority where the powers of the centre are said to be delegated through a variety of organizational positions and realized in the form of administration (following Weber, 1978). Managers in state-run departments or large corporations occupy their decision-making roles on the basis of their technical capabilities and competence to do the job. Authority, in that sense, comes with the position, and with that position comes the limits of what a professional or manager may decide or prescribe to others. There is nothing monolithic about the capabilities involved; where authority is exercised, this happens in an outward (and downward) fashion within the limits of the organization's rules. In the case of more flexible organizational structures, power may be distributed rather than delegated over space to secure potentially diverse geographical goals. In such instances, as for example in the case of large transnational firms, the distribution of powers between 'global' management, 'regional' partners and 'local' business dealings may be more problematic than is often believed (see Jones, 2002, 2008), yet the lines of authority, from point to point, retain their geometric integrity nonetheless.

Territory in this customary framework is not an undifferentiated landscape, but one partitioned and parcelled up into bounded units of spatial authority and control. Effectively, the flat surfaces over which power is extended are boxed up into administrative, regulatory or jurisdictional spaces, and often marked from the local and the regional through to the national and the global. Power, whether political or economic, in this geometric arrangement appears as authority *over* defined territorial spaces, although in practice the exclusivity of that authority or the stability of the boundaries drawn is often open to question, especially in relation to issues of political sovereignty and legitimacy (see Agnew, 1994, 1999, 2005a; Anderson, 1996; Paasi, 2003, 2009). In consequence, the strain between the ways in which power and authority are practised, on one hand, and the inability of territories to 'contain' the relationships extended, on the other, has been placed under extreme pressure. One outcome has been the steps taken to 'relax' the geometry, in the hope that there will be no subsequent loss of spatial integrity.

Scaled-up authority

In response to what are perceived as recent shifts in the global redistribution of power, there has been a greater recognition that the stability of bounded authority or the exclusivity of territorial scales no longer quite captures the more complex geography of power that has emerged. The privatization of authority, the shift from government to governance, and the proliferation of regulatory bodies are among those changes that have made it altogether more difficult to pin down the institutional geography of power, especially when it comes to tracking the decision-making processes that shape political outcomes. Neil Brenner (2001, 2004) and Bob Jessop (2005, 2007, 2009) are perhaps among the most consistent exponents of the view that state power has been liberated from the idea of both containment and contiguity, in terms of units of spatial authority seemingly piled one on top of the other. For them, state power has been freed from its territorial moorings and fixed co-ordinates, so that it is no longer plausible to think that a 'centre' of authority exists in the singular or that power is simply extended outwards. Instead, the geometry has been relaxed to accommodate the *rescaling* of power and authority. As Jessop puts it:

> National states have become even more important arbiters of the movement of state powers upwards, downwards, and sideways; they have become even more important meta-governors of the increasingly complex multicentric, multiscalar, multitemporal, and multiform world of governance; and they are actively involved in shaping the forms of international policy regimes.
>
> (Jessop, 2007, 196)

States, according to Jessop, thus increasingly face pressures from both 'above' and 'below', which have resulted in the displacement of their authority. Administrative and regulatory functions have, as it were, moved 'upwards, downwards, and sideways' as national states find themselves destabilized from above by the growth of supranational institutions and undermined from below by the devolution and decentralization of decision-making powers to sub-national institutions. On this view, the larger number of institutional interests on the political landscape, in particular the multiple sites of authority, from numerous quangos and private agencies to local administrative units, have undermined the notion that the central state apparatus is the prime locus of political power. In place of the conventional assumption that the central state is the only actor of any real import, the institutional playing field is now shared with non-governmental organizations, multinational enterprises and other supranational as well as interstate organizations. At any one point in time, the relative significance of each scale may change, in that the power can be scaled up or down through the different units of spatial authority, both transnational and sub-national.

This is an altogether different arrangement of powers from one that considers regulatory or devolved authority as something that is slotted into pre-given spaces, be it local, urban, regional or national. In recognizing that space is not simply an empty vessel into which power relationships are slotted, acting merely as a container within which things happen, the geometry itself becomes pliable, open to manipulation and modification. The lines of authority, as much as where the edges are drawn, and the scales of regulation, as much where their extension halts, are themselves the subject of political construction, relative rather than absolute in its geometry (Smith, 2004). Multicentric, multiform and multi-scalar are among the descriptors used to capture this new-found spatial complexity as the co-ordinates of power lose their territorial fixity and topographical bearings. But in a landscape where authority may now be 'upscaled' or 'downscaled' and power itself is deemed capable of 'jumping' scale (Smith, 2004; Swyngedouw, 2000), that is not all that has been lost. Arguably, so too has the spatial integrity of scale and territory itself.

The elasticity of scale in this political landscape is certainly not a property that Edmund Leach would have recognized, where a recalibrated metric is used to capture power's shifting geographies that, to all intents and purposes, actually cut across scale rather than reflecting it. In attempting to 'rescue' the vocabulary of territory and scale, it would appear that both Brenner and Jessop inadvertently end up overextending its use. By trying to explain too much through territory and scale, as I see it, they actually account for too little. My point here is not that territory or scale has been superseded or rendered obsolete, but rather that a notion of scaled-up powers is too blunt an instrument to grasp the shifting geographies of authority and leverage involved. But scale is not the only way in which territory has been re-thought when faced with questions over its permeability and consequent loss of spatial integrity.

Extra-territorial power?

A more nuanced use of the notion of territory is to be found in Stuart Elden's (2009) *Terror and Territory: The Spatial Extent of Sovereignty*, which attempts to work through why territory matters in an age when not only have boundaries become more porous, but state territorial sovereignty itself is increasingly under threat. Territory, or more specifically the connection between the state and its territory, is for him one of the key sites of struggle in the contemporary geopolitical moment. In line with Brenner, territory is not seen as a static backdrop with fixed co-ordinates, but as an arena through which particular geographies of fear, threat and division are played out. Elden's prime concern is with territorial integrity: the spatial extent of a state's sovereignty; that is, its effective political control over a given territory. Such integrity, he argues, has been fractured, as more or less failed states have had their sovereignty undermined by the international community in the name of security and the 'war on terror'. Yet, at the same time, that very same community has worked hard to defend territorial integrity in the interest of preserving stability and the right of states to exercise power legitimately within their borders. On one hand, the sovereignty of states has been drawn into question when they are deemed a threat to the vital interest of others, yet on the other hand, the spatial extent of their powers has been defended and their borders deemed inviolable. In the case of the United States, it is:

> looking for something other than straightforward territorial control ... a process of integration has emerged as the principal US foreign policy and security strategy. This is integration into a system of political and economic structures, framed by the United States. The economic structure requires geopolitical support, which has important implications in terms of territorial control because the very nature of US ambitions requires a double standard in its treatment of territorial issues. While it wants to completely enforce the inviolable standing of its own territory, and to reinforce and control that with whatever means necessary, it wants to assert the absolute contingency of sovereignty over territory elsewhere.
>
> *(Elden, 2009, 175)*

This, then, is clearly a landscape in tension; one in which territory as a 'container' acts both to depict the spatial limits of what a state can do and to represent the site under sovereign challenge. The image is one of territorial political actors, the more dominant of which extend their powers over the territory of others when 'global' danger threatens. There is no pre-givenness to territorial power and, as with Brenner, territory is conceived as an achievement, something that is actively produced. Unlike Brenner, however, there is less of a preoccupation with the redrawing of bounded spaces; with the need to continuously recalibrate spatial units of authority or, in Elden's case, territorial boundaries. Rather, the focus is more about the ability of certain powerful states to curb the powers of other states elsewhere and, in so doing, throw into sharp relief the making and remaking of territories. But, in assuming the extraterritorial nature of sovereign powers, it is possible that the geometry may have been relaxed a little too far.

To be fair to Elden, the extraterritorial nature of state power is implied rather than spelt out, but the extension of powers implied is not simply that of a set of capabilities radiating out from a central point. Nor is it of a force impelled outwards over a flat surface. For him, it is the character of the geopolitical moment which shapes his portrayal of territorial power, with events in New York and Washington, DC playing out in places such as Afghanistan in an explicitly territorial manner (Elden, 2009, xxviii), and vice versa. What enables US rule to be made present in a direct sense by embedded political and military agencies, and mediated through institutional domination, is reflected in the territorial strategies of Islamism, which reach across the globe through a diffuse network of contacts and operations. But such topological-style insights are not followed through or exploited for what they tell us about how different groups and political entities are able to make their leverage and presence felt from afar.

Which is all the more surprising really, given that in his expansive follow-up text, *The Birth of Territory*, Elden (2013) is adamant that territory be conceived as a bundle of political and legal relations that have taken a variety of spatial forms historically; conceived as a process not an outcome, one that is continually being made and remade over time. As such, territory's characteristic boundedness and exclusivity, for him, is a more recent incarnation, one shaped by the political technologies of calculation, measurement and geometry. On that basis, one would have thought that he would have considered how far such a notion of territory is appropriate to the contemporary moment, where extra-territoriality does not appear to grasp the political spatialities he describes so well in *Terror and Territory*. Having broken loose from a bounded sense of territory, it would have been a small step to explore how states are able to make their presence felt at a distance by composing the proximate and distanciated relationships involved.

Much the same concern can be directed at Saskia Sassen's (2006) *Territory, Authority, Rights: From Medieval to Global Assemblages*. For her, the mix of spaces and times that inhabit the national setting defines a new, overlapping geography of power within which different actors – state authorities and jurisdictional agencies, corporate firms and supranational institutions, civil society movements and transnational activists – jostle, co-exist and interrupt one another to gain advantage. As she sees it, the disembedding of state functions and the growing authority of non-state actors in the public realm, which Brenner also describes, opens up spaces within the formally exclusive territory of nation states where global firms are increasingly subject to new transversal forms of territorial authority. Parts of global cities such as New York and London, for instance, predominantly their corporate finance sectors, are seen to be partially detached from the geographically circumscribed authority of the state. This, however, is not a geography where some parts of national territory are said to hover or float above it; rather, such economic spaces remain firmly embedded in national territories, yet are subject to wider geographical authorities when it comes to regulation and control. While states remain the final authority over their expansive territories, the prevalence of such authority should not, as Sassen notes, be confused with dominance. On this understanding, states are both confronted by and are part of a new geography of power that does not have territorial exclusivity as its defining characteristic:

> The nation-state remains the prevalent organizational source of authority and to variable extents the dominant one. But … critical components of authority deployed in the making of the territorial state are shifting towards becoming strong capabilities for detaching that authority from its exclusive territory and onto multiple bordering systems. Insofar as many of these systems are operating inside the nation-state, they may be obscuring the fact that a significant switch has happened. It may take a while to become legible in its aggregate impact.
>
> *(Sassen, 2006, 419–20)*

Such a view, though, requires that we suspend belief in the assumption that state power and authority is extensive with the borders of the nation, as well as capable of uncomplicated reach. The detachment of authority from territory also brings into question the idea that borders are always at the edges of any given territory. For Sassen, this is clearly not the case, as borders are not so much redrawn as re-embedded within national geography, in line with the form of authority under consideration. New jurisdictional authorities, such as the World Trade Organization, can be seen to insert themselves as a kind of bordered transversal space inside national territories, in some cases overruling the national state or at least forcing it to sign up to its treaty laws. Such bordered spaces cut across conventional political borders, 'debordering' them in the process and embedding their own logics of power and authority (Sassen, 2013).

The disruption to a fixed geometry that such insights presuppose, however, does not lead her to problematize territory as a source of power, as Elden does, nor to question the nature of the geography that makes up the 'global'. On the contrary, the new transversal spaces are themselves seen as a novel type of territorial formation, one superimposed over the old order, without erasing it. Indeed, it would appear that although territorial or 'denationalized' authority may be 'lifted out' and 're-embedded', such practices seem to occur solely within national settings, with little thought for what happens between them, apart from the role of supranational networks, primarily digital networks, which are claimed to have the potential to destabilize existing hierarchies of scale. Instead, the language of territory and multiple border systems is used to 'save' a topography which is now increasingly marked by a network of connected points which extends within, between and across national territories.

The odd thing, though, to my mind is, having pushed up against the limits of topographical thinking on power, for both Elden and Sassen there appears to be little curiosity as to what lies beyond it. Networks, when mentioned, seem to be merely an additional part of an already complex topography, lines on a flat surface that can be drawn from one point to the next in a conventional cartographic manner. And, indeed, for many the portrayal of horizontal forms of power in this manner is less of a departure from many 'centre-out' accounts of power than they would otherwise have us believe.

Flattening-out power

Power within networks is not locatable in quite the same way that power within territories may be traced back to a given body, but both share a sense of power as something that can be extended, often straightforwardly, across a flattened landscape. In a world of porous borders and loose frontiers, extensive networks capable of uncomplicated reach tend to conjure up an impression of power as a more fluid, horizontal medium than the more conventional sense of delegated or devolved powers. Decision-making powers, for instance, do not seem to accrue to networks as much as the mobilization and transmission of all manner of power resources, from knowledge, information and ideas through to people and money. As such, networks provide a means of mapping the ties that connect territories and locations together on the basis of shared power resources. In this topography, power is extended horizontally from point to point, with the limits of its reach defined, not surprisingly, by the end of the line.

As with the territorial power, however, there is more than one way of conceiving networked relationships, and not all accounts fall back so easily upon the kinds of distance and extension that merely connect people and things across a largely flat landscape. An understanding of the significance that gaps and breaks represent for networked interaction, as well as the importance of the 'power to' construct the networks in the first place, has loosened a more rigid network geometry fashioned largely out of lines and connections stretched from point to point. But once again, for all that, it is as if that very vocabulary gets in the way of exploiting the implicit topological understandings gained, and thus the possibility of developing a spatial sensibility more in tune with power's shifting geographies.

Networks are hardly novel as an organizational space, but when powers are mobilized through networks it is the patterns of association and interaction which connect people and things together in the pursuit of certain ends that hold centre stage. A wide array of institutions and practices, from the broad sweeping alliances of geopolitical institutions and transgovernmental agencies, at one end of the spectrum, to the association of NGOs and political protest groups, at the other, connect people and places together over short or long distances. Differences in the make-up and dynamism between networks ensure that they reach out across space in different ways and to varying extents, in some cases cutting across established political boundaries and in others consolidating them. The proliferation of global concerns has, in turn, called forth organizational forms capable of extensive reach to meet them (see Thompson, 2003). On this view, power does not radiate out from any given centre, but rather runs along the length and breadth of a network, punctuated only by the points of connection; that is, the sites at which power and resources tend to cluster. It is, to all intents and purposes, a fluid medium that empowers particular groups and institutions.

When conceived in this manner, power networks may be understood in at least two ways: literally in the sense that new transport and communication technologies have enabled the greater movement of resources to control outcomes; or, in a more figurative way, as the organization and mobilization of different types of resources across space. The former is closer to Manuel Castells' (1996) sense of networks where they form open, interconnected structures, capable of unlimited expansion, through which resources flow: capital, information, technology, people as well as images, sounds and symbols. Domination through the networks, as some kind of resourceful mix, remains the goal of the networked elites in the new spaces of media communication (Castells, 2007), as it did before for the cosmopolitan elites circulating between the major global cities (Castells, 1996). The latter, in contrast, is nearer to Michael Mann's (1986, 1993, 2003, 2011, 2012) notion of power resources as organized and extended over space in loose or tightly orchestrated ways to achieve identified goals. In both these cases, however, networks represent a contemporary means of overcoming the barriers of distance to secure advantage for particular groups at specific locations.

In *Communication Power* (2011), Castells focused his attention more explicitly upon what he called network-making power; that is, the ability to programme the content of networks in line with specific goals, as well as to ensure a unity of purpose through the control of the points where different networks connect. Programmers and switchers, actors drawn from his earlier work on the nature of a network society, shape the communication content of networks that connect the local with the global and give them extensive reach:

> The programming capacity of the goals of the network (as well as the capacity to reprogram it) is, of course, decisive because, once programmed, the network will perform efficiently, and reconfigure itself in terms of structure and nodes to achieve its goals ... There is a second source of power: the control of the connecting points between the various strategic networks. I call the holders of these positions the switchers ... Programmers and switchers are those actors and networks of actors who, because of their position in the social structure, hold network-making power, the paramount form of power in the network society.
>
> *(Castells, 2011, 45–47)*

Thus for Castells different types of networks, political, financial, military and such, are said to interact, although each is programmed to achieve its specific goals across a range of interfaces. Mann (2003, 2011, 2012) too, in his account of the workings of power in the twenty-first century, utilizes his longstanding fourfold classification of power (re)sources – economic, political, military and ideological – to spell out their different scope and reach, orchestrated through either intensive or extensive organizational means. In theory, political relations are said to channel and institutionalize each of the other power resources over definite bounded territories, although in practice he details how powers are often poorly organized, uneven and incoherent, especially when it comes to his account of how US power in the contemporary period has extended outwards across the globe. Nonetheless, the ability of networks to span the local and the global remains for both Mann and Castells an intuitive assumption about how organizational or strategic goals are achieved, even if a more provisional sense of the arrangement often prevails.

This assumption works well for states as much as global business, but especially so in the case of transnational social movements (Della Porta and Tarrow, 2005; McDonald, 2006), as both Castells and Mann acknowledge. The ability to mobilize across borders, to conduct transnational campaigns through extensive activist networks, is a form of empowerment for both NGOs and social movements alike, in particular those engaged in environmental, human rights and sweatshop campaigns. The networking abilities of such groups to mobilize around and indeed construct the 'common good' effectively legitimize their right to interfere politically in the domestic activities of states (Beck, 2005; Cerny, 2009). Such empowerment, in part, is viewed as the product of newly forged connections, where the ability to span the globe from a local base is also suggestive of goals being secured by exercising power with others, rather than over others. As a fluid medium, power in this associational sense can expand in line with the resources mobilized, or it can diminish once collective, short-term goals have been achieved (Allen, 2003b).

There is, however, an underlying spatial sensibility to many such networked practices in an age of globalization, one that rests largely upon a geometry of lines and connections extended horizontally from site to site. Space in this framework is often akin to a lattice-like pattern mapped over a flat surface, where leverage and influence cut across nominally sovereign states. Authority is something that is seen to span the networks; it is used to exercise control *over* what is carried through them, rather than, as in earlier boxed accounts of authority, over bordered blocs of territory. Power, effectively, is conceived as the result of extensive interaction, where networks act as carriers of resources mobilized across multiple sites and locations. Yet such defined connections rarely capture quite how transnational actors have been able to exert an influence often way beyond their means. In part, this is because a concern for the control and co-ordination of resources across space tends to emphasize the organizational extent of power, as if the connections themselves were already drawn across the topographical landscape. Not all networked understandings work with such an inscribed geometry, however.

Net'work'ed power

Whilst power in most networked accounts does not pre-exist the connections forged, the impression often given is that the ties themselves, like lines on a map, are already etched. When the emphasis moves from the net to the 'work' of the networks, the focus shifts from pre-existing ties and connections to the construction of the net itself: to the mediated forms of interaction which effectively bridge, broker and connect people and things together in some provisionally stable pattern of relationships. Castells, in his recent work, nods in this direction, but broadly fails to develop the provisional, mediated quality of the relationships involved. Much of the groundwork for this way of thinking about networks has been put in place by actor–network theory, principally the contributions of Bruno Latour (1987, 1999a, 1999b, 2005) and Michel Callon (1986, 1992, 1998). In their hands, networks are sets of associations put together by actors who are able to enrol, translate and channel others into networks of meaning in such a way that they extend and reproduce themselves through space and time. In this kind of networked arrangement, well placed individuals or groups of individuals are said to be in a position to 'fix' an overall orientation or direction which, to all concerned, appears to be indispensable and irreversible.

The key to the success of this kind of arrangement, it would seem, is the ability to 'hook up' others to the process of circulation, to draw upon organizational resources to negotiate and persuade other actors to pursue certain goals. In that respect, the exercise could resemble the conventional process of resource mobilization referred to earlier, where control over others at a distance merely represents the capacity to muster contacts, artefacts and information of one sort or another as a means to exert power. By stressing the central significance of translation, however, Latour is able to show how the extension of networked arrangements involves more than the mere transmission of resources; rather it involves a mediated exercise of power, where distances are overcome by the successive enrolment of others to form what amounts to a single will across the network.

Latour (2005) also drew a distinction between mediators and intermediaries, where the former are an active force transforming and translating what is not connected into some form of association, whilst the latter appear to work towards stabilizing the network. It is difficult to adhere to such a hard-and-fast distinction, but its value lies with the different kinds of net 'work' involved. The 'power to' bridge what were previously separate and unconnected elements, to bring them into alignment, is suggestive of a loose form of networked interaction. The ability to forge associations and to broker relations through collaborative efforts does not have to resemble an over-connected view of networks already in place; rather the 'work' of spanning distances suggests a formation based upon the 'power to' hold associations together for a given outcome. Such partial connections are also suggestive of an understanding of distance that points beyond that of a series of mappable lines.

Extensive reach to those physically distant appears to involve more than a question of measurement, in whatever chosen metric. Indeed, what happens elsewhere, in far-off places, and what is drawn from the past to make the present possible, form part of what is obviously a topological equation, where presence does not have to be local, nor part of the same moment or time period, to be a link in a newly formed networked arrangement (2005). Having said that, in this flattened landscape, where the things that circulate across ever greater distances can be tracked and the patterns of association traced, it is all too easy to slip back into a topography of movement and extension. There is little that would be out of place in a networked topography of connected points where such ties can be tracked and traced. Latour's flattened topographies may not be intended to conjure up the flat surfaces of conventional geometry, but habit may work against that given the apparent spatial ambiguity. The powers of association may be conceived as a result of 'stretched' interaction, but they can just as easily be read as a series of lines and connections extended horizontally from site to site across an even landscape.

When the emphasis is placed firmly on the substance of the connections – on the *way* things are related, not on the fact of their connection or their extension – then the room for manoeuvre is likely to be less. In this topological landscape, relations of presence and absence are reconfigured so that the gap between 'here' and 'there' is bridged by the relationships involved, and distance itself is understood as a product of those relations, rather than anything measurable. Work by those pushing beyond actor–network theory (Callon and Law, 2004; Hetherington, 1997; Hetherington and Law, 2000; Law, 1999; Mol and Law, 1994) has amplified this sense of relational distance, where absent others perform an integral role in holding networks together in a stable yet changing pattern. What gives a network its integrity is pointedly the relationship between actors, rather than the location co-ordinates of their networked position (Law, 1999).

John Law and Annemarie Mol (2001) took this topological interpretation a step further by arguing that whilst metrologies of an infinite variety can hold a mobile world constant (see O'Connell, 1993), such constancy does not mean that something like authority, say, or any other object held together through a particular web of relationships, is the same everywhere. Rather, objects may retain their stability through shifting sets of relationships in a manner akin to something that changes as it moves, yet basically remains the same. Or, in the more classical language of topology, objects retain some kind of integrity or invariance despite being stretched or twisted out of shape. Insofar as the global is already present in the local, by virtue of the multiple relationships that cut across it, the likes of authority as an object takes on something of its surroundings. Quite simply, its performance is mutable and shifts in line with the ability of actors to make themselves more or less present in the here and now of spatial interaction. Or, at least, that seems to be the claim.

Certainly, for Law and Mol, the flattened landscapes that Latour describes are complicated by the mutability of what flows across them, but their navigation still appears to require more of the tools of topography than topology. As before, the vocabulary of movement and connection appears to get in the way of redescribing networks in a more composed, topological fashion. People and places appear to remain 'hooked' up to a process of circulation, no matter how mutable the things that pass through it; connections are still traced, despite, as we shall shortly see, the volatility of the associations which for them now seem to fan out in all directions. True, their relational sense of distance offers a non-metric account of connection, but the spaces described appear lop-sided in topological terms; more about rela-tionships *successively* altered as they circulate rather than, for instance, 'folded' in through near-instantaneous forms of reach, or 'twisted' through the shared experience of simultaneous exchanges at ever greater distances. In part, I suspect that this may be down to a lingering sense that the movement from 'here to there' is still only something that can be tracked and traced geometrically.

Novel redescriptions, easy geometries

If networks offer a more complicated topography of movement and connection than that of the more rigid geometry of territory and scale, both nonetheless can be mapped more or less faithfully across a flat, horizontal landscape. The flattening of power relationships seems to pull any novel redescriptions back into the landscape of connections where they can be traced only through their extension, not, say, through the twists and turns in real-time coercive relationships that give a heightened immediacy to their effect, or through the inducements folded in from those on the other side of the globe. It is not as if the 'twisting' or 'folding' of relationships is beyond our reckoning, yet the use of familiar words in unfamiliar ways often seems sufficient to fall back upon tried and tested vocabularies in order to make sense of them. Of course, invoking novel terms to describe spatial and temporal shifts is not an excuse simply to promote a nice line in enticing metaphors. There has to be an exploratory promise, by which I mean some kind of understanding has to be opened up for us by their use, but it is not entirely obvious why some spatial metaphors take hold and others fail to catch our imagination.

The very idea that connections may be 'twisted' or 'folded' over on themselves may seem, at first sight, distinctly odd, yet we seem at ease talking about the ability of local activist groups, for example, to 'jump' scale from, say, the local to the supranational without batting an eyelid; as if the meaning of the word itself is entirely transparent and obvious to us. In fact, we do much the same when there is talk of social interaction as 'stretched' over space, as noted before in respect of Latour's work, for instance, or in the earlier claims of Anthony Giddens (1981, 1984, 1990) that societies are 'stretched' over shorter or longer spans of space and time as a means of securing distant outcomes. The ability to regulate the timing and spacing of social activities from afar, through the employment and application of resources over tracts of space and time, represents for Giddens a 'stretching' of social relations that amounts to the actual generation and expansion of power which enables states and other actors to control events further afield. On both interpretations, 'stretched' interaction can sound a lot like acts that are extended over distance, or relationships that are mediated through a process of circulation, for there to be anything that could possibly surprise us metaphorically.

So why, then, should it be harmless enough to talk about societies that are 'stretched' or geographical scales that can be 'jumped' when no such acceptance is easily extended towards the idea that spatial relationships may be 'twisted' or 'folded' over onto themselves?

One possible answer to that, if we follow Rorty (1989), can be traced to the fact that the repeated use of words in unfamiliar contexts, over time, loses their power to jar. In short, they become dead metaphors; that is, they cease to surprise us when deployed because their habitual use allows us to cope with their new meaning within our existing vocabularies. The 'stretching' of social relations is a lot like the stretching of an elastic sheet over a given length or span. There is an easy geometry to the relationship; one that works for us when it comes to understanding what is new, say, about digital communications, or the novel side to real-time technologies. We have, it would seem, little problem entertaining the notion. And we entertain it, I believe, largely because we do not have to leave the world of flat surfaces, measured distances and extended connections. There is no pressure to break with existing spatial vocabularies, no obligation to change the way in which we talk about space and time.

Whether or not that was the intention of either Giddens or Latour in their metaphoric redescription of space as 'stretched', I am not entirely sure. But I doubt it, given that their writings include frequent reference to arrangements that enable distant actors to be present in terms of their influence, despite being physically absent, and for events elsewhere to have a direct impact upon the here and now of daily life. Even, in the case of Latour, the sense in which faraway interactions and materials play a direct part in what constitutes the 'local' is often described as 'folded' arrangements, usually in reference to past practices and objects which prop up the present or alter its meaning and significance in some way (see especially Latour, 2005). Intriguingly, the topological is never far away from disassembling the topographical in his work, although more often than not it is time that is 'folded' and dislocating in its effects, not space.

Perhaps we are more familiar with the notion that time may be 'folded', that the past, in the form of tangible objects or memorable events, can be enfolded or entwined in the present. A past history when spliced into the present has the potential to disrupt the current moment, or at least to disrupt any simple notion of history as a form of linear progress and continuity. The memory of past landscapes, centuries-old buildings juxtaposed to the new, can produce such a disruption, where a selective past can be tucked into a potential future. The language of 'present pasts' is never far away from matters of power and legitimacy, as Edward Said (1994) reminded us, when a memorable event or period is folded into the present to justify a particular way of doing or representing things. It seems as if time lends itself more readily to such topological interpretations, or at least the vocabulary seems to work well in conveying a non-linear narrative of history where the past plays across the present (see Hetherington, 1997). If we seem more relaxed about the possibility of time being folded *through* space, it seems odd that we have yet to fully embrace the idea of space being folded *through* time.

Breaking with topography?

The nearest equivalent in spatial terms, to my mind, is where proximity and distance play across one another to potentially draw some actors closer whilst distancing others. Space, when conceived in this manner, disrupts our sense of what is near and what is far by eliding notions of physical and social proximity. That sense of disruption to the near/far relationship is, of course, the focus of the much quoted conversation between Latour and Michel Serres (1995) which, by means of a handkerchief analogy, tries to evoke a landscape of rifts and folds precisely to break with existing topographical vocabularies (see Latham, 2002; Murdoch, 1998, 2006). In an explicit attempt to change the conversation around space and time, Serres presents the case for topology through the analogy of the crumpled surfaces of a handkerchief which, once folded and stuffed into our pocket, resembles a landscape that is no longer flat but distorted in ways that alter how we think about what is nearby and what is far off. If the flat, well ironed surfaces of a handkerchief stand in, as it were, for a geometric landscape of fixed distances and well defined proximities, the fabric itself, when folded, draws together weaves of cloth previously held apart and vice versa. Weaves that were once close are now distant from one another and, conversely, points previously at separate ends of the handkerchief are now in contact.

The apparent simplicity of the analogy is clearly a large part of its appeal, tempting others to think about separation, proximity and distance in a non-metric register, in much the same way that Leach talked about space and time as an elastic sheet, the edges of which, when pulled together, juxtaposed new worlds. Such analogies are enticing for the promise that they hold out for talking about space and time differently; that is, topologically. They evoke a landscape where the far-reaching powers of the state or supranational institution become graspable, yet – and this is the rub – only, it would seem, through the idea of a surface that folds backwards on itself. By their very nature, the initial premises of such analogies are topographical; the folding that is done consists of creases or bends in flat surfaces, where something like the institutional reach of a global authority remains by and large extensive. If not measurable in terms of miles and kilometres, the extended nature of that authority is still best understood in terms of its length, range and scope. Topography remains the default option. Or rather, the geometry of that power still seems the most reliable way to make sense of a spatial fold, even though the establishment of proximities over distance and the creation of distances through proximity have little to do with such a world of flat shapes and surfaces.

It does not have to be like that, of course, and in the same set of conversations Serres goes on to talk about topology in a manner that eschews such an interpretation. The ability to capture the turbulence in social relationships by tracing their movement and fluctuation seems to hold the centre ground for him, with the metaphors of fluidity and fire preferred over those of stretching and folding relations. A key allusion, for example, is to the ability of flames abruptly to send up great shoots, for them to join together, then fragment and die down just as quickly, so that the outline motion, as I understand it, is one of relationships cresting and falling the very next moment in some kind of ongoing pattern of turbulence:

> Look at how the flames dance, where they go, from whence they come, towards what emptiness they head, how they become fragmented and then

join together or die out. Both fluctuating and dancing, this sheet of flames traces relations. This is an illuminating metaphor, if I may say so, for understanding what I have in view – this continuing and fragmented topological variety, which outlines crests, which can shoot high and go out in a moment. The flames trace and compose these relations.

(Serres, 1995, 108–109)

The motion of the flames, as such, traces the line of the relationships as they constantly shift, together with their ill-defined edges, evoking a different way to understand the distorted shapes and juxtapositions of topological space. Indeed, Law and Mol (2001, see also Mol and Law, 1994), again with the help of Gaston Bachelard, explicitly draw upon such illuminating metaphors to sketch a number of possible ways in which connecting ties can be held together despite objects changing in both shape and character, in part, I suspect, to avoid backsliding into a portrayal of movements that can be mapped in simple topographic fashion.

In an attempt to capture the spatialities of globality, they invoke the fluidity of social relationships to emphasize the perpetual trickle of gradual changes, and that of fire to convey the abrupt, discontinuous movements involved. A flicker, an oscillation between the local and the global, where much of what is present is dependent upon absent 'elsewheres', forms part of what they term 'fire space', in contrast to the gradual, incremental movements of the naturally more flowing 'fluid space'. The intent, it would seem, is as mentioned earlier to capture the continuity of something that changes over time, or rather, in the language of topology, to convey how some things stay the same despite distortion, which in this case refers to the transformational or changing nature of the objects that circulate. If all this sounds quite colourful, complex, baroque even, then that is precisely what Law and Mol wish to get across. The heterogeneity out there is real enough and equally elusive to our grasp, especially when such globality itself does not assume the perceived rigidities of geometric shapes that take their cue from the clear-cut coordinates of Cartesian space. If the global is already included in the local, then, as mentioned at the start of the chapter, it is important to break with a vocabulary that no longer fits the bill. The employment of a new set of metaphors that enables us to see something differently or in a new light is precisely what we need to change the way that we talk about space and time.

But that does not give us a licence to come up with just any spatial redescription that challenges an easy geometry. It is one thing to multiply spatial metaphors that illuminate stability and movement, like those of fluid and fire space, to obtain some traction on what a topological account of globality might look and feel like, but quite another to continually reinvent the nature of topology. Rubber sheeting and, as it happens, handkerchiefs may not be judged serious attempts to grapple with the subtlety of spaces that cannot be defined by their metric surfaces and connections, but they do have the advantage of returning us to a vocabulary of twists and folds that has a central place in the mathematical roots of topology. There are, as noted in the opening chapter, inherent difficulties in borrowing a language from one discipline area and imposing it on another, but space and spatiality are a shared concern of certain branches of mathematics and geography, and for that very reason experimenting with metaphorical redescriptions of space, time and power should, I would have thought, fall within the ambit of that legacy. Talk of flickering or fluid spaces may prove persuasive for some, but not, it seems to me, where the aim is to explore the eye-opening possibilities that topology has to offer.

Lost in familiar spaces

If, as argued earlier in this chapter, Brenner, Elden and Sassen all push up against the limits of conventional geometric thinking in their efforts to account for the shifting landscape of power and authority, and Latour comes close to the topological disassembling the topography in his work, then Law and Mol, in their attempt to embrace topology, seem to lose sight of what is customary to it. They seem perfectly aware that landscapes are not flattened by what circulates across them or by the lines of connection drawn, yet rather than engage with what topology has to offer in terms of spatial insights, they choose to transcend them, focusing instead on the temporal dimension of continuity and change. In truth, this may well be because they are also only too aware that talk of bending, folding or stretching space is caught up in an older, topographical sense of those words which makes it just that much harder to shift the meaning. As novel as the 'folding' of the global into the local may sound, it is all too easy to imagine it as activity at a more expansive geographical scale having a direct impact on what happens closer to home. Likewise, the 'stretching' of relations of power and authority from 'here to there' is easily understood as extended lines that criss-cross the globe in some defined fashion. But if we want to cast something familiar in a new light then, as Rorty stressed, we have to use familiar words in new ways as a means of making us grasp things differently.

Rob Shields (2013) in *Spatial Questions* is well aware of such a challenge. In an explicitly topological text, he makes the case for a 'cultural' topology that foregrounds everyday life as a 'knotting of topologies that entwine local with the global, present with past and future' (2013, 158), without losing sight of its continuous flux. Yet, in his laudable quest to go beyond topology as a metaphorical appropriation, the topology that emerges from his account of its history and development tends to fall back on the borrowed vocabulary of mathematics itself, as if the language of topological neighbourhoods, nested manifolds and the knotting of spaces is transparent in its implications for engaging social and spatial questions. Rather than familiar words being used in new ways, an untranslated vocabulary is lifted from its topological roots and made to appear even less familiar. Whilst a fidelity to borrowed terms is certainly important, so too is a recognition that borrowed vocabularies require translation. Shields it seems has little problem breaking with topography, but has more difficulty in showing how a topological sensibility goes beyond scale and networks (see also Shields, 2012).

Let me be clear, this is not simply to argue that we should eschew territorial or networked understandings of power in favour of a topological interpretation. All, as I mentioned before, have their place in an understanding of power's geo-graphies, and much depends, as Shields reminds us, on the actual questions asked about power and its institutional settings. But I do think territorial and networked approaches have often been found wanting, mainly in respect of trying to account for too much, whether that be in terms of losing sight of what is and what is not an appropriate object of study, or by addressing questions that challenge the very geometric assumptions that such approaches, often unwittingly, rest upon.

Oddly, it seems that the very familiarity of our topographical bearings either masks the significance of the more prosaic topological nature of many routine exchanges practised by 'global' corporations, 'extended' government authorities and 'far-reaching' social movements, or it prompts a rejection of all that has gone before in favour of a pick 'n' mix selection of spatial metaphors. The importance of rethinking our bearings has little to do with the break itself and more to do with the fact that the language we often use to capture new developments is itself part of the same vocabulary that makes such a break with the habit of spatial geometry unlikely. Topology, in that respect, represents an opportunity for us to think again about what it actually means to say that events elsewhere are enfolded or woven into the political fabric of daily life, or how it is that actors are able to make their presence felt in more or less powerful ways that cut across proximity and distance, without, that is, falling back upon the comforts of a more elaborate topography of power or embracing the novelty of a nice line in metaphor.

3

POWER'S SHIFTING REACH

A topological distortion

If, when we talk about the stretching or twisting of relationships of power and authority, the tendency is to interpret them through the lens of topography, not topology, I suspect that is because such spatial metaphors are often seen as just that: an imaginative use of words, but at root mere decoration. The ornamental or heuristic function of metaphor has a long history of use, especially in literature and poetry, but that is not what is at stake here. As familiar as the idea of stretching an elastic rubber sheet or folding a handkerchief may be, the *process* of stretching or distorting something has a specific role in the mathematics of shapes and surfaces. In this and the next chapter, I want to give that role a new purpose, indeed to recast the process of spatial distortion and transformation in ways that I fancy would cause a mathematically minded topologist to raise an eyebrow or two. But I do think that we would share some common ground, not least an agreed starting point.

Topologists of a mathematical bent are content to twist and turn one shape into another, for instance, a rubber inner tube into a Klein bottle, so long as the end product is related in the same manner as the original (Barr, 1964; Gay, 2007). My interest runs directly parallel to that – for example, how the same relationship of power can be stretched or folded through time, yet what starts out, say, as an intentional act of authority may register as manipulation for those on the receiving end. In both cases, how certain *relations* reproduce themselves, yet change through the *process* of spatial distortion, is the prime interest.

Crucially, what matters for all concerned is not the actual shape and size of the things undergoing distortion, or indeed their length and breadth, as much as the effect that stretching or folding them has upon the ways in which such relations reproduce themselves differently through the one-to-one process of transformation. The process of distortion, as such, effects a transformation that owes nothing to the metrics involved. The physical distances between the points on a curve, or between powerful forces and those on the receiving end, do not indicate either their proximity or their separation. Neither proximity nor reach is given; they are part and parcel of what it takes for, say, the state to stretch or reach into our lives, to make its presence felt in a pervasive way, or for the likes of an NGO to fold in far-off injustices to mobilize a local campaign by reaching out selectively to distant harms. As we shall see, when the focus turns to how power relationships *compose* the distances enacted to place certain possibilities within reach, we are no longer in a landscape where the lines of control and constraint can be simply mapped by extension over a level surface, or the connections understood topographically.

Having said that, it is not altogether clear exactly what kind of landscape we find ourselves within when distant actors are, for instance, able to make their presence felt, more-or-less directly, by dissolving, not traversing, the gap between 'here' and 'there'. This, to all intents and purposes, is unfamiliar territory where power quite evidently does not come with its usual surface inscriptions or locational bearings. Inasmuch as it takes a leap of imagination to assume that the glass of a Klein bottle can be stretched and folded much like the rubber of a tyre's inner tube, it takes a certain jolt of the imagination to accept that relationships of power may be transformed through space and time as they are folded in or out on themselves. With the more defined positional and extended capabilities of customary power-geometries, we can pinpoint both their location and potential, but when power is understood topologically we lose much of the reassurance that comes with knowing where we think we can find it and what it may do. What we gain, I would argue, is a better grasp of how power is practised; that is, the manner in which it is exercised when *space is folded or stretched through time* to gain advantage. Such power-topologies, to my mind, are likely to come into view when the reach of actors jolts our understanding of what is near and what is far through, say, the practices of arms-length manipulation or the indirect leverage of authority and influence.

Of course, I cannot promise such a jolt, although in this chapter I hope that the redescription of the way that power works topologically acts as a spur of some kind. I start by contrasting two kinds of spatialized power, one based on geometry, the other topological, with the aim of recasting proximity, presence and distance in a more composed, topological fashion. Such a recasting also leads me to shape anew what it means to fold, stretch or distort a relationship of power through time to gain advantage. Finally, I try to show how such processes of spatial distortion enable centralized authorities and the like to reach topologically into local bodies and people's lives to get them to do things that they would otherwise not have done.

Before that, though, we need to be clear about the difference between power-geometries and power-topologies.

More to power than geometry

There is, as I have suggested, something reassuring about a geometry of power, yet that comfort seems to evaporate quickly when topology enters the picture. In part, that is because in the more-or-less bounded landscapes that I spoke about in Chapter 2, it is relatively straightforward to identify the centres of power through their concentration of resources and influence in what is effectively an uneven and unequal landscape. The location of such centres, at the heart of a given territory, may represent the apex of political or economic decision making or the very 'seat' of government, and as such we can draw confidence from knowing exactly what is in front of us and where it is to be found. But, as noted before, this spatial geometry can be something of a caricature, even though it does provide a useful shorthand for identifying blocs of power and figures of authority and influence in the context of an unequal geography of power.

It is the fact of this unequal geography that lies behind the kind of spatialized power that Doreen Massey has set out in recent decades, namely that of *power-geometries*. The notion of power-geometry was first outlined as a response to David Harvey's (1989) account of time–space compression and its perceived lack of differentiation in terms of those able to take advantage of the promised mobilities on offer and those effectively trapped by them. For Massey (1993), it was an opportunity for her to spell out what has now become a staple truth of the geography of the powerful and the powerless: that social groups and individuals are positioned differently in relation to their ability to move and circulate freely around the globe. Overcoming the barriers of distances is not open to all on an equal basis. More than that, some groups are in a position to take charge of the process, to initiate flows and movements, whilst others find themselves on the receiving end of such capabilities. There is an evident zero-sum geography to all this, with the relations of domination and subordination mapped onto a very uneven and unequal landscape.

In Massey's (2005, 2007) later work, it is not just social groups and individuals that occupy distinct positions within this unjust landscape, so too do places, institutions and authorities, each differentially located within a wider set of global power-geometries. The potential leverage and purchase that some places have in the global landscape is mirrored by those that lack the power to defend themselves from the inequities and injustices of globalization. There is a divide, which, although not absolute in itself, can be drawn broadly between those places that have the capability to secure outcomes in their favour by virtue of their position within a wider set of global interconnections, and those that possess little or no such ability to frame events. The located and extended capabilities of the former represent something akin to a veiled power, one that has the potential to take charge of the process of globalization and turn it to their advantage, much like the patterns of mobility mentioned before. One could view, as indeed Massey (2007) does, the power of the City of London in this way, and not only the ability of its financial institutions to grasp the lion's share of economic gains in the wider economy, but also their capacity to set down the rules of the game by which their dominance is secured and reproduced.

Or rather, with the benefit of hindsight, it is possible to chart the powerful manoeuvres that led to such an outcome. For what is portrayed here is a *latent* geometry of power, one whose shape and size in terms of the City's capabilities has the potential to place limits upon what is and what is not possible in the wider economy as a whole. As such, it tells us more about what institutional blocs of power like the City of London 'could do', given how well positioned they are to exert potential leverage over the political and economic landscape around them, but rather less about what they actually do; that is, how they respond and adjust to the contingency of events that confronts them. This is a more open question and one that cannot simply be 'read off' from a summation of all the capabilities in play or the concentration of resources at their disposal.

For that, we need to move beyond a simple geometry of located and extended capabilities to address the topological workings of power; that is, how power relationships are *mediated* through events, technologies and practices that enable them to be stretched, folded or twisted in such a way as to transcend a landscape of fixed distances and well defined proximities.

The difference that space makes

If Massey works with an explicit geometry of power, then somewhat disconcertingly her understanding of space and spatiality is often closer to that of topology, especially when it comes to a sense of space as surface (Massey, 2005, 2011). Despite her positional grasp of power, the world as she conceives it, or rather the spaces that comprise it, are understood as an ongoing product of social relationships, exchanges and interactions, rather than anything flat or horizontal which can be measured or crossed. There is, for her, a dynamism to the landscape across which the most powerful take charge of events, which cannot be accounted for by static lines of connection. This understanding moves her away from a straightforward geometry of spatial relationships towards one where space itself can be seen to make a difference to the way in which power works. Massey, though, does not take that extra step, despite her obvious inclination to do so. Such a step foregrounds what social groups, institutions, and authorities actually do 'out there', so to speak. On this view, how they practise power matters more than any inscribed capabilities, for the simple reason that outcomes are mediated relationally; that is, subject to the interplay of forces to be found in diverse settings which often play across one another.

Resources and decision-making abilities may well be concentrated in particular locations and places, in the HQs of financial institutions or at the seat of government, but this does not imply that power itself is centralized and only to be found at those sites. How actors *use* the resources and abilities at their disposal is, arguably, what matters most when power is understood as inherently spatial and subject to the contingencies of events and relationships, some of which may lie outside the immediate 'here' and 'now'. Both resources and abilities, when considered in practical terms, may be misused, wasted or applied to little effect; situations change, open up in unpredictable ways, and alter the ongoing course of events; what works in one context may fail in another or is only partially effective, and so on. The expediency of actors, the practice of manipulating wills at arm's length, or attempts to hold authority in place despite being stretched, for instance, lend themselves to more mutable, cross-cutting arrangements of power that cannot be fully subsumed under a spatial geometry that assumes size is all or that position matters above all else.

This takes us closer to the difference that space makes: namely, the importance of grasping that power is brought to bear in more ways than one and that space and spatiality make a difference to the way that power plays work themselves out. In contrast to Massey's zero-sum geography, the authority of 'centres' such as the banking and financial institutions of the City of London may be compromised by their dealings, not so much by a bloc of resistance as by other financial and political actors negotiating their own interests from afar, or by drawing within close reach those who are able to broker decisions in their favour. There is no spatial template to such exchanges, which suggests that centralized authority may be won or lost when exercised close up or indirectly from afar, only a landscape of power mediated by diverse groups of actors at various points of interaction.

Staying with the City, for example, what may start out as an authoritative position by one of its core investment institutions, say a bank's exposure to trading risk, may well be manipulated by others down the line to conceal their actual intentions or selectively to restrict the kinds of information flowing from the centre in order to balance their interests. As financial intermediaries, traders as well as brokers, for example, may exploit information asymmetries to their advantage so that the end point registers for the outside world as a rather different act of power from that of the original intention. Of course, this set of exchanges could be interpreted along the lines of Latour's (2005) mediated account of power outlined in the previous chapter, where networked interaction reaches out beyond itself. But, crucially, the issue is not one about the enrolment or construction of a single will, but rather its displacement through the concealment of intent. Moreover, if spatiality is to count at all in this mediated exercise, it is not so much the differently positioned actors who transform the power relationship from one of authority to one of manipulation, but rather the spatial twists and turns that enable the actual concealment to take place.

I am mindful of the fact that I have just dropped what could be seen as a spatial metaphor into the conversation, using a familiar turn of phrase, spatial twists and turns, to introduce a topological dimension. It is a Rorty-style gesture, but one with a serious intent which introduces the process of *spatial distortion* into the picture, one that rests upon a set of topological figures that are pretty much alien to geography, even though their spatial implications are not. In order to fully appreciate the difference between power-topologies and power-geometries, it may be helpful to look more closely at some of the figures that underpin a topological redescription of power and the role that spatial distortion plays.

Spatial twists and turns

No recasting of topology, it seems, can avoid introducing some of the iconic figures that hold sway in conventional mathematical topology. I mention just two here, the Möbius strip and the Klein bottle, for no other reason than that they have some bearing on the activities of the financial intermediaries just outlined. As is perhaps well known, we have August Möbius, a nineteenth-century German mathematician, to thank for the construction of a strip or band of paper that possesses only one side, even though to all intents and purposes it appears to be a two-sided figure. If this sounds odd, it is actually easier to demonstrate.

First of all, you need to take a strip of paper and give it a half twist (see Figure 3.1). Then, if you join the two ends together to make a loop, what you have in your hands is an object that seemingly jars with our understanding: you have a strip with one continuous surface, a one-sided band. It may look as if it has two sides, but if you trace your finger over the length of the band's surface it will return to the exact same spot where you started. The band has only one side, yet it also possible to place your thumb and forefinger at points on either side of the band. It is, as Rosen (1997, 2006) pointed out, both one-sided and two-sided in the paradoxical sense that what is seemingly impossible is possible.

For our purposes, what is of interest is that the two separate points on opposing sides of the band, whilst *different*, turn out to be *related* when the strip is taken as a whole. By giving the stretched relationship a half twist, the two corresponding points form part of a single continuous space. The latter manoeuvre, the twist itself, brings the two points into relation without losing what is distinctive to each. Now transpose that manoeuvre to the City of London example and what you have is a one-sided, continuous relationship of power, exercised by the likes of banks, brokers and other financial intermediaries in the City of London, that is transformed into a two-sided relationship as authority mutates into manipulation. In this topological setting, mediating professionals may draw upon a range of organisational and technological resources to displace authority or renegotiate the terms of a deal set down by their institution, yet remain part of the same relational arrangement. Institutional power, on this view, is mediated through technologies and practices that enable relationships to be stretched and twisted in such a way that one register of power is transformed into another without an actual break in the relationship. The Möbius-style stretching and twisting of the spaces involved effectively enables such a transformation of power relations to take place.

I say Möbius-style, but that is not to suggest some kind of analogy or modelling function, rather it is to convey the actual processes of spatial distortion involved. The point is not simply one of fidelity to the vocabulary of topology, but rather to the processes of stretching and twisting that are capable of transforming relationships of power over space and time, that is, between 'here' and 'there'. The paradoxical two-sidedness of the Möbius strip, in that sense, conveys a mediated power relation

FIGURE 3.1 Möbius strip

that reproduces itself differently. It also illustrates the possibility for register of powers to play across or run alongside one another, but that is to jump ahead of ourselves. Perhaps more familiar is the use of the Möbius strip to show how an apparently two-sided figure can mask what is in effect a continuous exchange between what happens internally and what takes place on the outside of an institution or social body.

We know this intuitively when we speak about the power of places such as the City of London as inextricably 'bound up' with external events elsewhere across the globe but, as argued earlier, simply pointing to external connections or net-worked relations is not the same as spelling out what is especially topological about them. In *World City*, for instance, Massey is explicit about the interdependence of places and the fact that the City of London is, as mentioned, positioned within a wider set of global connections. Linked places, she contends, occupy different positions within the wider power-geometries of neoliberal globalization. Indeed, she goes beyond the idea that the fortunes of places are merely linked to recognize that, in terms of a formative politics between places, it is possible not only to entertain the view that an 'outside can be found within', but also 'an inside that lies beyond' (Massey 2007, 93). Yet she stops short of reading places and power topologically, perhaps because her geometry of power only really works when it is understood as a capability that is produced between places, not as a series of practices mediated *through* them.

If she had gone further, then intriguingly the kinds of spatial distortion she invokes would actually have taken her closer to another topological figure: that of the Klein bottle, named after Felix Klein, another nineteenth-century German mathematician. For what she appears to be suggesting is an interpenetration of spaces, rather than merely an exchange between a place and its external surround-ings, and the spatial manoeuvres represented by the Klein bottle offer just that. The Klein bottle is a superimposed variation of a two-sided Möbius strip, and to represent it we have to fall back on a notion of surface that Massey herself would have doubts about. If this sounds a little abstruse, there is no easy way to put a Klein bottle in your hands and trace the folded relationships involved with your fingers. It takes a certain leap of the imagination to visualize the spaces involved and a break with simple topography.

Imagine a piece of elastic rubber sheeting, of the kind that Leach spoke about, which has been stretched out to form a cylindrical shape (a rubber inner tube vertically cut in two would fit the bill), with one end narrowed like the neck of a bottle and the other flattened into a base (see Figure 3.2). If you take the narrow end and fold it through the body of the tube, then flare it out to connect it to the base end, you have transformed a rubber tube into a Klein bottle. Effectively, the tube has been folded through itself to form a continuous one-sided surface, much like the Möbius strip, but unlike that figure the Klein bottle has no inside or out-side, no boundary line to distinguish one from the other. By stretching and folding the figure through itself, it penetrates itself: the inside has been folded in on itself to merge with the outside surface. Or, as Rosen rather challengingly puts it, 'rather than being contained in space, the Klein bottle may be said to contain itself' (2006, 34).

FIGURE 3.2 Klein bottle

Again, for our purposes, what is of interest is that although the figure has been transformed, there is no way of discerning Massey's 'inside that lies beyond' from an outside found within. By folding, not twisting, the stretched relationship, the single continuous space is 'bound up' with itself, in much the same way that the notion of places as 'bound up' with one another means precisely that – not linked together or merely brought into contact, but co-extensive with the presence of others acting elsewhere. This may take the form of a simultaneous presence established through real-time technologies, or one whose presence is forged through a kind of arms-length reach into financial centres such as London, but either way there is more to the relation than simply a surface connection or spatial tie. The sense in which institutions in financial centres are able to draw upon organizational resources to fold in others distant in space and time in order to exert leverage is itself a topological practice. The fact is that, when relationships of power are folded in like this, or rather enfolded, the actors involved may be more-or-less present in the here-and-now of mediated interaction. They may lack a physical presence in distance terms, but they are co-present in whatever power arrangement is taking shape.

More to the point, our familiarity with such co-present relationships belies the break with a world of flat shapes and surfaces that they actually represent. The man-oeuvre, the folding in of others distant in space and time, does not involve the folding *over* of a flat surface, as the folded handkerchief analogy mentioned in Chapter 2 depicts, but rather a set of spatial relationships folded *through* time. Whereas the former falls back upon a topographical interpretation of folds and stretches in order to make sense of them, the latter can be gleaned only if we suspend disbelief in the idea that a powerful presence can be achieved only by it being exercised over mappable distances. That idea, however, as stressed in Chapter 2, has a particular hold on our imagination: one that relies for much of its tenacity on the assumption that space is merely 'out there', where power is conceived geo-metrically as the result of extensive interaction. Once that assumption is relaxed, though, and the idea entertained that space may actually be composed by the relationships of which it is a part, the notion of intensive, as opposed to extensive, reach to others physically distant comes to the fore.

Intensive relationships of power

The sense in which powers are not so much located in space as inseparable from its composition is a distinctive feature of power-topologies. Massey, as we have seen, shares a compositional view of space and spatiality, yet when she sets out her positional stall on power she seems unable to see spatiality as itself imbued with power relationships – as something that composes the distances between the powerful and the powerless. The folded arrangements of power, those that enable distant actors to make their presence felt despite being physically absent, do not make an appearance in Massey's power-geometries. Nor, in consequence, does the idea that power relations themselves can take an intensive, as opposed to extensive, form where the barriers of distance do not necessarily dilute its potency or reach.

Intensity is all about focus and concentration, so when the intensive reach of governments or financial corporations is to the fore, the more familiar extensive arrangements of power, in the form of devolved bureaucracy, for example, fill in much of the diffuse landscape. Intensive and extensive, in that regard, are just two different ways of talking about power and space. Yet the familiarity of the latter can have the effect of *masking* the significance of the former. In much the same way that topographical bearings can mask the more prosaic topological nature of power relations, so too can the customary outward extension of power mask the kinds of topological reach that cannot be drawn on maps.

Perhaps this is best grasped if, first, we consider the often assumed trade-off between the extensiveness of power and its intensity, where the greater the distance over which power is extended, the more diffuse it is thought to become in terms of effectiveness.

Power trade-offs?

There is something intuitive about the idea that power lessens, that it becomes more diffuse, as it spreads outwards from a central point, be it the apex of a government hierarchy or a military HQ. In the 1960s and 1970s, Dennis Wrong, and others before him such as Robert Dahl (1961 [1974]), were keen to chart the nature of the trade-off between intensive and extensive powers. In doing so, they followed a well trodden path that assumed that control and influence naturally diminished in line with their extension over greater numbers across ever-expanding territories. Analytical in style, Wrong (1979 [1997]) spoke in terms of power-holders, chains of command, and the loss of control and compliance as the ratio of the number of people who held power over the powerless increased. The imagery recalls that of the boxed-in power highlighted in Chapter 2, although now with a clear emphasis upon the loss of concentration or intensity as authority and influence seep outwards across the landscape.

The concentration and intensity of power tend to work as synonyms in this context, drawing their meaning from either the density of the forces exercised or the types of power invoked. Both sets of meaning are present in the work of Michael Mann, whose fourfold depiction of power (re)sources – economic, political, military and ideological – was introduced in Chapter 2. Following Wrong, Mann implicitly acknowledges a trade-off between intensive and extensive powers, but he adds the recognition that such a trade-off works itself out differently in each of the types of power identified. Moreover, he argues that any one type of power is at its most effective when it combines intensive and extensive organizational means to achieve its goals.

So military power, for instance, is regarded by Mann as intensive in terms of its ability to tightly control those under its command through a form of 'concentrated-coercion', yet it also possesses a capacity for extensive strike power, of which none is more stark than that of drone warfare today (see Gregory, 2014). Likewise, economic power is said to blend the extensive power of global markets and trade networks with intensive control over the lives of working people. Indeed, in the final of the four-volume *The Sources of Social Power* (Mann, 2013), this combination is taken to new heights by Mann, with globalization believed to have deepened and broadened economic power structures as capitalism has spread to the far corners of the globe.

Throughout his voluminous writings on power resources, however, Mann has consistently subsumed each of the four types of power under two different power arrangements: one authoritative, the other diffuse in style. Authoritative power, as the term implies, takes its organizational shape from direct, centralized lines of authority and is considered typical of the way military and political power is organized. It is characterized as tightly orchestrated and concentrated in focus. In contrast, diffuse power is precisely that: indirect and dispersed in the manner of its execution. Its organizational means is loose and decentred, and is assumed to lend itself to the way in which economic and ideological power is organized. Not surprisingly, perhaps, the two arrangements bear more than a passing resemblance to extensive and intensive forms of power, in that extensive power is largely diffuse and intensive power is predominantly authoritative. In fact, they seem to operate more-or-less as a default position for Mann, although whether that was his intention remains unclear. Regardless, the result is a rather easy geometry of power that fits in with his taxonomic style of thinking, where the different resourceful powers fall into neat typological arrangements.

The difficulty with this position is that it makes it hard to envisage a situation where the concentration and reach of power are not involved in some form of trade-off. Any means of power that is focused or targeted is broadly assumed to have its intensity curbed over greater distances. There is no reason, however, why this should necessarily be the case, especially when attention turns to the exercise of power rather than the resources that support such practices. As stressed earlier, how actors use the resources at their disposal matters more than whether such resources are centralized or not. Political power, for instance, may be authoritative and centralized, as is often the case, but its authority, even its ability to coerce, may be exercised intensively, in a direct, more focused manner. Intensive authority, as we shall see, is relational not measurable in respect of its distribution; its reach can be more-or-less stretched depending upon the political ends sought.

Governments exercise both extensive and intensive reach in respect of their powers, but it is only the former that is readily affected by quantitative changes in the numbers governed and at what distances. The intensive reach of governments, the directness of their presence, by way of contrast, turns on more qualitative changes in its execution: on the mediated exercises of power which enable spatial relationships to be folded in such a way that, say, government authority can be made proximate, even though the officials themselves are distant in both space and time, or domination may be practised in real time, despite the physical distances that separate the parties involved. The two together, the extensive and intensive reach of governments, arguably goes some way to account for the more tangled arrangements of state power that have recently taken shape and forced a redescription of sorts, outlined in Chapter 2.

That the state's pervasive reach can be matched by its intensity should, perhaps, be of little surprise, yet the frequent conflation of concentration with the centralization of power can occlude its exercise. An extensive landscape of power that is already 'out there', with its recognizable scales and lines of connection, has the potential to mask the less familiar, the less intuitive. When understood topologically, however, distance has little or no part to play in the trade-off between the concentration and reach of power, and that, principally, is because the conventional metrics that spell out the distances at which power is assumed to be effective, or the size of resources required to have an impact, come into play only when power is conceived as a capability extended or distributed over space. When, however, it is conceived as a set of relationships that *compose* the distances enacted to place others within or beyond reach, it is the intensive nature of power relationships that takes centre stage.

We have Gilles Deleuze's *Difference and Repetition* (1994) to thank for drawing attention to the distinction between intensive and extensive differences, although you do not have to be a Deleuzian to appreciate that a key aspect of the distinction, as indicated, is that the intensive quality of something, a targeted act of power, for instance, does not alter when its size or shape changes. The force itself retains its concentration, its focus, whereas a marshalled capability is diminished when overstretched. Again, the distinction turns on the metrics involved: a change in the mass of resources mobilized, an increase in the numbers of people governed or in the expanse of territory taken under control, may diminish an effective extensive capability. When actors are able to make their presence felt close up at a distance in an intensive manner, however, no such loss of force or influence may be registered. The intensity and force of the power relations remains undiminished and that is because distance itself is conceived as a *relation*, not a metric.

Distance as a relation

Earlier, I spoke about power as a set of relationships which compose the distances enacted to place others within or beyond reach. When distance is understood as a relation like this, it is the relationships themselves that create the distance between things, not anything measurable. It recalls the sense of disruption or distortion to what is near and what is far that Latour and Serres' folded handkerchief analogy demonstrated, although now without the topographical baggage that their argument entailed. Having put that baggage to one side, it is possible to grasp that distortion as one produced through intensive relationships of power – relationships that are capable of establishing social proximities over physical distances and creating social distances through physical proximity. When things can be made proximate or distant like this, then that is precisely what it means to loosen defined times and distances.

By the use of the term 'made' in this context, all I wish to convey is that relationships, power relationships in this case, compose the spaces of which they are part; that is, they routinely reconfigure the gap between 'here' and 'there' to enable actors to make their presence felt. If this sounds a little like a throw-away line, having expressed it on more than one occasion, let's consider in a little more depth the kind of authoritative acts that Mann thought typical.

The key thing to note is that an act of authority, whether exercised on the basis of impersonal rules or acknowledged expertise, is effective only insofar as it is able to secure assent. In any of the types of organization that Mann listed, be they political, military or otherwise, authority turns on the question of recognition. Others comply because they acknowledge the right or the competence of those 'in' authority. Without such recognition, the relationship breaks down, and any semblance of authority with it. Authority's constant need for recognition, however, also carries with it certain spatial implications; not so much in terms of spatial proximity as of spatial *presence*. The more direct the presence of authority, the more intense its impact or force. A direct social presence may be achieved through face-to-face interaction, but it can also be made proximate by powerful institutions exercising arm's-length reach into the lives of those bound by its authority. Relational proximity, in such a context, is thus just as important, if not more so, than physical proximity. It gives meaning to the idea that distance is more than simply a set of calibrations concerned with length and extensiveness.

Referring to proximity and distance as relational, however, does not make a focused act of authority topological in and of itself. Authority may take a relational form, but for that relationship to be established directly at a distance requires certain topological processes to make it so. It takes us back to a point made earlier, about financial centres such as London, that for actors to be more-or-less present in the here-and-now of mediated interaction, to be co-extensive with the presence of others acting elsewhere, requires them to draw upon organizational resources to fold in others distant in space and time. Authority does not fold by itself, nor does it take it upon itself to stretch; rather it is transformed into a direct or indirect relationship by actors exerting *leverage* through such processes. The significance of topology in this respect is that such manoeuvres enable both the reproduction of power relationships through space and time, and the potential transformation of their intensity.

Mann, I suspect, would not approve of playing fast and loose with authority in this manner, either analytically or spatially. If authoritative power takes its shapes from direct, centralized lines of control, then its organizational reach is pretty much fixed in that mould. There is little wiggle-room, it seems, to adjust the account, even for new or novel circumstances. Once topology is introduced into the picture, however, other analytical and spatial possibilities open up, with the potential to disturb such neat thinking.

Chief among those possibilities is the fact that, in topological settings, the reach of authority is far from fixed. Authoritative power, when mediated through technologies and practices that enable relationships of assent to be stretched and folded, open up different ways of establishing a more-or-less direct presence. The use of real-time technologies to create a simultaneous presence in diverse settings is, for instance, just one way in which relations of presence and absence can be reconfigured so that the gap between 'here' and 'there' is bridged relationally. Another, less immediate, way to traverse the gap is to reach out to a dispersed population through a succession of 'authoritative' practices that mediate negotiation and assent. Both possibilities owe little to the shape and size of an actor's capabilities, or their inscribed position for that matter, and rely more upon what works to hold authority in place, despite being stretched across ever greater distances, or what enables it to be exercised close up at a distance.

Moreover, the mediated workings of power also draw attention to the topological processes through which relationships of authority not only may be held in place, but also may be subject to change and transformation. As we saw in the case of financial intermediaries earlier, and as would arguably be the case for other forms of mediated authority in the political and economic sphere, organizational and technological resources can be drawn upon to heighten intensity or to displace it. The former amounts to a transformation in the way that an authority's presence is registered, involving matters of degree, but the latter amounts to a change in the relationship itself, to a register of power other than that of authority. In such relational arrangements where, for instance, the inability to secure assent draws authority into question, the initial act of authority may mutate into a promise of inducement or fall back upon manipulative devices as a means of achieving consent. There is no easy geometry to any of this, no extensive mapping of figures across space, only a diagrammatic feel for reach and transformation.

Diagrammatic, that is, in the sense that intensive relations of power and authority are co-extensive with the mediated exchanges that compose the spaces of interaction. If that sounds a bit like a mouthful of words, in practice it comes down to the relationships themselves actually filling out the space, much in the same way that the Klein bottle was seen to contain itself. In a topological world, the notion of 'distant powers' or of a 'far-reaching authority' is complicated by the mediated relations which draw different groups, decision makers and institutions into a space of their own making. Authority and leverage, as such, are effectively reworked topologically so that the reach of different actors may be exercised in a variety of intensive ways to problematize what we conventionally consider 'near' and 'far'.

It is this ability to place others *within or beyond reach* to which we now turn to consider such topological possibilities.

Topological reach

'Reach' is one of those words that can mean a little or a lot. In conventional terms, the meaning of reach is fairly straightforward, in that it is tied to the extensive arrangements of power outlined earlier, where power is extended outwards, horizontally across the landscape. On this representation, the greater the distance that power is dispersed, extended horizontally from point to point, the greater its reach is assumed to be. As we have had cause to note, however, extensive reach can mask its topological counterpart. Its meaning, as for example in the case of the 'reach of government', can refer to extended lines of authority over defined territorial spaces, but it can also signify a more pervasive, intense quality where *reach is more about presence than distance*. The sense in which power can be exercised to place certain possibilities within reach, to draw others within its orbit to seek advantage, or, equally, to place certain possibilities beyond reach, speaks to the different ways in which a powerful presence may be registered topologically. Topology, in that respect, has a lot to say about both reach and presence (Allen, 2009, 2011).

At the top of that list of things to say is that presence, like reach, is not a given. Actors of whatever hue or variety have to make their presence felt, and make it felt in ways that, on the whole, retain focus. Relationships of power and authority do not, as stressed, reach out of their own volition; they are stretched and folded through time in order to register a presence. Power relationships are mediated through such topological processes and can be stretched just as easily as they can be compressed, depending upon the type of presence sought. Reach, on this understanding, is a form of relational distance – a space composed by the stretching, folding and distorting of relationships to achieve certain ends. As such, reach can be leveraged topologically in a variety of distinctive ways by cutting across proximity and distance to register a powerful presence of one particular kind or another. The quieter, more muted registers of power, increasingly prioritised by institutions and social groups alike, arguably owe much to such leverage. Before we consider such matters in the following chapter, however, it is important to be clear about how reach can be distorted topologically and the exploratory promise that holds.

Folding in reach

Earlier I suggested that a government's authority, its prescriptions and rule, could be made proximate. By that, I meant that its authority would have to be more direct, without the relationship necessarily experiencing any loss of focus. For that to happen, for central government to make its presence felt in this way, through its dealings with a wide array of public and private bodies, it would have to fold its authority in directly. There are at least two ways in which such *direct* reach may be leveraged topologically, both of which require authority to be mediated through specific technologies and practices.

The first involves the ability to draw political actors *within close reach* by establishing a broadly simultaneous presence through real- or, more accurately, shared-time technologies and embedded practices. Such a presence enables negotiations to be brokered directly, rather than from afar or across a spatial divide that places the 'centre' of political power above everyone else. The ability to broker and influence decisions directly through real-time engagements with a range of dispersed, semi-autonomous public and private agencies does not mean, of course, that the assent of such outlying agencies is guaranteed, only that such brokerage can have a significant part to play in turning 'authoritative goals' into more than pronouncements passed down from the 'centre'.

The parallels with Latour's notion of actors being 'hooked up' through some kind of successive enrolment, where the interests of others are bought into line and stabilized, are clear. Drawing others within close topological reach, however, has little to do with tracking and tracing movement and extension, and everything to do with the 'here and now' of mediated interaction. Crucially, the spacing and timing of such interaction takes place between people who, for the most part, are present in time only. Such leverage, however, is unlikely to be exercised in isolation from other means to directly establish an influential presence.

A second, more moderated means to achieve a first-hand presence is by 'lifting out' and 're-embedding' central forms of authority and expertise. This represents an alternative form of distorted reach, one that is capable of *reaching into* the politics of regional and local bodies on a different basis from that of real-time engagements. It, too, is characterized by mediated interaction with those physically absent, but the spacing and timing is different, as is the manner by which assent is sought. When government initiatives are 'detached' from the centre and 'lodged' in subnational institutions and agencies to secure compliance, authority is not so much consented to as embedded. The experience of directness is real enough, but the immediacy of the presence is mediated through those who by and large are detached; that is, present elsewhere. The effect, when successful, is to stabilize a pattern of authority at arm's length, by aligning local rulings and directives with those of the 'centre'.

What comes to the fore in this manner of delivering authority and control is the geography of political power that it illuminates; less the movement of authority delegated downwards, and rather more of an interplay between parts of central, regional and local authority 'lodged' at different sites and settings. Little really happens at a distance, on this account, because the authority of the centre has already made its detached presence felt in its dealings with the broadly dispersed officials and agencies across the formal political landscape. In opening up that authority to negotiation in a more direct fashion, there is of course always the risk that local administrative units and partnerships may reinterpret the lines of accountability or exploit any ambiguities inherent in the directives, but such risks may be reduced by a detached presence designed to seek compliance, if not agreement (Allen and Cochrane, 2007).

More significantly, it is perhaps important to note that the two ways of leveraging reach outlined, whether by drawing others within close reach to broker a political arrangement or by reaching into that arrangement, may work in tandem to secure the same outcome. The ends sought may be identical, yet the means of establishing proximate relationships of authority can draw upon quite different technologies and practices to achieve them. Topological reach is thus a malleable feast in respect of its spacing and timing.

If it is to work topologically, reach has to be leveraged through processes that actually distort the spacing and timing of the relationships involved. The ability to be more-or-less present in real-time negotiations of authority, for instance, occurs when others elsewhere are simply folded into the arrangement. The practice is commonplace, in the worlds of finance as much as government, even if the depiction of it is not. By describing the practice as a folded relationship, a single continuous Kleinian space 'bound up' with itself, as it were, all that I am drawing attention to is a *co-present* relationship that lacks physical presence. There is no particular mystery attached to co-present relationships or to the processes by which they are achieved. The *folding of space through time*, not over or by time, may sound less familiar, but it conveys one of the ways in which political and economic actors are able to make their presence felt through relations of proximity and reach.

In this heightened context, much has been made about the ability of communications and new social networking technologies to draw people together through real-time engagements. My point here, however, is a more general one about the shared experience of simultaneity as others elsewhere are drawn into the 'now' of mediated authority. The same holds for 'detached' forms of authority 'lifted out' and folded into the political interplay of central–local relations or the corporate bargaining process between scattered sites. The ability to reach into the political or economic affairs of more dispersed bodies to secure compliance may lack a real-time element, but the *detached presence* of the 'centre' ensures that they have a direct part to play in any negotiated outcomes. In that respect, the folding in of a shared presence provides a sense of 'nowness' to the arrangement that belies the physical distances between bodies.

Stretching to reach

Whilst folds may be the only topological practice recognized by the likes of Deleuze (1993, 1995), there are other topological processes by which power and authority may be made proximate. Reach, for instance, may be leveraged topologically in a less direct manner by central authorities through the exercise of decision-making practices and rulings that require the legitimacy of programmes to be acknowledged by others elsewhere. The *indirectness* of the leverage sought speaks to the stretched nature of the relationships involved. Authority in this case is stretched from 'here to there', not folded in from afar, but crucially the distances involved are not spanned in an extensive fashion. Nothing is extended over shorter or longer distances; rather the *stretching of space through time* enables a more intensive relationship of authority and obligation to take hold.

Again, the process resembles Latour's networked arrangement of well placed individuals who are in a position to 'fix' an overall orientation through the successive enrolment of others. Arguably, the ability to stretch such relationships through time is more in keeping with Latour's topological sensibilities, if only his vision of flat, extensive landscapes had not served to mask them. A misplaced vocabulary, in this instance, perhaps for the best of intentions, gave prominence to a form of stretched interaction over space and time, not one where absent others are interweaved with those present to bridge the distances involved relationally. In contrast to folded arrangements of power, when authority is stretched topologically neither space nor time is shared in any co-present or detached manner. But that does not mean to say that such relationships are any less pervasive in their reach. It is just that their reach is leveraged differently by virtue of the indirect tie-up involved.

Where, as mentioned above, a central government authority may *reach into* the politics of regions and localities by establishing a detached presence, to make themselves 'on hand', so to speak (Bulkeley, 2013), the same form of reach can also be exercised indirectly. This has less to do with bureaucratic protocols and delegated responsibilities, and more to do with the setting of priorities and incentives that percolate the culture of regional and local administrative units. The ability to steer and constrain agendas, to reach out to front-line officials through a succession of enrolling strategies, all work by attempting to write people into the scripts of the centre. Such attempts may not saturate a decision-making culture where agendas are mediated and translated for specific political ends, but they do open up the possibility of a more *intensive* arrangement of authority where reach can be stretched accordingly (Allen and Cochrane, 2010). As such, it represents a provisional means for the 'centre' to secure its outcomes at arm's length, although this time through the establishment of an absent, rather than a detached, presence.

The outcome is provisional because, in this topological setting, the highly mediated and indirect nature of the relationships involved also leaves authoritative statements exposed to reinterpretation and displacement. Insofar as all the governing bodies, from state-sponsored agencies and private agencies to local administrative units and partnerships, are part of the relational mix, the possibilities for political engagement are not only multiplied, so too is the potential for agendas to be skewed and incentives redirected in ways that may not have been fully anticipated by central authorities (Haughton et al., 2013). This is to suggest not that the political priorities of the 'centre' can be merely negotiated away, but that such priorities often require collaboration to be achieved, seemingly with an increasing diversity of actors and agencies. Indeed, in political and financial institutions alike, authority may be manipulated down the line by actors negotiating their own interests, effectively twisting institutional arrangements to their advantage without breaking the continuity of the relationships stretched to achieve a particular goal.

Whenever authority is stretched and twisted in such a manner, I perhaps should stress that this does not involve a form of horizontal reach, where power seeps away from those 'above' because it has been extended outwards. Such powers of extension are presumably evident in the standards and conventions of devolved bureaucracies. But nothing really seeps away from the more intensive arrangements of authority sketched here, because power is not so much 'up there' or indeed 'over there', but rather part of an interplay between those absent every bit as much as those who are present. Arm's length reach, in its topological sense, is about the establishment of an absent presence, not the lack of any kind of presence. When the reach of authority is stretched in this manner it begins to take on all the trappings of pervasiveness that James Ferguson and Joe Painter, following Timothy Mitchell, have spoken about so graphically.

Mitchell (1991), for one, has argued that the sense in which central government, the state and its apparatus of authority is geographically 'higher up' is itself a reification, an effect of the state's claim to spatial authority. That claim, as both Ferguson (2004, see also Ferguson and Gupta, 2002) and Painter (2006) have shown, is supported by the mundane practices of authority by which governments instantiate their spatiality and, indeed, reach. The embeddedness of registration, certification and administrative practices, for example, and the weighty impression that they convey of authority reaching down 'from above' and encompassing all in its path, masks a more precarious achievement: that of a central authority continually trying to establish its presence in a variety of different settings and sites. Whilst the insights of such authors chime with the topological description of reach outlined here, individually they stop short of its spatial and temporal implications, preferring instead, it would seem, to fall back on topography.

In that respect, the ability to leverage reach topologically, to establish a detached presence, of the kind noted earlier, or one where absent others are interleaved with those present, does not figure in their accounts of spatial authority, even if their understanding points in that direction. As such, it also makes it just that much harder for them to conceive of authority and the demands made upon it as something that could also be placed *beyond* reach.

Placing beyond reach

There is nothing particularly remarkable about the notion that some things, authority among them, can be placed within or beyond reach. If indeed governments are able to fold in their authority directly to make their presence felt, or achieve it indirectly by stretching such relationships, then it seems only plausible that such topological processes can work the other way too. What can be folded in can be folded out and, in terms of leverage, what can be drawn within reach can also be placed beyond or out of reach. They are simply two sides of the same topological equation. But again, if topological reach, as suggested, is more about presence than distance, then there is more involved than things simply disappearing over the horizon and being reliably further away.

Central government bodies, for instance, may distance themselves from the need to take particular decisions or meet particular demands on their authority by displacing them, either by pushing them further away in real time to quasi-public bodies operating at a different political 'scale', or by lifting them out and re-embedding policy pressures within a different jurisdictional framework. The spaces themselves are institutional and, although they may appear to be stacked hierarchically in geographical terms, the distances between them are relational, not physical. States, in that sense, are not simply confronted by supranational institutions or constrained by them, they can also use them and the growing range of private authorities in the international arena to *fold out* political demands. That does not imply that states can somehow avoid these pressures by adopting such spatial tactics, merely that they may establish a more direct, *displaced presence* through their use.

At most, there is an interplay of forces involved, with the different elements of central, regional and local authority responding to the actions and demands of the other, and leveraging their reach accordingly. When the political demands of one set of actors is lifted out by another and placed beyond reach, all that is really involved in topological terms is a different way of reconfiguring spatial authority so that the relational distances involved are just that much greater than before. It may sound at odds with conventional senses of displacement, but in spatial terms it amounts to the fact that the relationship between proximity and presence, in this instance, has been corrupted by the close at hand being made distant.

The same topological distortion can be achieved in other ways too, most notably by 'lengthening' the exchanges involved so that any challenges to the authority of the centre are mediated in a more circuitous manner. The more convoluted the forms of mediation, the more indirect the exchanges involved, the greater is the likelihood that demands for political arbitration or acceptance of responsibility can be placed out of reach. Again, the distances involved are relational not physical, but here leverage may be obtained by *stretching out* the exchanges between actors and multiplying the possibilities for intervention. In a topological setting, the kind of relationships that underpin a state's enactment of its authority and rule can be stretched just as readily as they can be compressed when challenged from 'below'. Responsibilities, even liabilities, may be outsourced, so to speak, to private forms of authority and effectively displaced, or perhaps even misplaced.

Such a topological manoeuvre offers a different angle on what it means to disrupt our sense of what is near and what is far, in this case by potentially eliding physical proximity with relational distance. The ability of actors to 'distance' themselves from the demands of others is a more familiar refrain, but it fails to address the reconfiguration of spatial authority that has taken place. Ferguson, and I think Painter (2008) too, have an intuitive grasp of the leverage involved, even if their topographical vocabulary is out of synch with the process itself. The rituals of spatial hierarchy and encompassment that both authors illustrate may well mask the manner by which governments actually establish an authoritative presence, yet they also mask how such a presence can itself be displaced when challenged. As such, it masks an altogether different act of power, one achieved by leveraging reach topologically.

Topological sensibilities: take one

This chapter is paired with Chapter 4, and my intention here was always to provide what is, in effect, a one-sided topological redescription of power, where the emphasis has been upon what it means to *fold, stretch or distort* a relationship of power through time to gain advantage. The ability of more-or-less powerful actors to leverage reach through such processes, to fold in a *direct* presence or make their presence felt *indirectly* by stretching their authority, for example, recasts, to my mind, proximity, presence and distance in a more composed, topological fashion. Such topological sensibilities may represent a less familiar landscape than one where the size and extended capabilities of power are easier to chart, but an outlook of intensive forces and relational distances is arguably more in tune with power's shifting geographies today.

But such concerns do nonetheless represent only one side of a topological redescription of power; one that has drawn attention to the spatial processes of folding and stretching rather than to the effects that such distortion can have upon a transformation in power relations, where they may shift from one register to another, or overlay one another. This is the other side to a topological redescription of power, where the focus is upon how power relationships are *reproduced in different ways*, depending upon the relational arrangement of which they are a part. I touched upon this side in the spatial twists and turns that financial intermediaries may be subjected to, where their authority can mutate into straightforward manipulation, yet their power to engineer financial solutions to their advantage remains intact. Here, any jolt to our understanding comes from the disruption to our sense of continuity and transformation in the ways that such financial intermediaries may register their power and presence.

Once again, though, the obviousness of such topological disruption is not always in evidence given, in this case, the often taken-for-granted nature of financial power and its institutional expression. If, however, as I have suggested, topography and its extensive trappings can mask an intensive topological spatiality, then perhaps so too can the seemingly enduring dominance of banking and financial institutions mask the possibility that their power is a more tenuous achievement than many would have us believe. If so, it masks the possibility that power relationships themselves can undergo transformation, yet by and large remain fundamentally the same, in spite of the spatial twists and turns. Such a possibility switches attention to another key concern of conventional mathematical topology – what changes through the process of spatial distortion and what survives it by staying the same.

4

POWER REPRODUCED DIFFERENTLY

A topological practice

In one sense, the other side to a topological redescription of power is all about continuity, although to leave it at that would be misleading. Mathematical topologists are fond of talking about continuity, but only in the context of shapes and surfaces that survive the process of distortion. If the previous chapter was concerned to show how the process of folding or stretching space through time enabled powerful actors to leverage their reach and presence topologically, along the way the power relationship involved was also shown to reproduce itself, often in a different guise or register. Whereas the ability to get others to do something that they might otherwise not have done was more or less a constant, the manner in which that relationship was reproduced differed depending upon the political or economic arrangement in play. It is the ability of power relationships to be *reproduced differently* that forms the central focus of this chapter. Such a focus has less to do with the actual *processes* of spatial distortion and rather more to do with how they enable a *relationship* of power to undergo transformation yet remain fundamentally the same.

Another way to capture this shift in focus, from process to relationship, is to consider power as what topologists call the invariant in the relationship between figures which have undergone spatial distortion, or for our purposes the relationship between 'here and there' established by a continuous powerful presence through space and time. From the point of view of a mathematically inclined topologist, what is of especial interest are the properties of contorted figures that basically remain the same despite such figures no longer bearing any resemblance to their original shape. Turning a rubber inner tube inside out and folding it through itself to fashion a Klein bottle may result in an altogether different object, but topologically they are deemed to be the 'same'. The transformed figure is still an object with a continuous surface and a single opening, although significantly its curves are now a different shape, as is the opening itself. I say significantly, because in the one-to-one process of transformation that has taken place the figure has reproduced itself, albeit in a different guise. It has *changed* shape, yet fundamentally remained the *same*.

Again, it takes a certain leap of imagination to accept that power relationships, when stretched and folded through time, may shift in register despite maintaining a continuous presence. We glimpsed as much in the last chapter, but here I want to move towards a more explicit *pragmatist* account of power which reveals something of its expedient nature, where the practised ability to leverage reach to maintain advantage involves actors and institutions responding to the contingency of events in a more-or-less improvised manner. It is the actual workings of power, its mutable arrangements, that I wish to explore in this chapter, not only to show how a powerful presence may be reproduced between 'here and there', but also to reveal how such a topological presence may be registered in a variety of different ways, some *quieter* and more muted than others.

First, however, I want to set out what is at stake topologically to claim that something like power may change yet remain fundamentally the same.

The changing same of power

Among geographers, in particular, it is probably fair to say that those attracted to topological approaches have focused on its spatial and temporal possibilities, at the expense of what I have referred to as the other side of topological redescription: continuity and transformation. There has been a tendency to overlook the fact that when one figure is stretched or distorted into another, the less rigid approach to distance, size and shape entailed is only one of its attractions. The other, perhaps more awkward to accommodate, is the fact that certain features remain unchanged after deformation; they remain invariant aspects of whatever shape a figure may have morphed into. Invariance, as a term, is not likely to have immediate appeal to many working in today's more nominalistic-inclined social sciences, but its neglect in favour of a more composed spatiality is to miss the coupling of continuity with change that survives the process of distortion.

Derek Gregory's (2003, 2004) topological imaginaries, for instance, when projected onto the border relationships between Israel and the Palestinian West Bank, offer a rich account of the spatial and temporal distortions of everyday life in Palestinian towns and villages, but the continuities of exclusion and inclusion that underpin his power-topologies are broadly sketched. The changing forms of such exclusion and inclusion are registered, but not centrally considered as part of what makes the continuous presence of an occupying power possible. It might have perhaps helped if he had taken a leaf out of Gilles Deleuze's (1994) *Repetition and Difference* and his concern to show how things get 'repeated' through difference as part of transformations that produce variation. Repetition, here, in its Deleuzian rendition, it should be said, is not about something that continually reappears over and over again, like the proverbial 'bad penny' that repeatedly turns up at the most unwelcome of times. Rather, its sense is closer to a phrase that I used earlier, that of things being reproduced differently. On this interpretation, repetition has the force of procreation, but only insofar as that force has itself changed through transformation. Repetition entails transformation, as such, a process of mutation rather than one of replication.

What reproduces itself, if we return to the question of power, is not power in the same shape and size, but power in its different guises, in its specific modalities. There is more than one way for actors and institutions to reach into people's lives, to make a constraining presence felt, and what may start out as an exercise in domination, with efforts to erode choice, can quite easily mutate into attempts to manipulate by concealing intent, or combine with efforts to seek compliance by the assertion of authority, should initial efforts to constrain choice prove fruitless, for instance. In the distorted territories of the West Bank that Gregory outlines, for example, the instrumental control exercised by the Israeli domination of the land-scape, through border constraints and checkpoint impositions, could be said to reproduce itself, both through coercive acts of military violence as well as through the arbitrary manipulation of transit permits designed to frustrate routine travel movements. Something as simple as a daily travel routine, in that sense, can be the focus for a variety of constraining practices, each involving its own distinctive mode of exercising power.

In such arrangements, the evident mutability of power, the different ways in which it can be practised, speaks to power as always of a particular kind. And yet, to all intents and purposes, it remains power. It is the same constraining force, getting people to do things that they would otherwise not have done. But not always, as it were, in the same way. Power, in topological parlance, is the same, but different, or, put another way, there is something of the 'changing same' to power relationships when topology enters the frame.

Same, but different

I have skated over what it really means to be the 'same' in conventional topology, by way of reference to the features that remain invariant when one figure is twisted and turned into another. Rubber inner tubes and Klein bottles are perhaps too readily thrown into the mix when it comes to illustrating topological invariants, where one is stretched and folded into the other to reveal the same arrangement of surfaces and openings. But whatever iconic figures are drawn upon, or indeed even if it were simply a series of mundane shapes undergoing distortion, the main point that topologists wish to convey about 'sameness' is that it is evident when there is an *equivalence* between the two figures; that is, certain characteristics and features of one, such as the number of points at which they are connected, can also be found on the other. They are directly related or equivalent to one another through such shared characteristics (Barr, 1964; Gay, 2007).

Mathematically minded topologists will tell you that they are not interested in every shape or figure, only those that can be fashioned into another without recourse to cutting or breaking. It is perhaps for this reason that materials such as rubber, elastic and even clay frequently feature in topological illustrations, given the need to demonstrate topological equivalence. As Ivars Peterson (1988) points out in his snapshots of modern mathematics, anyone who has stretched a clay pot's mouth by pulling on its rim has some sense of how mathematical deformation works, where the eventual size and breadth of the opening is of no consequence, so long as the original opening corresponds directly to its newly moulded counterpart. The metrics do not come into play, only the relational distance between one opening and the other.

Topologists have a word which captures this one-to-one correspondence between figures that have been twisted and turned into another. Such figures are said to be *homeomorphic* to one another; that is, despite having been distorted every which way, they remain related to one another by possessing a similarity of form. That similarity may be evident from their corresponding features, for instance in terms of the surfaces, openings or connections that on one figure are likewise to be found on the other. Crucially, though, what matters about such corresponding features is that they remain *related in the same way* despite a process of continuous deformation. Or, put differently, the same relationship is reproduced in a different arrangement.

For our purposes, what is interesting to note about what counts as the 'same' in mainstream topology is that such invariance draws attention to the continuities of *relationships* under transformation. It is not so much the figures themselves that hold centre stage as what remains related and how equivalence is reproduced. As with the constraining force of the Israeli border practices documented by Gregory, what remains related despite the contortions of the border itself is a system of exclusion and inclusion. The powers of exclusion and those of inclusion are reproduced through mobile borders as much as fixed boundaries, temporary closures as well as permanent checkpoints, military deployments in addition to outposts of radar surveillance. While the topography of this occupied landscape has been designed to separate and divide, the topology of the border reproduces the forces of exclusion and inclusion from one point of displacement to another, from one moment of dislocation to the next (see Weizman, 2007).

Such forces of exclusion and inclusion clearly resemble that of the two-sided Möbius strip, with an inside and outside masking what amounts to a continuous relationship of power, despite the obvious constraining edge of power that the border itself represents. But that resemblance may be particular rather than general, given that state borders today, in Europe and the United States at least, appear to be less about constraining lines at the edge of territory and more to do with securing movement of the right sort of people (Balibar, 2002, 2004). Increasingly, the shift seems to be towards the establishment of border processes that regulate the movement and circulation of people, rather than simply the erection of border lines and territorial fences, as indeed Gregory's account points towards. In that sense, if Didier Bigo (2001) is right, the Klein bottle, as outlined in the previous chapter, may offer a better account of contemporary bordering practices at work. In his words:

> Sovereignty no longer defines borders. The agencies of security have expanded into a space that no longer respects sovereign borders. Topology of security in democracies is no longer the elegant cylinder but a complicated form, the Klein bottle. The opening of sovereign borders destroys the security construct of a homogeneous society. Once freedom of movement of persons has been accepted, the construct of the sovereign cylinder is no longer adequate. In this case, freedom is limited by a new security device: the monitoring of minorities and of diasporas. Identity fences replace territorial fences. While people are allowed to move, their identities must be constructed and controlled.
>
> *(Bigo, 2001, 115)*

The clear lines of the sovereign cylinder, with its opposing internal and external sides that plainly separate those allowed legal entry from those excluded from such a status, has on this understanding morphed into a more ambiguous shape. The Klein bottle, with its continuous one-sided surface that merges inside and outside, no longer admits any fixed border lines but delineates a space where inclusion and exclusion are matters of degree, relative not absolute. Migrants, especially those seeking low-skilled work, may find themselves included for the purpose of temporary labour, yet excluded from welfare, citizenship and other social rights. They may embody a physical presence on the inside, yet find themselves outside the protection of employment law, for example, or denied access to housing and other welfare benefits. Sovereign borders may be more porous than before, more ambiguous in shape, but that does not mean that entry protocols, residency rights and welfare benefits are the same for all who move across borders (Popescu, 2012).

It would be a mistake, however, to regard this shift as simply the replacement of one set of rigid fences by a more flexible set of barriers. Perhaps the key point to note is that the transformation from border lines to border processes is a continuous one, not a break from one regime to another. In effect, the powers of exclusion and inclusion are reproduced differently, through more subtle arrangements that regulate the movement of people and their legal identity. Equivalence is established between seemingly closed and open borders by processes that exclude and include in more differentiated ways (Mezzadra and Neilson, 2012). On a pragmatic, if not entirely transparent, basis, the manipulation of people's legal rights, the control exercised over their length of stay, and the coercive policing of routes and channels of entry work alongside the more straightforward border practices of domination and constraint that high walls and fences represent.

On the face of it, the transformation simply amounts to the reproduction of border relations in a different arrangement, one focused on mobility and circulation rather than physical debarment. But that, I would argue, is to lose sight of the other side of the topological equation: namely, the processes of spatial distortion that enable border relations to reproduce themselves in a different guise. Borders have altered not just in terms of function; the spacing and timing of border relationships have been stretched and folded in ways that distort any connection to a sealed or boxed-in territory. The outsourcing of immigration controls, the creation of 'waiting zones' in third countries, is one such practice where border controls have been stretched out to make access harder to negotiate (Vaughan-Williams, 2012). The lifting out of borders, in that respect, works to place entry for some further out of reach. Likewise, the folding in of borders such that those who have gained entry find themselves excluded from all manner of legal and social rights transforms what it means to be included, in terms of residency and citizenship (Coleman, 2012)

In making a case for the diffusion and extension of borders, as intimated in Chapter 3, it would be easy to leap to the conclusion that such practices would inevitably lead to a loss of intensity in terms of control. That, however, would be a misreading of the situation. When grasped topologically, as will become apparent in Chapter 7, the outsourcing of border controls represents an intensive exercise of power, where the state makes its presence felt regardless of the physical distances involved. The gap between a centralized authoritative power and the exercise of that authority perhaps far removed from territorial borders is bridged relationally, mediated through technologies and practices that enable a more-or-less direct presence. On that reinterpretation, the central state and its border agencies compose the spaces of which they are a part; the folding out of borders does not preserve the exact distances between centre and outpost, only their relationships to each other. That does not rule out, however, the possibility that relationships of formal authority may mutate into something more manipulative or coercive in terms of control, only that the powers of exclusion and inclusion remain the same.

Difference through mutation

The use of the term 'mutate' above was not simply a slip of the tongue, for it conveys the sense in which power may change register as a result of spatial distortion. Relationships of power, such as those of exclusion and inclusion, as I have had cause to stress, may remain a continuous presence in any particular arrangement, yet change in terms of their actual content. As glimpsed, the folding out of border controls, or their ability to be stretched through time, may also be twisted in such a way that lines of authority and constraint mutate into arbitrary acts of manipulation to deny certain groups limited entry. In fact, similar kinds of mutating relationships are common to many institutional arrangements of power. The closing down of possibilities, the erosion of choice, the threat of force, the manipulation of outcomes, and acts of inducement − that is, rewards for compliance, may all be drawn upon by different actors in response to changing pressures. Power in that sense is both one and many, capable of being reproduced differently. But there is a little bit more to say than that, at least in terms of how power relations are more likely to mutate in situations that lack predictability or where they have clearly proven inept.

The apparent neatness of many an institutional arrangement often belies the more mutable nature of power relationships when situations change and open up in unpredictable ways. As actors adapt to new or unforeseen circumstances, so too may the manner in which power is exercised. Adaptation and mutation are, in that respect, two sides of the same coin.

Charles Tilly (2002) has helpfully drawn attention to what is involved, in his case to the significance of improvisation in the 'in-between' workings of power when centralized authorities come up against unforeseen consequences or unexpected obstacles. By improvisation here, I take him to mean the ability of actors to adapt to changed circumstances, to react to the moment by trying out what works best to achieve a given end. Adaptation, in the context of governments seeking to make their presence felt at-a-distance, involves aligning local interests with those of the centre, twisting a situation to their advantage where possible by, for example, manipulating behaviour when their authority passes unrecognized, or threatening coercion when persuasion falls on deaf ears. It is not only different registers of power that may be improvised in such a context, however; so too may the reach of government.

Improvisation, drawing certain possibilities within reach when other ways of making their presence felt have fallen short is, in that sense, a topological tactic open to governments seeking to secure compliance. In Chapter 3, reference was made to the possibility of central authorities leveraging reach in both direct and indirect ways, either by folding in their presence directly or stretching relationships to bridge the distances involved. Co-present and detached relationships, as well as the establishment of a more indirect presence, represented different ways of achieving what may well be the same goal. Should one means founder, should such authority come unstuck, those 'in-between', so to speak, may resort to other forms of leverage or draw upon different technologies and practices to make their presence felt. Compliance may not hold firm on such a basis or be secured only in the short term, but the spatial twists adopted may enable alternative registers of power to be drawn upon.

An altogether different twist is also highlighted by Tilly: that of the polyvalent performance, where the mediation of authority between central and local interests works to secure what may often be contradictory ends. Here an act of authority can play itself out in different ways to different audiences, to reconcile what are in effect opposing wants and needs. Where those at the centre of government may read a particular authoritative gesture by a regional public body as a directive reinforcing its own objectives, those at the local level may read the same gesture more as advice, a form of guidance about how best to secure their own goals given the constraints imposed by the centre. One side recognizes the gesture as a rational-legal style of authority, while the other believes its compliance is being sought through consensus and expertise. This, then, is less the mutation of one register of power into another, and more a twist in meaning as the performance of authority deliberately opens itself up to ambiguous readings.

Perhaps the key insight to draw from these types of performance is that, as with all mediating practices of power, it is a response to the circumstances confronted. There is an element of *pragmatism* involved, as there would appear to be in many mutating relationships, about knowing how to adapt to the context as well as the contingency of events.

Power registered in practice

Context, it should be said, amounts to more than simply knowing that times and places are different from one another. In a topological world, the immediate 'here' and 'now' is not something that can be ring-fenced, bounded in territorial terms and shown to be different and separate from elsewhere. The reason for that is quite straightforward, insofar as there is an interplay of forces to be found in any context or setting, some of which will have been folded in by others acting elsewhere and may involve messy co-existences and awkward social juxtapositions. Indeed, not only may the actions of those not present be critical to how such forces work themselves out in practice, so too will be the responses of those seeking to gain advantage from the newly configured context (Allen and Cochrane, 2014). Power can be brought to bear in a variety of ways, and the leverage of different actors can make a difference to the way that such power plays work themselves out.

Such leverage is not reducible to the resources and capabilities of actors but, as stressed, to how they are used; that is, how they are put to work to gain advantage by, say, stretching their authority to establish a detached presence or, if that should fail, by folding it in, in real time. The leverage of reach in such contexts, in new or perhaps unanticipated circumstances, highlights the practised rather than the positional nature of power. It draws attention not only to the improvised, adaptable character of power that I have just spoken about, but also to its *tenuous* nature. In contrast to a simple geometry of predetermined outcomes based upon the unequal distribution of resources, when power is understood as a tenuous achievement it is something that is made and remade, reproduced differently to sustain an ongoing presence.

It may seem obvious enough that what people *do* matters more than simply the size of the resources at their disposal, but such obviousness is often obscured by its conventionality. In part, I believe this is because in much pragmatist thought power is often unrecognizable as something that is wielded at somebody else's expense (Allen, 2008a). The somewhat ingrained idea of power as a force to be reckoned with, something that is held over others, is displaced in the thought of John Dewey (1930, 1934; see also Bernstein, 1960, 1966) and other like-minded pragmatists by the looser notion that power is one among a number of practical tools used to get things done, to secure an outcome. Power, on this view, is seen more as an enabling tool than an instrument of constraint; a means to an end rather than a means of control. Whilst it is important to distinguish, as I will go on to show, the 'power to' make things happen from the more familiar exercise of 'power over' others, there are at least two ways in which a practical account of power can serve both enabling *and* instrumental ends.

One is that, from a broad pragmatist standpoint, power is always exercised with a purpose in mind: be it the pursuit of a particular goal to bring about change or the drive to get people to do things that they otherwise would not have done. It makes no difference whether the outcome is one of empowerment or of constraint, so long as power as a practical means serves a given end. Another is that whatever the purpose in mind, some ways of exercising power always seem to work better than others to secure it. Power may be a useful means to get things done, but some actions appear more suited to given ends than others. Leverage in such circumstances can thus be something of a hit-and-miss affair, a more tenuous achievement than often appears to be the case.

When I spoke earlier about mutable arrangements of power, where different registers of power may combine or play across one another, it is the expedient nature of power that perhaps best captures what is involved. Quite simply, what works best in any given situation cannot be known in advance, only *in practice*.

Power without guarantees

One of the comments that Richard Rorty makes about Michel Foucault's enabling notion of power in *Consequences of Pragmatism* (1982) is that it is not markedly different from seeing power as one among any number of practical tools that people use to meet their needs and desires. The belief that many things in life, our ideas, language, even pragmatism itself as a philosophy, are useful tools for coping with the world and its challenges is a core thread in pragmatist thinking from Dewey onwards. Rorty remained strangely mute on the subject of power and its workings, even in his publications that struck a political note (Rorty, 1998, 1999), but the idea of power as a kind of trial-and-error tool, seeking out what works best for certain purposes, is in keeping with his comments on new and existing vocabularies, underlined in Chapter 2. Some means work better than others to achieve particular ends, but what works best to meet the needs and demands of the moment is often a question of expediency. There is an element of hitting upon the right course of action, whether to draw others within close reach to bring them into line, for instance, or to establish a more proximate authority by a different relational means.

To highlight this sense of expediency, however, is not to glorify the indeterminacy of all things related to power. Everything is not simply down to accident or chance. The use of trial-and-error tactics, knowing for instance whether the arm's-length manipulation of behaviour on the part of governments may work better than direct inducements by front-line agencies, forms part of a calculated intervention. Such interventions, however, whilst taken with a purpose in mind, are likely to be decidedly uncertain as to their actual, as opposed to their intended, effects. Looking back over such arrangements, the means that were more suited to a given end may appear somewhat obvious and more certain than was ever actually the case at the time.

Governments and many other institutional bodies have to weigh up means and ends as part of a routine practised ability, but this is perhaps especially true for organizations such as NGOs, which often mobilize around singular purposes. Campaign groups that rely upon the activation of moral and political energies to effect change around factory sweatshop exploitation, human rights, or any number of environmental goals, for example, may treat power less as a useful tool and more as a series of interventions of which they are capable (Feher et al, 2007). They are more likely to gauge what works best to enliven public debate and tailor their campaigns to suit either the compassion or indignation of audiences in order to exert an influence often way beyond their means. Knowing when and where best to apply pressure to achieve the desired political ends, in that sense, is a form of practical expediency (Tilly, 2002).

As such, the mobilization of distant and dispersed 'publics' around issues of global justice, the ability to reach such publics, turns on the question of leverage. The ability of activists, for instance, to link the actions of governments and corporations directly to the abuse of impoverished communities elsewhere in the world, or to issues faced collectively such as climate change, ecological disasters, food risks and sweatshop exploitation, resembles both a topological and an expedient practice. In the case of consumer campaigns, for example, NGOs such as Oxfam and War on Want have been known to fold in distant harms, drawing them within close reach, by fixing upon company logos and linking the actions of branded retailers directly to abuse overseas (Allen, 2008a). The big fashion retailers on the high street, much to their annoyance as we shall see in Chapter 6, have all been on the receiving end of such tactics, designed principally to persuade consumers of the need to right particular 'wrongs'.

When, however, such tactics have proven less effective than anticipated, NGOs have tended to focus their energies upon the indirect tie-up between, say, what people eat and the exploitative conditions under which the foodstuffs are produced elsewhere. This kind of topological reach, where the responsibility for such exploitation is stretched from 'here' to 'there', not folded in from afar, by and large represents an attempt at manipulation rather than persuasion, although should the circumstances dictate it, both may be exercised in combination. Far from mindless trial and error, it would seem that NGOs and campaigning groups leverage their energies and reach to achieve the most telling impact. They hit upon what works best for them, given the political moment and context (Allen, 2008a).

Of course, there is always the possibility that campaign groups may misjudge the political moment or misread the situation and their efforts come to nothing. In many respects, this kind of political activism resembles *experiments* with power, as Dewey (1916) might have thought of them. Even though power may be exercised in such moments with a purpose in mind, the difficulty of matching means to ends implies that the outcome of their actions is always likely to be provisional.

The articulation of the possible, experimenting with possible ways of mobilizing a 'public' in the case of consumer campaigns, for instance, may involve a sequence of interventions along the length and breadth of a commercial supply chain. There are no guarantees as to the success of such manoeuvres, and all actions are hedged by the contingency of events where circumstances may turn out quite differently from those anticipated. Trial and error, to reinforce the point, means just that. If persuasion peters out or fails to win over hearts and minds, or should the 'public' fail to recognize their responsibility to a far-off form of exploitation, NGOs may have little option but to trial a different use and leverage of their abilities. But they do so in a context where they are more likely to have taken on board the lesson of past trials and tribulations. What is new, each time, is their achievement: that NGOs have been able to skilfully leverage whatever spatial reach they can to take advantage of a given situation (Feher, 2007).

In that regard, things are not entirely dissimilar to governments and corporate institutions that actively reproduce their power by exercising it in different ways at different times depending on the situation at hand. If the purpose is to establish a continuous powerful presence in a particular political or economic arrangement, then one way to achieve that continuity is precisely to adapt to changing contexts by skilfully bringing different registers of power into play. When power relations work in such topological fashion, an ongoing institutional or group presence is effectively maintained through such continuous transformations. Put another way, when power is leveraged topologically to maintain advantage or establish an influential presence, the ability to reach people on a prolonged basis works precisely by actors exploring the different options available to them to meet the demands of change-able situations. Such transformations are part and parcel of what it means for power relations to be reproduced differently under contingent circumstances.

That reproduction, however, is not always readily apparent to those on the receiving end of such instrumental actions. The issue is complicated by the fact that, for much of the time, what may actually pass for institutional or group power is not the kind that, on the face of it, bends the wills of others to gain advantage. In no small part, this is because power is often exercised simply as a facilitative means for securing outcomes, more an enabling tool than an instrumental one, along the lines that Dewey envisaged. This looser sense of the 'power to' act can be spun out in a range of different directions, designed to secure what to all intents and purposes are mutually beneficial ends. What is less obvious perhaps is that the 'power to' make things happen in this way can all too easily flip over into the 'power over' others; that is, closing down rather than opening up possibilities. In such moments, though, power may not be experienced as anything like an instrumental force.

'Power to' secure outcomes

When conceived as a means to an end, power as such does not have to serve any particular interest or be tied to practices of domination and control. Power of whatever kind can work for people or it can work against them; it can block social change as well as smooth its path. Seen from more than one angle, the 'power to' act may look suspiciously like the power that is exercised over others to stop them from acting. As a practical medium, the power that is brought to bear upon people's actions may be experienced in a positive, benign register as much as one of covert direction and disadvantage. Inducements, for instance, whereby positive-sum gains are held up for all, may in retrospect skew rewards more to some than others. Positive-sum gains do not automatically amount to equal-sum gains, and some gains may turn out to be illusory. It is in that sense that the 'power to' secure outcomes may not be quite the innocuous tool that it is sometimes held up to be.

Not so long ago it was possible to conceive of the 'power to' act as a general precondition for all kinds of action, of which the power that is wielded at somebody else's expense is a particular type of constraining action (see Giddens, 1977). On this view, the ability of the weighty institutions of the world to hold 'power over' others reduces itself to one way among others of acting in the world. Of late, however, this subsumption of instrumental power under a more general, catch-all, facilitative notion of power has given way to a sharper distinction between the two usages (Clegg and Haugaard, 2009). Whereas the habitual sense of power as something that is held over others broadly remains the default option in the social sciences, in tandem, so to speak, is the idea that power is more about the ability to make things happen, to exercise power with, rather than over, others. The pragmatic roots of this conception are perhaps plain to see, but the particular associational spin given to it is of more recent origin.

The powers of association can be traced back to the writings of Hannah Arendt (1958, 1970), in particular to the idea that power is something experienced through other people, through the formation of a common will. More enabling than instrumental in its purpose, on this view, power is something that springs up between people when they come together in mutual collective action. But this account of associational powers has arguably been eclipsed by the more instrumental version set out in Chapter 2, namely the networked understanding of association put forward by Latour and others in the actor–network mould. In their hands, as we have seen, the 'power to' bridge, broker and connect people and things represents a mediated exercise of power, one where distances are overcome by the enrolment of others into arrangements that may offer the potential of gains for all involved. Leverage, on this understanding, is achieved through association, through the continual translation and channelling of interests, rather than by recourse to imposition and constraint.

But that is not all that is at stake here. Interests may well be brought into some form of alignment, stabilized, and associations held in place through means that involve acts of facilitation. Yet such means may just as easily be directed towards instrumental ends, where the 'power to' secures an overall outcome that may benefit one group at the expense of another. If we only think about what it takes to secure the network, it is possible to miss the avenues closed off or the choices that were limited or never proffered. Persuasion and inducements, as registers of power, may drive such networked associations, but running alongside them may well be the possibility for manipulation and dissimulation which can skew rewards in favour of some but not all. Even the persuasive channelling of interests through a negotiated settlement may 'fix' a network orientation so that those who accept it as irreversible may lose out.

I shall return shortly to the significance of such quieter registers of power, in contrast, that is, to the more strident forms that usually pass for instrumental power. The point for now is that treating power as something that is sustained through patterns of association which bind people together can close down as many possibilities as it may open up. And, significantly, for those involved the situation that confronts them may not be experienced or grasped as one of manipulation and constraint. Experience, as noted before, does not arrive with all its social and political implications on display (Eagleton, 2005).

Any experience, memorable or otherwise, requires interpretation, and the experience of being on the receiving end of an artful piece of manipulation or a persuasive gesture that masks its real intentions has first to be grasped if it is to be understood. How things really are and how we experience them are not necessarily one and the same thing; power that is exercised to gain advantage can be mis-understood and misinterpreted, especially if the intentionality is unclear or ambig-uous. If confronted by a power that, on the face of it, is simply a means to get things done, to make things happen or to secure an outcome, it would be easy to assume that both means and ends are fully on display. Yet, as will become apparent in later chapters, when NGOs set out to mobilize and enrol a 'public' to back a particular campaign, it is not the manipulation of sympathies that is on display. Likewise, when financial intermediaries in New York or London channel investor interests towards a particular deal, it is not necessarily the exorbitant fees and commissions earned that make the headline banner.

'Enablement', in such contexts, takes on a rather different shade of meaning and hue of interest. It is the point at which the 'power to' make things happen or make a difference turns into the kind of power that is held over others, often at their expense. The more provisional sense of power argued for here, as an expedient, practical means exercised with a purpose in mind is, I would have thought, well suited to such transformations taking place. Besides, when one turns to the ability of corporate institutions and the like to reproduce their power differently it is hard not to notice the gains to be had from working through the more subtle, quieter registers of power at hand. Not least because they are enabled by a form of lever-age and distorted reach that can be used to get people to do things they would otherwise not have done without, it seems, them actually experiencing the 'hard', constraining edges of power.

Quieter registers of power

The harder edges of power, when brushed against, leave a mark. When someone is on the receiving end of an imposing act of authority, or a coercive threat, or the constraining efforts of domination, there is an undoubted rawness to the experi-ence. Those on the receiving end of an edict abruptly issued by government offi-cials, or those who find themselves threatened with arbitrary violence or excluded at a border crossing point, know that they have come up against a powerful body of some kind. Such acts have the look and feel of a powerful force, and are responded to as such. Authority has to be conceded before it is complied with; coercion has to be suffered if the threat is to mean anything at all; domination leaves people with no choice but to submit to the situation they face, and so on. Often there is a certain bluntness to such acts, which leaves the recipient in no doubt that some force or other is being held over them. But power, as we have just seen, can work in ways where nothing is actually held over anyone.

Power does not have to be loud and in your face for it to be effective. People can end up doing things that they did not really set out or want to do, not through compulsion or duress, but through inducement, seduction and manipulation, in particular. These quieter registers of power have, I would argue, come to the fore in recent times, precisely because such acts can turn open-ended situations to particular advantage without recourse to more overt displays of authority and restraint. The very fact that such acts may appear insubstantial or low-pitched should not lead us to conclude that those on the receiving end are not subject to some form of control and influence. Indeed, it is the modest nature of such actions, paradoxically, that underpins their strength. Because there is less that is overt to show the imbalance of power and who is plainly doing what to whom, the effects are just that much harder to discern.

A case can be made, for instance, that the quieter, more impalpable registers of power can be as, if not more, insidious precisely because they may pass unrecognized. The prospect of gains that are too great not to want, that lie behind the pull of inducement, as already indicated, may draw people willingly into arrangements that work directly against their interests. The exploitation of information asymmetries in financial dealings, where outcomes are engineered to suit some but not all interests, is one such instance. Yet those drawn in may find out only after the event. Likewise, the manipulation of social and political outcomes by definition involves the concealment of intent so that only one side gains at the expense of the other. But the practice of dissemblance or dissimulation involved means that the pretence may never be apparent or recognized by those deceived. In such situations, where no actual force or arm-twisting is in evidence, the more subtle ways in which power can be exercised holds the potential to *mask* the instrumental character of the relationships compromised.

Let me be clear about the nature of my argument here. None of what I have said about the more wily practices of power is meant to gloss over the fact that blanket acts of domination, the enforcement of authority and the blunt use of violence remain the most conspicuous registers of contemporary power. My point is simply that there is more to power than its more manifest forms of control and constraint. In particular, as noted earlier, what passes for the 'power to' secure outcomes can often obscure the fact that today more subtle means of control and influence may be employed to achieve similar ends. It is not, I should stress, that I wish to claim that quieter registers of power have simply replaced those of a more blatant variety, or that manipulation rather than domination is the order of the day. Rather, my argument is that topological shifts have altered many of the ways in which leverage over others can be achieved today, enabling actors to register their presence through quieter acts that previously lacked spatial reach.

This is the critical point. The ability to draw others within close reach, to establish relational proximities over distance, or to place others out of reach by distancing them, opens up many more possibilities for less strident registers of power to be exercised. In practice, there are simply more means to draw upon that may best suit a given end. Where a distant act of authority may no longer command consent, for instance, the ability to exercise authority among rather than over others through closer collaboration holds out the possibility for actors to bring everyone more or less into line through the powers of negotiation and persuasion. The ability to establish a broadly simultaneous presence through real-time negotiations of authority, for example, is possible when others elsewhere are folded into the arrangement, be it one of corporate financial networking or a similar exercise on the part of the global political establishment. The point is not that authority from afar is no longer a viable option, although a case can be made, but rather that it has been reworked to be exercised with other, more supple means of control and influence. As the spatial and temporal dynamics of reach have shifted topologically, so too have the ways in which power is reproduced.

The likes of US banking houses, Goldman Sachs or JP Morgan Chase for instance, their investment managers in particular, perhaps know this only too well. In fact, they have never really 'done' corporate domination on its own or relied solely on their financial authority and expertise. Inducements have long played a part in connecting previously unrelated investors, holding out the prospect of profitable returns should they be persuaded of the credibility of the offer placed before them. The lure of a win–win situation and the authoritative management of risk projected may be sufficient inducement, although the difference in the quality of information enjoyed may skew the rewards disproportionately, allowing those 'in-between' to capture the larger share of the economic gains. Such asymmetries are not new, as will become apparent in Chapter 5, but the intensive, relational reach enjoyed by the investment houses is of more recent origin and enhances the ability of managers to mould the actions of others in more pliant ways across ever greater spans of distance. Tilly, I suspect, would have regarded them as an exemplary example of improvisation at work. Indeed, he might even have considered investment managers as among the most skilful of polyvalent performers.

In such financial situations, talk of rewards, incentives and double-digit returns or the proficient management of risk may appear to be all that is involved, yet actually conceal the fact that the risks of a particular venture have been passed on to those least able to bear them. As we shall see, the investment houses are aware of their role in this kind of double game, but are unlikely to openly acknowledge that manipulation is the flip-side of inducement. The concealment at the heart of such actions, where the underlying motives are never fully revealed, implies that those on the receiving end remain unaware of the control exercised over them. Should the deception be revealed, to follow Tilly's line of thinking, then a new means of twisting a situation to the advantage of management is likely to be improvised. In such quiet, unassuming ways, the continuity of the arrangement is reproduced by different means.

More quiet than soft

Having raised the fact that certain registers of power are felt and experienced as 'hard', namely those of domination, coercion and authority, it may seem churlish of me to talk about 'quiet' rather than 'soft' power. Joseph Nye (2002, 2004, 2011) has done much to draw attention to the significance of what he calls 'soft power'; that is, power which works through attraction, shaping the preferences of others so that you get them to want what you want. The merit of this argument is that it recognizes that 'hard' power, the kind that relies on threats and constraints to get people to do things that they do not want to do, is a limited means of bringing people into line. It may work well as a blunt instrument when force bends as well as breaks the will of others, but in the longer term, if an arrangement of power is to be maintained, 'softer' methods of power and persuasion are likely to be part of the arrangement.

Nye's account of soft power was formulated with his eyes firmly on the so-called relative decline of US power and the conduct of its foreign policy in an interdependent world, so the term itself is meant to convey what the US should exercise more of, if it is to stay ahead of the curve. In place of confrontation, soft power is said to work through co-option, where the emphasis is placed upon exercising power with rather than over others. Enticement and attraction are the means through which others on the world stage are drawn into a sphere of influence, their preferences shaped by a willingness to adopt what are perceived to be a credible bundle of values, norms and institutions worthy of emulation. Imitation, in this context, is less a form of flattery and more a tool of indirect influence. If others admire your values and want to follow your example, it becomes just that much easier to influence their behaviour to get 'others to want the outcomes that you want' (Nye, 2004, 5).

As with the quieter registers of power that I have outlined, the more subtle means of securing outcomes is a thread common to both accounts. But there are some significant differences too, which hinge upon the *instrumental* nature of power that Nye describes, yet seems to shy away from. The prime difference is that there is nothing particularly 'soft' or understated about using indirect means to shape the preferences of others or frame their interests in ways consistent with one's own. Imitation may be a more pleasing way to talk about getting others to want what you want, but incitement and manipulation are probably a more accurate description of the means involved. Marshalling the wants and preferences of others so that they align with your interests involves channelling them in ways that make other choices appear unattractive or less credible. Better still, the mobilization of bias can rule out some values and preferences by ensuring that they never actually reach an audience.

As many will know, the 'mobilization of bias' is a term drawn from the work of Bachrach and Baratz (1962), and was popularized as the 'second face of power' by Steven Lukes (1974) back in the 1970s. Nye (2004) draws an explicit parallel between his sense of soft power and its 'second face', which for him involves the framing of agendas to ensure that only some messages get across. It is the indirect means to get what you want that appeals to him, where the editing and restricting of choices closes down the range of possible preferences. If not quite suppression in Nye's case, the understanding that some values and ideals can be 'organized into' politics while others can be 'organized out', is a practice clearly known to him. Yet despite this grasp of the manipulation involved, he seems to distance himself from its duplicitous consequences. It is as if he chooses to gloss over the instrumental intent of 'soft' modes of power, whose purpose is to *limit* the preferences of others so that they want what you want.

The stress that Nye places on co-option, however, exercising power with others rather than over them appears to suggest otherwise. Though what Arendt would have made of this, one can probably guess. It would be disingenuous, I think, to claim that Nye's sense of co-option is akin to the formation of some kind of common will. Power for Arendt is associational not instrumental, empowering of those taking part, rather than directed towards aligning the interests of others with your own, as is clearly the case with 'soft' versions of power. In many respects, it is possible to regard the shift in emphasis towards more subtle means of power and influence, seduction and persuasion, manipulation and dissimulation, as just the latest in a long line of expedient measures. Given the acknowledged drawbacks of 'hard' power to meet all situations and the challenges noted by Nye (2011) of a world where power is more distributed and uneven, such measures may simply represent a better instrumental means of dealing with such a geographically neb-ulous state of affairs. But, for me, it seems misplaced to refer to such calculated interventions as 'soft'.

All this may be a little too fussy for some, given that both Nye and I are pretty much talking about the same means of power. But to describe such means as 'soft' is to lose sight of their instrumentality: that they are exercised with a controlling purpose in mind, often behind the backs of their intended audiences. In fact, for the most part, the motives that lie behind acts of persuasion and seduction may remain deliberately obscure and, in the case of manipulative ploys, they are unli-kely even to be recognized as such. Indeed, should such deception be revealed, the credibility of the whole exercise is likely to be lost. That makes such acts, as pointed out earlier, more not less insidious. Their often unassuming nature as a means of influence belies a deceit that leaves no imprint and an instrumental end that remains inconspicuous. A quiet influence, in fact, which works as a means to get others to want what you want and thus act in ways they might not otherwise have done.

The logic of seduction, for instance, works through enticement and attraction. Contrary to what is often thought, it does not involve telling people what they should want or indeed what is best for them. Rather, seduction seeks to influence by diffusing values and standards that are already in circulation, but have not yet been widely adopted. In the context of US influence, Nye and others have spoken about the values of liberty and upward mobility, as well as choice and openness, as part of what is attractive about American popular culture and its institutions. Such values would be hard to contest. Set out in broad terms, they appear to be to the obvious benefit of all. Yet when framed in a particular way, they direct sensibilities along certain lines and not others. Freedom and mobility speak to personal freedoms and individual mobility, not to social contracts and collective advancement. Choice and openness give us free markets and private enterprise, not equal opportunities and public services. Seduction in that sense exploits existing tendencies and frames them in ways that restrict other possibilities and influences (Allen, 2006).

With seduction, as with quieter registers of power in general, people may end up going along with things that ordinarily they would not. Their will is not broken, nor bent even, just directed, channelled into particular arrangements which may close down as many possibilities as they open up. As such, the 'power to' attract others to what you want, so that their interests align with yours, turns into a form of influence over others. Seduction is thus one of the more subtle ways of gaining influence by instrumental means, helped in part by the greater reach afforded it today.

Influence and reach

Quiet power has much to do with gaining and maintaining influence, but it is not only its instrumentality that sets it apart from many conventional accounts of how influence plays out. It is also the manner in which quieter modes of power can be leveraged topologically. Acts of seduction do not aim for complete control, rather they seek to win over hearts and minds to bring into sharper definition the aspirations and wants of those in their sights. They work, as noted, through enticement and attraction, drawing in people through suggestion in the hope that it becomes more difficult for them not to follow suit. The broad indeterminacy of seduction as a mode of power is, paradoxically, its strength. Those subject to its overtures can simply resist them or affect indifference, but its unassuming qualities disguise the fact that embryonic tastes are being exploited and options restricted. That very same indeterminacy also gives seduction a topological reach that enables it to be folded in from afar, either by drawing others within close reach or reaching into audiences elsewhere.

Likewise, manipulation may be leveraged topologically in just such a pliable fashion, but not for the same reasons as seduction. As a clearly focused act, it lacks the indeterminacy of seduction, but its one-sided nature leaves those on the receiving end unaware of the control and influence exercised over them. The ability to mould the preferences of others, to edit their choices, without having to reveal the underlying motives, gives those engaged in acts of manipulation the possibility of placing them within or beyond reach in a variety of ways. If the nature of the influence is concealed from you, outcomes may be engineered at a distance by actors either folding in their presence directly or stretching the duplicitous relationship by more indirect means. There is no question of resisting such influences or simply walking away from them, precisely because they remain covert. By that, I do not mean that some kind of false trail is laid down to exploit others, but rather that certain things are held back to conceal the real nature of the advantage sought.

Manipulation is more likely to be exercised in situations where the open-ended qualities of seduction or persuasion fail to gain traction or prove difficult to 'fix' in their line of suggestion. Getting others to want what you want by dissimulation often involves holding back what is fully at stake, with the express purpose of taking people in a particular direction that is not always in their best interests. The risk of being found out, however, may mean that such acts are not best suited to work alongside the suggestive ploys of seduction, and that the rewards of inducement may well work better in tandem as a means of establishing a more prolonged influence. Or, alternatively, the deployment of sound, expert advice may be better suited to back up the less substantive, more hit-or-miss nature of seduction, as a form of authority held among people, not over them. The potential for improvisation and the adaptation of one or more means of influence in response to the circumstances confronted is always present.

I say always present, but that only really holds for those means of exercising power that are pliable in their reach and composition. The more conspicuous methods of control and influence – that is, attempts to impose authority over others, threaten excessive force or constrain through domination – by virtue of their manifest aims, lack the supple leverage of those means of influence exercised in a quieter, more unassuming register. The former, largely extensive means of control are more likely today to be exercised in combination with intensive measures that can more effectively reach and hold an audience, either through the directness of their presence or through a presence that is more indirectly leveraged. Quieter means of influence, such as seduction and inducement, and indeed manipulation, which can be leveraged topologically in a variety of ways that cut across proximity and distance, offer just such an adaptable tool. More pointedly, they enable powerful bodies and institutions to reproduce their influence through different means, as part of what it takes to sustain an ongoing presence.

Consider, for instance, the widespread influence that neoliberalism, as a set of ideals around the role of markets and competition, has had in recent decades. Projected as a liberating force by international financial institutions, an army of private sector consultants and any number of government agencies, the market values which underpin neoliberal practices have been held up as the key to economic prosperity and freedom. The prising open of restricted markets, the making over of social relationships in the likeness of the market, speak to a set of power arrangements whose influence over city, regional and national economies has been beyond question. There are a number of ways in which such influential arrangements may be understood, one of which relies upon the more pronounced forces of domination and coercion to account for the uptake of market-orientated policies and thinking (Peet, 2007).

On this understanding, cities and regions across the global South and North would have had little or no choice but to fall into line with the interests of the international banks and financial institutions. Despite reluctance, formally free agents, government officials and politicians alike would have been unable to resist the imposition of market-based policies, especially when backed up by the threat of withholding financial aid and investment. A combination of economic domination and political coercion would have placed local officials and politicians in a situation where they had no choice but to open up their markets to international competition. Such an opening up of markets has clearly taken place in a number of countries across the globe in recent decades. What is less clear is whether political threats and the removal of economic choice are wholly responsible for neoliberal values and practices taking hold.

It would, after all, require the dominant financial institutions and governing agencies present elsewhere to exercise near blanket reach over the markets in the subjected economies, and for the external funding threats to be continuously renewed despite opposition. It is difficult to know for sure, of course, how effective the reach of such measures have been, but the widespread adoption of market values hints at other means of influence behind the traction gained for liberal thinking and the ongoing hold of market reasoning.

Chief among them is the seductive appeal that markets can deliver on the question of economic growth and development. The ability of not-so-distant market advocates to frame the benefits that follow from the adoption of neoliberal strategies by bringing into sharper definition what they can deliver in terms of value for money, efficiency and competitive positioning has had strong resonances among city politicians, for instance. Jenny Robinson (2011a), for one, has shown how those involved in urban politics and policy making may be persuaded of the merits of competitive markets where there are obvious perceived benefits for local interests, or the attraction of private capital can be used to meet alternative political ends. Although expediency rather than conversion to market-orientated solutions may have led to their initial take-up, arguably the seductive combination of viable growth strategies and rewards for compliance helped pave the way for policy imitation and emulation.

The role of brokers of one kind or another, international advisors, private consultants, think tanks, urban policy professionals and managers operating on a worldwide stage have been critical to the framing of market-based futures. By attempting to exercise their authority among rather than over officials and politicians, their collaborative role enables them to align city interests to strategic visions that find a place for cities in a challenging economic world. Able to conceive of neoliberal visions as a whole, they simultaneously offer an array of choices, editing and translating possibilities for different cities and negotiating the often conflicting interests involved. Influence in such contexts comes from the quiet advice and authority behind such translations, held in place through practices of inducement and negotiation, and directed, if need be, by the manipulation of possibilities that suggest some futures whilst others are held back.

Robinson hints at the topological interplay of relationships that can be involved in such arrangements. The reach of market-driven strategies when translated by outside brokers may be folded in directly, through real-time engagements to establish a proximate authority, or by agendas 'lodged' in city contexts to influence local decision makers, often both at the same time. In much the same way, such strategies may be conducted at arm's length, in a more indirect fashion, where consultants and other brokers reach out to officials and politicians through a succession of enrolling practices to establish their authority and presence. When authority is stretched in this way, however, the lack of direct interaction leaves their judgement and counsel more exposed to reinterpretation and displacement downstream by local political interests – some of whom may reach out beyond their city to fold in alternative agendas formulated elsewhere, that frame events differently (Allen and Cochrane, 2014).

When the 'outside' of cities is not distant in terms of miles or kilometres, political actors near and far may make their influence felt in a variety of relational ways. Such interplay of forces speaks to the adoption of market-orientated policies as a more tenuous achievement than many straightforward domination scripts would acknowledge. The distorted reach in such contexts highlights the different ways in which actors may bring their influence to bear, reacting to the forces present by attempting to work out what best suits a given situation and adapting their means accordingly. Quieter registers of power and influence are more likely to be part of that adaptable mix precisely because of the greater reach that they afford, in terms of the number of ways that they may be leveraged topologically. Not, as I have had cause to stress, exercised in isolation, but as part of what it takes for economic and political actors to gain purchase; one that is reproduced differently to register a more durable influence.

Topological sensibilities: take two

This chapter, as mentioned, is paired with Chapter 3. It represents the other side of a topological redescription of power, a second 'take' as it were, with a more explicit focus upon how power relations are reproduced differently. I chose to split the redescription into consecutive chapters because the two sides of the topological equation broadly lend themselves to separate treatment, one focused on the *processes* of distorted reach, the other focused on the *relationships* of power transformed by those very same processes of distortion. If the aim of Chapter 3 was to outline the processes of folding and stretching space through time that enabled powerful actors to interact directly or indirectly with others elsewhere, the intention of this chapter was to show how such topological leverage may be used to register a powerful presence, often in different and diverse ways. Continuity as well as change, sameness as well as difference, the changing same of power, in that sense, both form the topological centrepiece of the present chapter.

Having said that, quieter registers of power and influence have, to my mind, assumed greater significance in today's more broadly topological world, where the gap between 'here' and 'there' is frequently bridged in ways that exhaust our geometric descriptions. Distant acts of political seduction, as noted, may rarely be what they seem when folded in to frame the benefits of economic prosperity, while acts of manipulation exercised from afar may not be recognized for what they are, as closing down alternative avenues to prosperity. Those on the receiving end of such practices may find themselves having to adjust their bearings; that is, by acknowledging such 'connections' as composing the spaces of which they are a part, not simply as lines drawn on a map. Relational proximity and distance, together with topological reach, in that sense, have to be seen for what they are, as familiar words used in new ways that enable us to see things differently.

If we alter our spatial understanding of power to one of a set of relationships stretched and folded through time, however, we also need to conceive of power as a practical tool. It is what actually happens out there that matters, which practical means work better than others given the situation and how actors adapt when such measures fall short. This more provisional set of arrangements, where power as a relationship is actively reproduced between 'here' and 'there', its reach distorted topologically, is explored in greater depth in the remaining chapters of the book.

PART II
Powers of reach

5

THE FINANCIAL ENGINEERING OF ADVANTAGE

Power that defies maps

Much has been written about the greed and exuberance of the financial sector both before and after the global financial crisis of 2007–08 (see for instance Stiglitz, 2010; Tett, 2010; Wolf, 2014). Coming across the words 'manipulation' and 'finance' in the same sentence these days is hardly the stuff of shock and horror, especially after the fallout from the manipulation of Libor and Euribor lending rates, the Foreign Exchange market-rigging scandals, as well as concerns over money laundering and tax evasion more generally. Few, I would have thought, have been deeply shocked by the ongoing revelations about money markets and their fraudulent antics. But such proscribed wrongdoings are not the focus of my attention here.

Rather, in this chapter, I want to look at how, with the onset of financialization, the moneyed elites, bankers, brokers and investment managers among them, have been more-or-less successful in actively *reproducing* their power in a variety of *different* ways to skew rewards in their favour. I say more-or-less successful, because, as intimated earlier, the practised ability of these groups to turn financial transactions to their advantage is a tenuous achievement and as such they risk losing that advantage. Much hinges upon how they exercise their power and influence to skilfully exploit whatever opportunities for advantage arise. Dissimulation, the ability to quietly present yourself as you actually are without revealing all, I would argue, has been central to that exercise. It represents a subtle way of concealing what one is up to without the need for disguise and, more pointedly, it has been made possible by the distorted reach leveraged by such moneyed elites.

Indeed, to my mind, financialization and the rise of the shadow banking system has provided the context for acts of dissimulation to take hold. By that, I do not wish to attribute any systemic power to finance, but rather to the fact that, for the best part of the past two decades, the volume of transactions conducted outside of the regulatory banking system has afforded opportunities to traditional banks, along with hedge funds and other financial actors, to reward themselves seemingly at the expense of others (Epstein and Jayadev, 2005; Sayer, 2015). In short, with the burgeoning of deals off the balance sheet of banks, such actors found themselves well placed as intermediaries to exploit resource and information asymmetries to reproduce their power to gain advantage. Not, it should be stressed, by illicit or fraudulent means, but by quietly manipulating deals in their favour, tempting investors to enter arrangements not wholly transparent in terms of actual benefits, and persuading others of deals that, on the face of it, look too good to pass up.

Of course, such rewarding practices are not new to financial markets. But what is new is the innovative means employed as banking has been pushed into the 'shadows', not just in terms of credit derivatives and such, but the topological means to place financial activities out of regulatory reach in 'offshore' locations. The disembedding of financial risk across regulatory borders is a characteristic of recent topological shifts in the architecture of global finance (Haldane, 2009). The 'lifting out' and 're-embedding' of financial risk that involves indirect interaction with those physically absent is one version of this shift, as is the composing of spaces 'elsewhere' to escape the territorial controls where the financial activity is actually taking place. Both shifts are not so much concerned about whether financial actors have become more or less networked through the latest in mobile communications technologies, as they are with how certain ways of leveraging reach topologically have enabled them to make their proximity and presence felt regardless of the physical distances involved. Such topological activities seem to defy actual mapping, where for instance brokers, dealers and the like attempt to reproduce their power and advantage by directly *folding* in their influence from afar or by indirectly *stretching* their authority through time to engineer less-than-equal outcomes.

But, as often seems to be the case, this is not how the contemporary landscape of finance and power is always experienced. This, I believe, is largely down to the fact that what actually passes for power in the financial markets is not the kind that bends the will of others to gain advantage. In no small part, this is because the power exercised by financial intermediaries is largely directed at making things happen: making deals happen, aligning interests and brokering outcomes (Folkman et al., 2007). This, as was argued in Chapter 4, is the kind of facilitative power that may look innocuous enough, yet actually obscures a more instrumental goal.

In this chapter I want to show first, how the 'power to' engineer outcomes has been used by financial actors to skew rather than share rewards and, in so doing, has reproduced their advantage in financially novel and spatially innovative ways. After that, in the second half of the chapter, drawing on the example of a privatized water utility in the UK, Thames Water, I attempt to show how, over the past decade or so, an international consortium of financial players, led by the Australian bank Macquarie, set out to engineer household water for financial gain in the UK, seeking to reproduce their power and advantage in the process. In particular, I draw attention to how the consortium leveraged their powers in topological fashion to place others within and beyond reach and, in so doing, skewed financial rewards in their favour.

'Power to' skew rewards

In the context of financialization, if shadow banking did not exist, you would have to invent it. On the back of financialization, the crucial intermediary role long played by banks grew in significance to draw in a host of financial actors alongside banks, from private hedge funds, security dealers and private equity trusts to corporate lawyers and asset managers (Eturk et al., 2008; Pike and Pollard, 2010). In the 1980s and 1990s the proliferation of financial players eager to act as go-between for those willing to lend money, and those looking for money to borrow, was matched by ever more sophisticated techniques for managing the risks associated with the accelerated volume of borrowing and investment. Driven by competition between financial middlemen, new financial instruments emerged to cope with the increased uncertainty of a momentum-driven system (Bryan and Rafferty, 2006; Montgomerie and Williams, 2009). Rather than eliminate risk, however, techniques such as securitization and swap-based derivatives, it is now acknowledged, led to its transmission and diffusion, and the collapse of the lending boom in 2008 (Tett, 2010). It is also understood that shadow banking, the name given to many of the innovative techniques and those who practise them, brought about that collapse and the subsequent financial crisis. What seems to be less well understood is that shadow banking remains a crucial part of finance today, indeed vital, it seems, to its operation and its reward structure (Fein, 2013).

Shadow banking, as a description of financial activity, is something of a misnomer in that it tends to convey the idea of a parallel, almost spectral set of operations to those of traditional banking. While there is some truth to that impression, it is perhaps more important to recognize that much of what passes for shadow banking is conducted by traditional investment houses or bank holding companies, either directly or indirectly through subsidiaries and affiliates (Pozsar et al., 2010). Many of these unregulated activities take place behind a legal architecture that distances them relationally from the bank proper, even to the extent that they are registered 'elsewhere' for operational purposes in 'offshore' locations (Palan and Nesvetailova, 2014). Nonetheless, such activities and many of the leveraged techniques that underpin them are integral to the business of the regulated banks and do much to help create liquidity in the markets, as well as pass on risks to those thought most willing to bear them.

Such activities and techniques, however, are also fundamental to the skewed reward structures that have enabled a number of banks and other financial intermediaries to extract a disproportionate share of the benefits (Blackburn, 2006, 2008). An outcome which is odd, really, for a business that is said to work for all parties involved: that is, investors, borrowers, shareholders and all those sitting in between. Perhaps even more so, given that the business of banking presents itself as a veritable positive-sum game.

Positive-sum games?

Positive-sum games, as mentioned previously, play to the advantage of all concerned, so that the allocation of capital and the management of risk performed by those in between results in a 'win–win' situation. No-one in the shadow banking world need be compelled to join a positive-sum game, in that the prospect of predictable gains is normally sufficient inducement. Nothing, though, is guaranteed, and a positive outcome is predicated upon the effectiveness of the 'work' that is put in by those mediating the financial arrangement. Returns may even be negative-sum, where all parties lose out should the deal fall through or the expertise of those acting as 'middlemen' turn out to be misjudged. In today's complex, dispersed global economy, the application of informational resources and market expertise to bring people together, to manage interactions at a distance, foregrounds skills that have more purchase in collaborative, negotiated arrangements. Such mediating skills are at a premium if financial outcomes are to play to the advantage of all parties.

Bruno Latour (2005), as noted in Chapter 2, drew a useful distinction between mediators and intermediaries, which goes some of the way towards describing the 'work' of financial intermediation. Mediators, for him, are an active force transforming and translating what is not connected into some form of association, while intermediaries work towards stabilizing the arrangement. In the context of financial markets, the distinction is blurred somewhat, but its analytical usefulness stems from its depiction of the different kinds of skills involved in the act of mediation. Both types of activity are required to form patterns of association that bind people together in the pursuit of agreed ends. The 'power to' bridge what was previously separate and unconnected elements, to bring them into alignment, as noted previously, is the kind of thing that he had in mind. Crucially, the ability to forge associations and to broker relationships through negotiated efforts resembles not a set of financial networks already in place (see Burt, 1976, 1992), but rather a looser arrangement held together for a given purpose, namely the promise of positive-sum games.

Such an arrangement, though, tends to obscure more than it reveals. As stressed in Chapter 4, the issue does not boil down simply to whether gains are either positive or negative, for those are not the only possible outcomes. Positive-sum games, after all, do not have to equate to equal-sum games. Certainly those placed along what is sometimes a surprisingly long chain of financial intermediation seem to possess the means to benefit from ostensible positive-sum games. Indeed, the instrumental nature of the mediation involved reveals itself through something more than just plan brokerage skills; namely the ability of bankers, fund managers and other intermediaries to make themselves *indispensable* to the deal.

Whether through the powers of artful persuasion, subtle inducement or the establishment of their authority and expertise, the ability to impress upon investors, borrowers and the like that they cannot obtain what they want by themselves, given the risks involved, represents what has become known as an 'obligatory passage point' (Callon, 1986). Having signed up to a deal that is seemingly hard to resist, those on board may have little choice but to go along with the bundle of fees and costs tucked away in the detail of the arrangement. What cannot be passed up, in that sense, has to be passed through. High fee options may be justifiable on the basis of the uncertainties faced, but once the difficulty of going it alone seems indisputable, there is likely to be no going back or retracing the steps of investment. There is a point at which a deal becomes, to all intents and purposes, irreversible. When that point is reached, other ways of arranging the deal are closed down, choices are restricted to only those on offer, and so on.

If this all sounds a touch overblown, that is because, in part, it is. Having argued that the ability of bankers and other financial actors to turn situations to their advantage is a tenuous achievement, it would be fanciful of me to claim otherwise. People, investors included, do not necessarily stay persuaded, authority can be questioned, and deals can unravel when obligations are not fixed. Charles Tilly's observations on the 'in-between' workings of power perhaps come closest to the kind of 'improvised work' that has to be put in by financial intermediaries, if the outward impression of indispensability is to be sustained. Knowing how to adapt when things do not stay fixed, you may recall, is the hallmark of situations where more than one set of interests is in play or their alignment poses particular problems. Working out what works best in the context of a financial deal may require the adjustment of interests from short to long term, for example, or rates of return to be altered to fit a new situation. The ability to improvise, the ability to keep a deal on track by adapting to changed circumstances, often requires such practical negotiating and bargaining skills (Konings, 2010).

That said, negotiations in such situations are not always even-handed, and bargaining does not necessarily imply give-and-take between evenly balanced interests. In a context where more than one set of interests is in play, Tilly (2002) also refers to the process of 'accommodative bargaining', where the concerns of more than one set of players may be exploited, while simultaneously accommodating the interests of other groups. Governments and taxpayers, for instance, may lose out from what appears to be a positive-sum arrangement, while some investors gain a more than adequate rate of return, and those orchestrating the deal benefit by charging fees all round. Bankers and fund managers may negotiate and bargain with others to achieve a desired end but, as stressed earlier, the end itself may not benefit all parties equally. Acts of dissimulation, as will become apparent later in the chapter, may conceal to one or more parties the self-serving nature of a financial arrangement, or limit the margins for manoeuvre in a bargaining situation for one or more parties. In such subtle ways, the 'power to' bring a set of varied interests into alignment may mask the fact that not all returns are of equal value, and those orchestrating the deal may benefit whether it goes ahead or not.

Strange power

Susan Strange (1974, 1994), a dogged commentator on the self-interested nature of power-bargaining arrangements, would have recognized the asymmetric dependence of investors and borrowers alike on those who attempt to make themselves indispensable. No bargain lasts forever and concessions, often minor, form part of any brokered deal, but once an 'obligatory passage point' has been reached, the banks and financial players holding the arrangement together are in a position to 'game' all sides. By 'game', I simply mean that those holding the ring, advising and negotiating the best possible outcome for all involved are in a position to exploit whatever financial opportunities arise. Strange (1998) recognized early on that financial innovations, devised by bankers, brokers and dealers in the 1990s to reduce uncertainty in the marketplace, changed not only the financial 'products' they had to offer, but also the balance of power.

Observing developments at a time when shadow banking had yet to be named as a set of unregulated financial activities, she recognized that the ability of banks and others to side-step territorially-based regulatory controls represented a shift in the balance of financial power. As the turnover of financial securities traded across the globe began to rocket, so too did the number and type of risks. In that context, the development of the derivatives markets, to hedge possible interest rate changes, for example, or swings in currency exchange rates, was an obvious means to offset the escalation of the very real risks involved. What was less clear at the time, as she pointed out, was that the innovation and use of a bundle of related financial 'products' would tempt investors to enter into more obscure hedging arrangements or would persuade them that the potential risks could be managed only by such 'products'. The subsequent manipulation of deals, so that swaps and options, for instance, entered into the frame as a means of further reducing liabilities, in that respect only added to the opacity of the financial arrangements.

Opacity, of course, is a relative term and what appears incomprehensible to some may be reasonably well understood by others. What may appear as artifice or contrived, on closer inspection, may turn out to be less a means of powerful influence and control, and more a useful tool, albeit a sophisticated one, for distributing and hedging risk. Strange's way of teasing out what, if any, play of advantage is involved was to ask the simple question: who benefits? What purpose do the improvised practices of much of what falls under shadow banking serve and who benefits most from their use and deployment?

Take the 'product' or rather the technique of default swaps, for example. This type of credit derivative serves to further distribute risk insofar as it enables banks and other financial players to sell to another party the risk that someone it has lent money to might default. That party is then liable should the borrower default, or be likely to default on the debt should their credit rating drop. The risk is 'swapped' for a payment akin to a type of insurance premium and all parties, including those brokering the deal, may be said to benefit: the latter through the fees charged for the 'product', those swapping the risk on one side from an insurance premium, and on the other from the assurance of a risk apparently well managed. Left at that, default swaps are simply a technique to reduce uncertainty. As a financial 'product', however, they represent an opportunity, together with other novel means to reduce risk, for substantial gains to be realized by those who sell them. The greater the number of ways in which a deal can be financially engineered, the greater the variety of ways in which a debt can be refinanced, for instance, the more opportunities there are for financial intermediaries to repackage and resell a vast and growing array of potential risks.

What lies behind all this engineering of financial 'products' is the drive to get more out of the business of trading, to increase turnover and momentum. The faster the turnover, the greater the trading in assets, the easier it is to extract more in the way of fees: fees from holding financial assets, from moving assets and from trading assets. Assets – that is, debts, bonds, loans, bills, stocks and the like – do not move freely by themselves, however. They need a little help to become 'marketable', to be bought and sold, and there has been no shortage of innovation directed at changing the characteristics of an asset so that it can be more easily traded. Perhaps the best known innovation designed expressly for that purpose is the technique of securitization.

Securitization, for want of better way of phrasing it, is a means of liberating value. As a technique, it involves turning a tangible asset into a tradable financial security by breaking it up into separate earnings packages, assigning each package a risk profile, and then selling the securities on to investors willing to purchase or trade them. What effectively is being traded here is the earnings packages, that is, a claim upon a future repayment or revenue stream, and the risks associated with them. The projected streams of money are the underlying asset and the value from them is freed up when the owner of the asset, a company with a pile of debts, say, or a bank with a student loan portfolio, is able to remove those debts from its balance sheet and replace them with the cash raised from the sale of the securities.

So, to invoke Strange's question, who benefits from a technique such as securitization or, for that matter, from default swaps or credit derivatives in general? Such 'products' clearly exist for a purpose, which conventionally is to pass on risk and increase the 'marketability' of assets so that turnover and trading is increased, which, in turn, is said to lower costs and promote efficient pricing. Whilst that may have all the trappings of a positive-sum outcome, as we have seen, it does not necessarily imply that all parties benefit equally. Strange clearly believed that the development of innovative techniques designed to by-pass territorially based regulatory controls pointed to the ability of those practising them to benefit at the expense of others. Who exactly is 'gamed' by such practices is less clear-cut, although governments, taxpayers and shareholders come into her frame. Moreover, the rapid turnover of the financial markets that she documented also presented opportunities to those working 'in-between' to exploit the new rules around managing risk and the possibilities to create value seemingly out of next to nothing (Dodd, 2011).

Strange (1998, see also 1994) was writing a decade or so before the global financial crisis of 2007–08 and setting out a raft of techniques and practices that now, as mentioned, make up what has become the shadow banking system. The power relationships that she identified reflected her long-held assumptions about the self-serving nature of financial practices, even to the extent that those looking out for themselves did not always recognize their own self-interest in the improvised schemes. Indeed, the asymmetric dependencies that she considered to be a critical feature of financial intermediation have been shown to be a persistent feature of that exchange, where trading in debt and risk products, above all, continues to work to the advantage of bankers, brokers, fund managers and the like (Blackburn, 2008; Ford, 2008).

Dariusz Wojcik (2011, 2012a), in particular, has drawn attention to the powerful relationships that underpin practices such as securitization, especially in the US finance sector, and the ability of those who manage, advise and broker the process to skew rewards in their favour. He documented how many of the financial techniques identified by Strange were used to increase the turnover in the packaging and selling of risks that comprise the different elements of a securitization transaction. Putting all the elements together, linking investors, individuals as well as institutions with the issuers of securities and, in turn, connecting investors to each other in the marketplace created opportunities for those 'in between' not only to exploit information and resource asymmetries, but also to make themselves indispensable to the outcome. Enticement and persuasion, as well as inducement, some of the quieter registers of power, all come into play in such dissimulated arrangements and are implicit in Wojcik's account of power and influence in the securities industry.

On the back of financial inventiveness and advances in computing technologies, he went on to show how the control and influence of the investment houses and bank holding companies, together with the likes of hedge funds, grew in line with demand for the products of shadow banking. The ability to keep innovative transactions off the balance sheet and to avoid regulatory oversight of the risks involved gave them a competitive edge over their more regulated brethren. For shadow banking to operate, however, it needed to be outside of the jurisdictional authority of the central banks. Or not so much 'outside' as merely *out of reach* of the territorial controls exercised by nation states. As already mentioned, the entities that made up the shadow banking system simply had to be registered 'elsewhere' for operational purposes. On such a basis, a novel topological fiction came into being: offshore finance.

Topological fictions

Offshore financial markets, contrary to what is often thought, did not originally come about as a means to avoid the payment of taxes. Such markets owe their existence to an anomaly which can be traced to the development of the Euro-markets in London in the 1950s and the regulatory barrier that UK banks faced at the time over lending outside the sterling area. In order to deal with this regulatory anomaly, the Bank of England, in a Tilly-esque improvised manoeuvre, proposed:

> to treat certain types of financial transactions between non-resident parties and denominated in foreign currency *as if they did not take place* in London.

Paradoxically, the bank created, in effect, a new regulatory space outside its jurisdiction, and a new concept – offshore finance.

(Palan and Nesvetailova, 2014, emphasis added)

What started out as a condoned solution to an unexpected obstacle faced by UK banks, however, turned into something much more significant when US banks operating in London used this new space of offshore finance to circumvent their own US banking and finance regulations. While the UK authorities were looking the other way, so to speak, US banks took full advantage of the fact that the 'offshore' nature of the Euromarkets enabled them to behave as if they were conducting transactions 'elsewhere', and thus beyond the regulatory reach of the US government. The 'elsewhere' in question, however, is in practice a topological fiction, a legal fabrication that allowed financial institutions to carry out their business in one place whilst recording the transactions in another, in a location free from any kind of political regulation or interference by their own governing authority (Picciotto, 1999). Without the customary constraints of keeping sufficient reserves to meet potential withdrawals and other imposed trading restrictions, banks operating in the Euromarkets thrived on the competitive advantage.

The improvised fiction, the condoning of a practice that works on the basis of a continuously composed space, is perhaps the key point to hold onto here. The pretence, accepted by all the players involved, that transactions conducted in one location would be looked upon as if they took place elsewhere, is itself a form of financial engineering, albeit one of spatial rather than purely financial innovation. Nonetheless, the same purpose is served, which, as Strange observed, is to take profitable advantage of the cracks and chinks in financial regulatory systems that are territorially based. She would, I think, have been aghast at the sheer scale of offshore finance today, if not entirely surprised by the degree of manipulation and concealment involved. Despite limited attempts to bring banking out of the shadows, the ongoing use of derivatives to distribute and hedge risk, the continuing use of securitization techniques to free up value, as well as the accepted need to boost investment and liquidity, seem to require the topological fiction of a space 'elsewhere' to function.

Palan (2003) and others writing along similar lines have described 'elsewhere' as nowhere in particular, so long as the fictional space serves the purpose of financial transactions remaining unaccountable to the tax or regulatory authorities. The offshore world of finance, the Cayman Islands, Jersey, the British Virgin Islands, Monaco and Delaware, to name but a few, are obviously actual locations, but their specific geography, even the fact that they are not all, in any sense, 'offshore', is besides the point. Whether onshore or offshore, what matters is that the financial transactions recorded in such locations are outside of the jurisdictional domain where they are actually taking place (Roberts, 1994). In that sense, arguably, what matters above all is that such financial arrangements are placed beyond the reach of the regulatory regimes which would throw a legal spotlight upon them.

The point, and indeed the practice, is an explicitly topological one, not one of geometry or the actual circulation and flow of monies around the globe. No disguised caches of money actually move; rather, transactions are merely registered elsewhere in order to avoid regulatory oversight and control. Moreover, nor are any physical distances traversed when such transactions are recorded digitally. The distances involved are *relational*, not metric; they are composed of the relationships between the operation, transaction and registration of the financial activity, and electronically recorded in different locations *as if* the monies moved elsewhere. The topological fiction enacted takes the form of a continuous exchange between what happens in the different locations, despite the fact that more than one jurisdictional space is involved. As such there is no actual break in the financial relationship, only different sides to the same transaction.

Any resemblance to the figure of the Möbius strip discussed in Chapter 3 is clearly intentional on my part. The paradoxical two-sidedness of the Möbius strip neatly conveys the actual topological distortion involved when a financial transaction, say a securitization deal, is conducted in New York but is recorded as having taken place in the Cayman Islands to avoid regulation. By *stretching* out the financial relationship between 'here' and 'there', by 'lengthening' the process of intermediation in a more complex, circuitous manner, the intent is plainly to escape regulatory controls in the former location. Such circumvention, however, requires a jurisdictional twist, so that the by now complex, mediated financial relationship is transformed into a two-sided relationship spanning more than one jurisdictional authority. In this topological setting, the deal itself is displaced, registered as having taken place in a location different from the actual transaction, yet it remains part of the same securitization arrangement.

Stretching a financial relationship through time, however, is not the only means of placing a securitization deal beyond the reach of regulatory authorities. A more direct form of topological leverage is to wrap the deal into an 'investment vehicle', detach it from its actual location, say London, and re-embed it within a different jurisdictional framework in the British Virgin Islands, for example. What is kept off the balance sheet of a financial institution as a separate legal vehicle is, in that way, further displaced by its registration offshore (Wojcik, 2012b). The distance between London and the British Virgin Islands, in this instance, is purely relational, intensive not extensive in its reach, as part of the process of continuous exchange. The securitization deal that is put together in London, within the bounds of UK regulatory controls, is effectively displaced directly, *folded* out as a legal entity from one domain to another to avoid the regulatory oversight of the UK banking authorities.

The fiction of a space 'elsewhere', an offshore location, is obviously critical to the operation of shadow banking and the financial innovations that it has spawned. Without such a topological fiction, banks and other financial players would have found it increasingly difficult to take on more risk. The ability to place such risks beyond reach, through acts of legal manipulation and spatial distortion, nonetheless requires that such reach be leveraged. Susan Roberts (1994) once usefully suggested that offshore financial locations are both on the margins and at the centre of contemporary capitalism, but perhaps a more accurate depiction would have been to say that such locations are topologically equivalent. The *same* financial relationship is reproduced, but in a *different* spatial arrangement. Topology, in that regard, enables us to grasp how financial actors, despite being physically absent, can have an impact at, or in spite of, the physical distances involved. The advantages engineered defy any simple mapping because 'elsewhere', as Palan argued, is really nowhere in particular (see also Belcher et al., 2008).

How such advantages have been actively reproduced by bankers and investment managers by the skilful exercise of their power in diverse arrangements is the focus of the rest of this chapter. For that, we turn to the case of a privatized water set-up in the UK, one financially engineered from well beyond its territorial shores, yet brought directly within reach.

Reproducing financial advantage

In 2006, a German-owned water utility in the UK, with some 14 million customers in the South-East of England, was acquired by an international consortium of investors led by the European arm of an Australian bank, the Macquarie Group. Quite what an Australian bank, together with an assortment of Canadian, Dutch, Spanish and Australian pension funds, as well as a Spanish private equity fund and a Portuguese investment vehicle, saw in the privatized utility, Thames Water, beyond a relatively stable, long-term investment, was not obvious at the time. The clue lay in the monopoly provision of water supply in England and Wales, the predictable nature of the revenue streams captured from households who have no choice over their water supplier or indeed the amount that they have to pay for their water. Such characteristics, conventionally, amount to little more than a dull, safe asset, with earnings to match the profile, but to the new owners of Thames Water, especially the Macquarie Group, a guaranteed revenue stream over time represented an opportunity to extract value from the water business, skewing rewards more effectively towards investors and intermediaries alike (see Allen and Pryke, 2013).

In the hands of financial intermediaries such as Macquarie, a stable regional water utility in a conventional operating system was effectively 'lifted out' and placed into the risk-taking world of financial innovation and offshore finance. In topological terms, the utility figure of Thames Water was stretched and folded into a distorted corporate holding structure, much of which was 'elsewhere'. Despite the topological distortion, however, a relational equivalence was established between the utilities and the corporate figures that enabled Macquarie to reproduce its financial advantage. What remained related was the power to skew rewards through a securitized arrangement put together 'onshore' in London but consolidated 'offshore' to escape regulatory oversight. Indeed, one could argue that the financial advantage in this instance was folded into the very fabric of Thames Water and its dealings.

At root, Macquarie used its knowledge of financial products and debt-refinancing skills to piece together investor interests in such a way as to 'fix' an overall orientation that appeared to more-or-less suit all involved. Their practised ability to fold in a group of globally diverse investors and keep them *within reach*, to broker their concerns and align their interests, made it credible for them to capture the revenue streams by securitized means. Once enrolled to such practices, the use of offshore locations, in this case the Cayman Islands, to raise the securitized debt ensured not only that the risks were concealed from view, but that they were placed *out of reach* of both the UK's financial and water authorities. The re-embedding of such risks within a different jurisdictional framework stabilized a debt structure at arm's length, without a break in the continuity of the financial relationships under transformation, and engineered a water business to their advantage.

That advantage, however, has not shown itself for what it really is. The cash that flows from household water bills in the South-East of England now and in the future is the financial asset in question, not water as such. Thames Water's 14 million bill-paying customers underpin the securitization of revenue streams, yet little if any of the financial engineering has ever been disclosed to its customers, nor the full extent to which such revenues have been diverted to pay off the money borrowed by the Macquarie-led consortium to buy the water company in the first place. As an exercise, this has little to do with overt corporate domination and everything to do with the ability to practise dissimulation as part of a continuous, yet changing, arrangement of power. Holding back what is fully at stake, not revealing the self-serving nature of engineering water bills, whilst getting others to want what you want, is one of the more subtle ways in which Macquarie quietly reproduced its power and advantage.

Dissimulation and financial manipulation

Dissimulation, as an act, is probably best thought about as a form of manipulation. Whereas manipulation, as noted previously, involves the concealment of intent so that advantage is gained by the lack of exposure, dissimulation draws attention to a particular means of concealment. If the real motive behind the Macquarie-led consortium's acquisition of Thames Water was to extract value from the water business, not all the parties involved were engaged in some kind of cover up and none, I think it is fair to say, was pretending to be what they were not. The European, North American and Australian pension funds would have been tempted by the predictable returns that such an investment offered over the longer term precisely because it matched their long-term liabilities. That is their economic function and there would seem little point in them going out of their way to project anything different in terms of investment motives. Macquarie too, as an investment bank, did not disguise the fact that its interest in the deal lay in the returns on its proprietary investment funds and the fees earned from trading on behalf of others. But disguise is not the issue here, for there are other, more subtle ways to conceal one's intentions.

Dissimulation does involve a pretence of sorts, but it is the kind of pretence that diverts attention from what you actually are, or indeed your actual motivation

(Runciman, 2008). If the extraction of value from Thames Water reminds you of asset-stripping, no-one involved in the consortium, least of all the pension funds, would sign up to such a strategy. But nor would they disguise the fact that, as an investment bank, a pension fund or a private equity fund, their intent is to extract the best possible return that they can from their capital investment. There is an element of 'hiding in plain sight' involved, whereby a practical way of concealing what one is up to is to consciously avoid disguising it. Disguising one's actions carries the risk of being found out, whereas not actually revealing all there is to know about yourself or your motives leaves you free to be open about your role in the public domain. As such, there is no necessity to conjure up a false impression or leave a false trail, only a need to be less than fulsome in your disclosures.

Macquarie's role in the Thames Water deal never required it to pretend to be anything other than the broker it actually was. As an investment broker, it facilitated a deal between interested parties that could lead to a win–win situation all round, for the UK government and the customers of Thames Water, as well as for the global array of investors lined up behind the deal. Equally, Macquarie never hid from view the fact that it intended to leverage the debt used to buy Thames Water through a securitization arrangement. Nor did it bury the reason for pursuing such an arrangement, which was to simplify its capital structure by reducing the peaks and troughs of its debt repayments. As mentioned earlier, securitizing your debt has the effect of freeing up the value from the underlying asset, in this case the revenues raised by household water bills, and having the cash raised from the sale of securities at your disposal. What Macquarie failed to reveal, however, was that not everyone benefited equally from such an arrangement, and some, namely itself, considerably more.

One year after acquiring Thames Water, in 2007, the Kemble Consortium, as the Macquarie-led group of investors is legally known, transferred all its existing debt, some £2.9 billion, into a securitized vehicle and raised a further £1.2 billion of debt. This arrangement virtually doubled the company's debt at the time and set the pattern for debt refinancing up to and including Thames Water's £1 billion debt issue in 2012. In the five years between 2007 and 2012, the Kemble Consortium had packaged together some £7 billion of debts, issued bonds against them, and sold them on to willing investors. As stressed, securitization represents a claim against an underlying asset, in this instance the cash that flows from household water bills; that is, money for which Thames Water's customers have yet to be billed. It is a claim on not just tomorrow's bills, but revenues stretching way into the future, 2062 to be precise for the latest tranche of securities. A host of financial intermediaries, from the banks issuing the securities to those hedging the risks involved and those providing working credit facilities, benefited from the arrangement through the fees earned for their services, but that is not the point here.

The point is that the money freed up from the sale of billions of debt turned up in places far removed from the pockets of Thames Water's customers in the form of lower water bills. A financial product designed to simplify Thames Water's capital structure, which should benefit customers through reduced water bills, was turned to a new purpose, namely to pay a higher shareholder dividend to the consortia of investors and to pay back interest on intra-company loans and interest on external debt, that is the money borrowed previously to buy Thames Water (see Allen and Pryke, 2013). Effectively, the Macquarie-led consortium, through the use of leveraged debt, was able to bring forward future income streams to skew rewards more to themselves than to Thames Water's households. At the same time, Macquarie, as the lead member of the consortium, used part of the cash raised from the securitized revenue streams to pay down interest on its own debt, much of it borrowed at attractive rates through its own holding companies that comprise the mainstay of its spatially distorted corporate structure.

Why would Macquarie pay back interest to its own companies when it could pay more out to investors in the consortia? Well, the obvious point is that interest repayments can be used to offset or reduce Thames Water's tax bill to the UK government. But perhaps a more significant point is that paying down interest on debt enables the consortium to run its debt-driven model, so that it can continue to pay sizeable dividend payments over and above actual profits earned; that is, payments out of the money borrowed by the securitization of customer's water bills. The intricacies of a model based on maxing out on debt can at best be only glimpsed through company accounts, as can the engineering of benefits more towards investors than customers. In part, this is because the financial manoeuvres are indeed complex by any accounting standards, but also because of the relational distance created between the water business run by Thames Water and, as we shall see shortly, its financial operations elsewhere in the Caymans. While the latter offshore operations strictly speaking are not a cover-up, nor are they particularly revealing in terms of the distribution of benefits.

What comes to mind is Tilly's 'accommodative bargaining' arrangements whereby more than one set of interests is in play, yet not all are rewarded equally and some may benefit at the expense of others. Clearly, the consortium of investors behind Thames Water has benefited through higher rates of return, arguably at the expense of both Thames Water's customers and the UK taxpayer. But Macquarie, as a well placed intermediary, has used its financial engineering skills to exploit the deal to reproduce their advantage even further. Dissimulation, as I have had cause to stress, involves the ability to manoeuvre oneself into situations that best suit your interests without revealing all, even to the extent of diverting attention away from one's actual intentions. Macquarie's ability to be all things to all people, investors and governments alike, whilst not disclosing the self-serving nature of an arrangement, perhaps best approximates to what Tilly had in mind. It is certainly what James Meek (2014) had in mind when trying to tease out Macquarie's interest in Thames Water. Dismissing the idea of Macquarie's capture of Thames Water as a simple story of capitalist exploitation, he is of the opinion that:

> It is a tale of clever middlemen. On one side, millions of Thames Water cus-
> tomers, paying an inflated private water tax; on the other, millions of Dutch,

Canadian, Australian and British pensioners, dependent on their pension funds in their old age, and millions of Chinese and Emirates, powerless to influence their governments' disposition of national wealth. In the middle, an international fraternity of fund managers, telling the Thames customers what a brilliant deal they have with the Thames thirteen as their tax collectors, and telling the world's pensioners what an extraordinary return they're getting on their stake in Thames Water, so extraordinary that they, the private planners of the fund manager class, need to be rewarded with fat fees, options, salaries and bonuses. It's not possible for both messages to be true.

(Meek, 2014, 115–116)

Leaving the rhetoric to one side, Meek is drawing attention to the unrealistic nature of the positive-sum game played by Macquarie, where not everyone can benefit equally from the financial arrangements put in place to run Thames Water. The 'clever middlemen' that he refers to, Macquarie in this instance, are able to get others to want what they want without disclosing everything that is at stake, in particular their own set of interests and 'exit' game. With the UK government that task was made somewhat easier by the belief that only private finance could deliver a better deal on the supply of household water (Cave, 2009). Only increased competition and innovation in water markets, it was assumed, could deliver lower household water bills, a better service and environmental sustainability, and Macquarie was hardly likely to disabuse them of that notion. Nor, however, did it fully reveal the fact that the financial engineering of household water bills would, it turns out, be one of the main means adopted to achieve such desirable outcomes. Or that, in order to so, the restructuring of Thames Water's debts would be used to benefit Macquarie and its investor group at the expense of households and their rising water bills or, as Meek would have it, the inflated private water tax that they have no choice but to pay.

It perhaps needs to be said that it would be surprising if the UK government was unaware of a company like Macquarie and its innovative financial practices. But so long as the financial activities of Thames Water's parent company did not prejudice the managerial viability of the water supply business and it had sufficient financial resources to support that business, the government's regulatory body chose not to probe further. What the UK government had no reason to seek, Macquarie had no reason to hide. If indeed there was more at stake in the private ownership of a UK water company, there was no pressure upon Macquarie to reveal what that might be. Whilst falling somewhat short of Meek's 'brilliant deal' for Thames Water's customers, Macquarie's message to them never included the desirability of packaging and selling their households as a captive revenue stream.

What Meek puts his finger on is that 'middlemen' like Macquarie practise a form of dissemblance, saying different things to different groups or sets of interests over time. The different messages are in part scripted to suit the particular interests, be it a government or investor, and 'edited', as it were, to reveal details that chime with their needs and requirements. The pension funds invested in Thames Water to which Meek draws attention, for instance, may well have been tempted by returns too great not to want, or at least by the prospect of solid, predictable returns from a monopoly enterprise. Yet the extent to which the pension funds were party to a debt-driven model that hides risks within its own distorted corporate structure and uses that debt to distribute sums greater than profits alone generate is perhaps less obvious. The major benefits of such a model, as Strange might have concluded, are realised by the major shareholder which, at the time of Thames Water's purchase, was Macquarie – in this case by orchestrating its own funds and generating revenue from its client base through a range of fees, as well as the overall costs of running the consortium.

None of this happens, however, without the likes of Macquarie interacting directly and indirectly with its investor and client base. Relational proximity and distance, the ability to draw others within close reach and hold them there, is part of what enables Macquarie to piece together its investor interests and make its presence felt. Its skill in placing itself in situations that suit its interests, without revealing all the risks and rewards at stake, in that sense, involves it in leveraging reach topologically, as much as it does leveraging debt.

Drawing investors within close reach

There is a surprising amount of disparate geography behind the Kemble Consortium (see Allen and Pryke, 2013). In addition to the original group of Canadian, Dutch, Spanish and Australian pension funds, from late 2011 and early 2012 the consortium now includes two sovereign wealth funds – the Abu Dhabi Investment Authority and the China Investment Corporation – as well as British Telecom's pension funds. The Macquarie-managed assets, some of which were sold to accommodate Abu Dhabi's interests, comprise six separate funds, of which Macquarie's two European Infrastructure Funds account for the largest share, although this itself has been further diluted by the sale of 13 per cent of its shares to British Telecom. China's sovereign wealth fund acquired its 9 per cent stake in Thames Water when the Spanish and Portuguese investment funds chose to sell up. Overall, an investment stake of around 10 per cent is pretty much representative of the groups involved, although some have as little as 2 or 3 per cent. Macquarie remains the lead and dominant partner of the consortium with a 26 per cent stake in Thames Water, down from its original 48 per cent at the time of purchase.

In terms of holding all this together, there is much to suggest that the kind of mediating work described by Latour is apparent, that is, the 'power to' bridge and align interests. The tenuous nature of such an achievement, however, when a variety of interests have to be settled, requires the kind of 'improvised work' that Tilly described if an outward impression of indispensability is to be sustained by Macquarie in its lead role. There is more involved here, though, than attractive propositions circulating between global investors at ever-greater distances which can ultimately be tracked and traced. The sense in which Macquarie is able to topologically place certain possibilities within reach, to draw investors within its orbit to seek advantage, suggests that it is able to *fold* others in directly through real-time negotiations, as well as *stretching* to reach interested parties through a succession of enrolling practices. Both sets of relationships are capable of establishing relational proximities over physical distances; both involve mediation to draw in pension funds, sovereign wealth funds and the like into a space of their own making.

Negotiation and persuasion over fees, the level of appropriate return and risk levels, require actors to be more-or-less present in the here-and-now of mediated interaction. Inducements of the kind that are tailored to the specific needs of particular investors require a form of simultaneous *co-presence* if uncertainty is to be minimized or at least reduced (Clark and Monk, 2013). Face-to-face interaction is one means of achieving a direct social presence, but so too is the ability of organizations such as Macquarie to draw upon resources to establish near-instantaneous reach through a variety of telecommunication and media technologies, for example (Crang, 2007). Such means are not mutually exclusive and relational proximity runs through both regardless of the physical distances involved. Drawing a group of dispersed and somewhat diverse investors within reach topologically also allows Macquarie to assess the extent of its investment expertise and how far it can go with its own line of authority without losing credibility (see Jones and Search, 2009).

The quieter means of influence, the lure of more than solid returns, the attraction of what appears to be relatively low risk, the persuasive counsel backed up by reputation and expertise, lend themselves to topological transformation in a way that more conspicuous methods of control fall short of as a powerful tool. Attempts to impose authority on a deal at a distance may meet with limited consent, and seeking to dominate the members of an investment consortium by overtly restricting their choices may prove ineffectual in the longer term. The ability to turn open-ended situations to particular advantage without having to fall back on displays of authority or dominance as the lead partner is likely to prove more effective in situations of close, relational proximity. That said, proximity on its own is no guarantee of effectiveness. For that, the *intensiveness* of the relationships between Macquarie and its consortium partners is a factor in its own right.

Certain places can heighten the intensity of financial relationships, and one of those places is undoubtedly the City of London, with its dense clustering of skills and expertise in finance, law and banking (Sassen, 1995). The concentration of such specialist activities brought together in one location, together with access to European markets, played its part in Macquarie building up its investment banking and infrastructure operations in London from the late 1980s onwards. As its European HQ, the City provides Macquarie with an opportunity to monitor investment opportunities, of which Thames Water was one among many, and, with an eye to local regulation, translate them into deals suitable for different types of investor worldwide. The intensity of exchanges produced through such a combination of people, knowledge and expertise, however, is not merely the outcome of an 'internal' London effect. It is as much a product of its constitutive 'outside'; that is, investors and others acting elsewhere who, in co-present fashion, are already part of such exchanges. In that respect, we are back with Massey's notion of an 'outside (that) can be found within', although now more fittingly understood as a topological expression.

As such, the metrics of size and distance are only one aspect of the way that Macquarie manages its investment relationships. Their often intensive character is not something wholly dependent upon the number of financial transactions that pass through the City of London, but rather upon their immanent, focused quality. Concentration and reach, as argued in Chapter 3, are not traded off in such situations; there is no significant dilution of Macquarie's ability to fold in investors from as far afield as China, North America and the Middle East and keep them within reach. In topological terms, the barriers of physical distance do not necessarily restrict Macquarie's ability to attract and influence its diverse range of institutional and private investors and, in the case of Thames Water, frame the benefits in specific rather than general terms, so long as their reach is more or less leveraged intensively.

In fact, Macquarie's skill in being able to draw and hold the Kemble Consortium of investors together, within reach, is in part down to the manner in which it seeks to exercise its authority *among* rather than over them. As the lead member of the consortium, its debt-driven model provides a blueprint for the way that Thames Water should be run, with the different time horizons and risk profiles of investors accommodated under its broad investment umbrella. As I have underlined, there is no real secret to this arrangement. What is manifest, though, is that any collaboration between Macquarie and its consortium partners is not exactly among equals. Whether intentional or not as a strategy, the significant number of nominal investment stakes in the consortium gives Macquarie considerable latitude over the make-up and organization of Kemble.

In terms of minority stakes, the two Dutch pension funds hold just 6 per cent of Kemble between them, the Queensland Investment Corporation has upwards of 9 per cent and the Australian Super Fund considerably less at 2 per cent, and the British Columbia and Alberta Investment Corporations have stakes of 9 and 3 per cent, respectively. The fragmentation of ownership, with Macquarie in a position to broker and influence investment opportunities, makes it difficult to see how those nominally involved in Thames Water can obtain what they want, in terms of returns, by themselves. The difficulty of going it alone for such investors is perhaps evident, although that still leaves Macquarie with the task of aligning the multiple interests and keeping the overall project on track. It would be an exaggeration to suggest that Macquarie's 'power to' achieve shared outcomes benefits the smallest as much as the largest interest, but that does not detract from the play of authority, negotiation and persuasion that holds the leveraged arrangement in close proximity and in line.

Those with minor investment stakes in Thames Water experience restricted margins for manoeuvre, although not in any sense comparable to the hundred or so clients in Macquarie's own investments in Thames Water: its two European

Infrastructure Funds. Accommodative bargaining is pretty much beside the point when it comes to Macquarie's own managed funds, insofar as it exercises considerable discretion over them, controlling the purchase and acquisition of assets as well as the access investors have to their own capital. The advantage of investing through separate funds is that it allows Macquarie to spread its borrowing rather than consolidate it at the holding company level which, in turn, serves to insulate the parent company from risk, and to earn revenue from the fees it charges clients to handle and operate their assets (Jefferis and Stilwell, 2006; O'Neill, 2009). This diversified structure serves Macquarie well, enabling it to generate base and performance fee income from its two managed funds, while the Kemble Consortium as a whole, in turn, derives benefit from the financial products engineered by Macquarie to capture the revenue streams generated by Thames Water's households.

Whilst much of that financial activity, once revealed, can be grasped for what it more-or-less is, the same cannot be said for the risks and rewards displaced 'elsewhere' in topological fashion. Manipulation, here, involves such risks and rewards being placed beyond the reach of the UK's financial and water authorities by the Macquarie-led consortium.

Placing risks and rewards beyond reach

If Macquarie exercises its power to draw investors within its orbit of influence, placing certain possibilities within reach, it also exercises it to distance itself from demands that would limit its ability to extract value from Thames Water. Again, the means of concealment are subtle, not demonstrative: nothing is covered up or disguised, yet not all is fully revealed either. There is nothing particularly secretive about the fact that Thames Water has a distorted corporate structure, with numerous holding companies each tucked one inside the other; or the fact that it uses an offshore location, the Cayman Islands, to raise its securitized cash (Standard and Poor's, 2008). But nor is it entirely transparent about why the operational side of the water business should be so far removed, in terms of relational distance, from its financial side. Or about why the risks and rewards bound up in this arrangement are effectively *folded* out and placed beyond reach.

On the face of it, Macquarie, as stressed, has nothing to hide. The corporate structure of Thames Water resembles that of a wedding cake, with the global owners, the investors that comprise the Kemble Consortium, at its apex. Below that, in turn, are a series of holding companies, some with the name Kemble affixed, others with Thames Water in their company title. Each holding company is a wholly owned subsidiary of the one above, with the parent company, Thames Water plc propping them up. None of them, however, is the actual regulated water company, the business that supplies the water and fixes the leaky pipes. That is Thames Water Utilities Limited, and this company sits at the base of the structure, alongside its two financial offshoots. The role of the two finance offshoots is to raise cash in the marketplace which, as noted earlier, has involved them in the securitization of household revenue streams. One of those finance companies, Thames Water Utilities Cayman Finance Limited, as the name indicates, is based offshore in the Cayman Islands.

Why go to all that organizational trouble if you have nothing to hide? Well, in the first place, Macquarie will tell you that separating the parent company and its investors from the actual water business is a way of ensuring that any financial risks that the former may be exposed to are 'ringfenced' from the company responsible for delivering the water and sorting the sewage. The last thing that the UK water regulator wants is for the Thames Water business to be brought down by what goes on in another, riskier part of its parent's operations. For much the same reason, having Thames Water's financial subsidiary based in the Cayman Islands is a way of legally separating the business of raising cash from the operational side. The fact that Cayman Island companies are untouchable, in a legal sense, protects them from possible claims made by Kemble's investors on the securities held offshore (Standard and Poor's, 2011).

On this view, the intricate corporate structure of Thames Water and its use of offshore finance serves a purpose, namely the protection of Thames Water's 14 million customers and the water supply business from the threat of financial exposure. When put like that, the Macquarie-led consortium is not pretending to be other than what it is. The separation of the parent company from the actual water business makes sense in terms of avoiding undue risk, as does the legal separation of the finance business from the day-to-day running of a water company. But if the owners of Thames Water are not pretending to be something they are not, nor are they actually revealing all that they are.

The untouchable nature of Cayman Island companies is double edged; it can serve to protect the likes of Thames Water from a risk-taking parent company, but it can also make it harder to discern the build-up of debt in a company as a whole, where it ends up and why. The level of debt in Thames Water, as it currently stands, amounts to around four-fifths of the company, which, when you consider that it was debt-free at the time of UK's water privatization in 1989, gives you an idea of how little value there is left in the business. Of the sums raised in the Cayman Islands by Thames Water through the securitization of water bills yet to be paid by its customers, as outlined before, much of it found its way into the pockets of the Kemble Consortium, but also into the various holding companies in the shape of layered debt and the high interest payments required to service it. Debt is cheaper to service than equity and has a tax advantage, but a less than transparent debt-driven model, with its feet, as it were, 'elsewhere' in the Caymans, has the greater advantage of concealing the potential rewards realized through financial engineering.

Perhaps one of the more intriguing aspects of the use of the Cayman Islands to raise funds is that Macquarie, and everyone else involved for that matter, acts as if the whole arrangement did not take place in London. The topological fiction that Thames Water's securitization deal was somehow 'elsewhere' works not only to remove the debt trail from regulatory oversight, but also to obscure where the sums end up. Effectively, one part of Thames Water, a corporate investment vehicle, has been 'lifted out' topologically from one jurisdiction and set down in another, in this case the Caymans, to create a legal distance that places the financial engineering of household water bills beyond the reach of the UK's financial and water authorities. The displacement itself is relational, part of a process of continuous exchange between the different legal entities that comprise Thames Water's corporate group structure, rather than one of actual physical distance.

At the risk of belabouring the point, there is no cover-up involved in such a displacement, no false trail laid down to put regulators off the scent, so to speak. The use of offshore finance as part of a distorted corporate structure by Thames Water works more as a diversion, a means of averting the eye from the funds siphoned off, but also as a way of concealing the full extent of the risks involved. After all, if rewards can be displaced by such relational means, then so too can the risks.

Meek's account of Macquarie's attempt to portray Thames Water as a kind of positive-sum game suggested that it was in fact too good to be true and intimated that there were potential risks attached. In fact, the agreed formal separation of Thames Water plc and its holding companies from the operating business is a tacit admission by Macquarie of the latter, if not the former. On that basis, the UK government's regulatory 'ringfence' that separates the two sides, the financial from the water supply side, places at one remove the elaborate corporate set-up of Thames Water and its offshore debt-refinancing arrangements. Responsibility for any financial dangers exposed is placed by the regulatory authority squarely on the shoulders of Macquarie and the Consortium. Yet, in practice, the risks that arguably matter most to the running of Thames Water have already been placed out of reach of the authorities. Their presence has already been displaced topologically, folded out, both temporally and spatially.

As mentioned earlier, recent securitization deals enacted by Thames Water are underpinned by the predictable cash flows of household water bills for the next thirty to forty years. The time frame itself conjures up significant unknowns, not least the possibility of Thames Water's debt being downgraded if the cash flows should be curtailed by regulatory price reviews. There are safeguards in place should such a situation arise, however. But the safeguards are not the issue; while they remain intact, the Kemble Consortium for now and in the foreseeable future will continue to extract value by means of debt leverage from Thames Water's customers. For as long as the topological fiction of an 'elsewhere' is maintained – an offshore location where Thames Water plc can raise further debt and funnel it upwards through its layers of holding companies to service high-yielding intra-company loans and channel dividend payments – the opportunity to financially engineer water to its advantage remains.

In the absence of full disclosure of the debt layered in at the holding company level, the debt-driven model based largely on the securitization of revenue streams is only ever partially revealed. When you operate in one location, whilst registering financial transactions in another less transparent, less accountable domain, the topological sleight of hand provides a means for companies such as Macquarie to shift both risks and rewards beyond regulatory reach. This act of concealment, the quiet manipulation involved, which never fully reveals the self-enriching nature of the arrangement, however, is not only beyond regulatory oversight. As a powerful practice, the concealment is far removed from the everyday world of leaky pipes and the water bills that land on the household mats of Thames Water's customers. Unbeknown to them, in part as a consequence of the relational distance created, they have morphed into the very asset upon which the whole exercise in financial engineering is based.

Powers of financial reach

As the first of three chapters designed to tease out the actual topological workings of power, in this case those exercised mainly by banks, investment houses and financial intermediaries, it would have been all too easy to imply that a systemic bias operating in the favour of moneyed elites ensured that they reproduced their dominance and advantage. After all, if money is the bedrock of the whole economic system, then those in a position to control it naturally could be assumed to have an in-built advantage. Indeed, many may have already convinced themselves that such financial hubris equates, if not to the amount of power held, then certainly to the enjoyment of a dominant economic position that others have to confront. That rather straightforward geometry of financial power, as I hope is apparent, is not one that I share, principally because it takes for granted an achievement that is far from predetermined.

As I see it, financial intermediaries like Macquarie and other money-brokering institutions derive their power from their practised ability to engineer opportunities to their advantage, notwithstanding the fact that they could always lose out or misread a situation. In hindsight, the engineering of Thames Water for financial gain may not always look like a tenuous achievement, but the adaptable means and innovative methods by which Macquarie made itself an indispensable part of the financial 'gaming' of the privatized utility is testament to a skilful exercise in power and manipulation.

The success of such an exercise is undoubtedly helped by the fact that the instrumental nature of such power is often practised behind a facilitative veil. Deals are brokered, interests are aligned and divergences are bridged, all in the name of the 'power to' make things happen. The subtle nature of the arrangement is mirrored by the means adopted to achieve financial advantage, with acts of dissimulation at their core once control over the deal is secured. Not disguising an investment and trading interest, while not revealing all that there is to know about it, provides a more subtle means to engineer financial advantage. In such mutable arrangements, power may initially be registered as quiet authority and persuasion, supported in turn by rewards and inducement, and finally secured by manipulation and the closing down of possibilities to obtain compliance. Or it may be secured by other, different combinations. The point is not one of simple variation in the range of powers drawn upon and exercised, but rather that for the most part financial actors have been able to *reproduce* their economic advantage by registering their power in diverse, often mutable ways to skew rewards in their favour.

Their power, as such, represents a continuous relationship that is transformed through processes of distorted reach. The ability of banks, fund managers and other intermediaries to draw investors and the like within their orbit of influence, to draw and hold them within reach topologically, not only plays to their advantage, it is also one of the means by which indispensability is achieved and maintained. The folding in of others in real time, the ability to engage others in the here-and-now of mediated interaction, enhances the likelihood that those persuaded or seduced by what is on offer remain 'fixed' in their persuasion. Doubtless, Strange would have understood the self-serving nature of the power relationships involved, if not their topological means. She would, though, have easily grasped the practice of risks and rewards being placed out of reach of the regulatory controls of nation states, displaced 'elsewhere' so that financial players such as Macquarie are able to distance themselves relationally from demands that diminish their advantage. Indeed, if proximities can be established over distance, global or otherwise, then so too can jurisdictional distances be created through proximity despite the obvious spatial fiction involved. Topology has a way of altering how we grasp such relationships.

6

FOLDING IN DISTANT HARMS

Spatial experiments with NGO power

One of the revealing consequences of living in an interdependent world is the recognition that the ties that bind people and places together often do so in unequal and unjust ways. Vast numbers of people on the far side of the globe, as Onora O'Neill (2000) reminded us, may be harmed by our actions or indeed inaction, and distance itself is no barrier to the responsibilities involved. The fact that others are far away, distant from our lives, is not reason enough to cut ourselves off from consideration of their plight. Indeed, it has become harder to miss the fact that the lifestyles of richer nations, if not the direct cause of suffering elsewhere, may benefit at the expense of others less fortunate or render their livelihoods unsustainable. Nothing, it would seem, is far enough away not to care about or too 'global' to escape taking some kind of responsibility for the harms done.

It would be comforting to suggest that such concerns are simply 'out there' among the more fortunate, but that, I think, would be misleading. Perhaps a more accurate description of the concern displayed for the plight of others often thousands of miles away would be to say that it is something that has been *mobilized by* groups and organizations, that is, produced among and between people by NGOs intent on exercising their 'power to' make a difference.

Power, for NGOs and activists bent on making 'publics' present around such issues as rainforest destruction, human rights or overseas sweatshop exploitation, is understood in much the same way as by banks and hedge funds: as a practical tool. Campaigning groups leverage their energies and reach to achieve the most telling impact, taking advantage of political opportunities when they arise by seeking to exploit them. The main difference between bankers and the campaigning groups that sometimes oppose them, in that respect, is one of the ends sought, not so much one of the means adopted. Lobbying, brokering alliances with interested parties, adopting legal positions and making representations in the public arena are characteristic features of non-governmental politics and have their counterparts in financial games-play, as do artful persuasion, the dispensing of authority, and even the quiet manipulation of wills. If the trial-and-error tools are often quite similar, though, the purposes to which they are put by NGOs, and the task of mobilization itself, are fundamentally different.

NGOs and campaigning groups are basically in the business of *claims-making*; that is, claims-making that makes a difference to people's lives, be it claims for equality, claims for justice, claims for a more sustainable future, and so forth (Tilly, 2008). In order to make such claims 'stick', however, organizations such as Labour Behind the Label, Oxfam and the Fairtrade Foundation have to mobilize and enrol public support for their claims, largely by seeking for them to take responsibility for, or at least care for, others at-a-distance. Without the demonstration of an engaged public presence behind a particular claim, little of the lobbying and advocacy politics mentioned above is likely to come to anything. The challenge for such organizations is how to make the spectacle of distant suffering matter to those *not* present. Or, put another way, the task faced by NGOs is to oblige people to take responsibility for events elsewhere, to identify with the plight of others remote from their lives, and thus be moved to act. To my mind, this places NGOs and campaigning groups squarely in the domain of topological politics, where success is measured principally by their ability to establish an *equivalence* between distant harms and the benefits enjoyed by others far removed from them.

In this chapter, I want to spell out the nature of that topological equivalence, drawing attention to how social movements have enhanced the scope and reach of their power by experimenting with ways of making 'publics' present around hardship and distress elsewhere in the world. Central to this process of spatial experimentation, as touched upon in Chapter 3, is the ability to *fold in* claims for justice and fairness by lifting out and re-embedding remote harms, or by *stretching* the indirect ties of responsibility to exploitative practices elsewhere. In the latter part of this chapter, I dwell in particular upon the ability of the anti-sweatshop movement to collapse the distance between producer and consumer by drawing within close reach the exploitation that the marketplace and its fragmented supply chains have effectively obscured. The skilful leverage of reach, which distorts the spacing and timing of the relationships involved, is shown in this case to work intensively, as a focused exercise in topological claims-making.

First, though, I want to set out how the business of claims-making rests upon the practised expediency of NGOs and campaigning groups, and their skill in bringing different registers of power into play.

'Power to' make a difference

For those such as Hannah Arendt, it is the power to act together that is capable of making a difference in the world of public affairs. Power, for her, as noted previously, is a collective or group thing, a set of solidaristic ties, which, as set out in *The Human Condition* (1958), is the product of mutual action, of people acting together to pursue common, agreed, 'public' goals. Such mutuality, you may recall, is rooted in the powers of association, something that is experienced through other people. As such, it is more about exercising power with others, where the power to act is empowering in and of itself. On this view, power not only comes into being through mutuality, it is what holds people together in their quest 'to make a difference'. Conversely, the point at which such a common will starts to dissolve, or the moment that the ties of solidarity begin to melt, power itself can be seen to evaporate – as would, indeed, the capacity of being able to make a difference in the world.

The rub here is that mutual action can be fleeting and ephemeral, something that can peter out unless sustained. Matters of concern for the plight of others across the globe, as NGOs are only too aware, can be short-lived, liable to dissipate, unless facilitated in some way. Wells of feeling and compassion among the more fortunate around poverty and suffering in faraway places is not the same as people acting in concert to bring about change. Constituencies of support have to be built, opportunities have to be created for people to express their indignation, ties of solidarity have to be brokered and, above all, the capacity to make a difference has to be mobilized. A 'public' presence, in that sense, has to be generated to back a particular campaign, so that pressure can be brought to bear to spur wider political change.

John Dewey knew as much almost a century ago when, in *The Public and Its Problems* (1927), he drew attention to the loss or 'eclipse of the public', as a more atomized, fragmented culture in North America at that time threatened to overshadow the possibility for collective political action. As Alan Ryan (1995) noted in his assessment of Dewey's life and times, it was a problem of 'finding a public', knowing how best to express the diverse goals of a dispersed and increasingly mobile public. NGOs, lobby groups, charities, justice movements and ethical trading organizations that campaign to make a difference today have all learnt that lesson well. It takes concerted effort to mobilize a pluralized and dispersed 'public' on the basis of shared experience and there is no guarantee of success; political claims for equality or justice have to be generated and kept alive by whatever means work best (Barnett, 2008).

In that respect, how best to actualize the power of mutuality and its collective capabilities is often down to a form of practical expediency. The leverage of such energies and experience by social movements, the ways in which they are channelled to address worldly 'wrongs', forms part of an instrumental purpose that turns largely upon the political moment and context. The concerted effort involved, however, is no less enabling of sorts despite that.

An enablement of sorts

The qualification is intentional on my part, as it is debatable just how far attempts by activist and campaigning groups to set 'wrongs' right are enabling of *all* those involved. If some members of the public have to be persuaded or co-opted into the belief that they have the 'power to' make a difference, it begs the question as to the extent of the enablement involved. I suppose the question can be answered in at least one of two ways. If all that is really at stake here is a simple alignment of interests and a facilitation of ties so that more people are able to express their views on the wider, global stage, then the potential for empowerment is evident. If, however, the main purpose of the persuasive tactics is to demonstrate to overseas governments, global corporations and other relevant audiences the support and intensity behind a particular campaign, then the extent of empowerment is likely to be limited, at least on Arendt's terms.

But perhaps a fuller answer is one that recognizes that both outcomes are possible? Let me rehearse what that might involve.

On one hand, organizations such as War on Want, Christian Aid and Labour Behind the Label have to be responsive to the embryonic political concerns and dispositions that are already present among members of the public, local associations and other collective organizations (Barnett et al., 2011). This has less to do with the direct or covert steerage of views, and more to do with the framing of injustices or grievances in ways that mesh with existing or emergent political leanings. People are drawn to a set of claims, enticed, as it were, because they can identify with the political sentiments expressed (Melucci, 1996). They may or may not feel implicated in the wider political claims or feel the need to act on them, yet may still be persuaded, even moved in some way, that they ought to act. This is another version of being 'organized into' politics, which we first met in Chapter 4, although here it is the NGOs and campaigning groups that are shaping people's preferences, facilitating ties and aligning interests. The framing of such responsibilities may still, nonetheless, be empowering in and of itself.

On the other hand, NGOs do the work of framing and persuading for a purpose, and that purpose extends beyond merely enabling the public to express themselves politically. Far from simply an exercise in public awareness, the purpose of mobilizing a public presence behind a particular campaign is to demonstrate the legitimacy of an NGO's claim in the eyes of others. If a campaign is to be taken seriously at all, NGOs have to justify their right to speak and act politically, and they do so largely by underlining the strength of support behind a particular claim, the degree of unity and commitment shown by those enrolled, and the obvious worthiness of the cause (Feher, 2007). Numbers and fierce passion matter, not only to give credibility to the claims made, but also to make it possible for campaigning organizations to lobby and intervene to right the wrongs suffered by those living far away. What starts out as an exercise in persuasion and enticement around existing dispositions of care and concern becomes the very means by which NGOs lend authority to their public voice and legitimate threats to bring about change (Bulkeley, 2013).

I will resist the temptation to say that this means–end relationship is straightforwardly topological, but the two-sided exercise of power outlined does nonetheless possess a certain equivalence of form. Insofar as the 'power to' make a difference has first to be mobilized and then used to bring pressure to bear on those able to effect change, wherever that may be, there is a certain continuity in the relationships of power under transformation. Once empowered and enrolled into a particular campaign or movement, members of the public provide NGOs with an organizational resource that can be deployed to influence wider political debate, even to force the hands of those elsewhere blocking or resisting change. Such an achievement, when understood as a series of different moments across a variety of dispersed locations, forms part of a single continuous space where the 'power to' make a difference is *reproduced differently*.

More often than not, this continuity is understood geometrically as a kind of extension that connects a 'local' campaign, or a series of 'local' campaigns, to the wider 'global' stage, where states and corporations are frequently targeted for whatever harmful or intolerable practices they may be caught up in. Such topographical connections tend to emphasize the organizational extent of so-called 'collective power', either as a movement from the local to the global scale (Fraser, 2008; McDonald, 2006) or through a series of extensive networked ties (Diani and McAdam, 2003; Nicholls, 2009). Such 'collective power' and its extension over space, however, tends to mask the mutable arrangements of power put in place by NGOs that enable them to register their presence in different ways by drawing 'publics', authorities, and a suffering or exploited population into a space of their own making. Perhaps the easiest way to show how NGOs compose such topological relationships is by way of an example: in this case through the spatial and temporal manoeuvres conducted by the Fairtrade Movement.

The Fairtrade Movement, like most social movements, is made up of a mixed bag of political and social groupings, including activists from charities such as Oxfam and Christian Aid, volunteers from Tradecraft who buy and sell fair trade products, as well as the Fairtrade Foundation itself which has the demanding task of trying to keep the campaign against trade injustice speaking with a singular public voice. The movement's claim is for trade justice, so that producers of, say, tea, coffee, cotton or bananas in poorer parts of the world get a fair deal, and it is that overriding sense of 'fairness' that frames the movement as a whole. 'Fairness' works as an enrolment tactic, enticing those so disposed to sign up for the Fairtrade campaign, who, in turn, are encouraged and persuaded to become part of a wider, global lobby for change in the rules of trade and purchasing worldwide. How that process of mobilization takes shape at the grassroots level and draws people into wider arenas of public participation that have global reach is the subject of a study conducted by Clive Barnett and fellow researchers (2011) into the politics of Fairtrade in Bristol in the UK.

What is striking about the Bristol study is the attention paid to the actual mechanisms of recruitment and involvement in Fairtrade issues, where, for example, Bristol's legacy as a trading port was carefully calibrated by activists to equate with fairness in trading practices at the global level and the alleviation of poverty in places as far away as Central America or West Africa. Although the authors do not go so far as to show how activist and campaign groups drew together a Bristol 'public', the trading authorities and a distant set of smallholding producers into a spatial and temporal arrangement all of their own, they do point up the crucial mediating role that NGOs perform in such an arrangement. In practice, they show how NGOs use their powers to mobilize in support of claims made on states, corporations and authorities in far-off locations. The different registers of power that are skilfully deployed by activists, first to persuade and enrol a membership, and then to use that membership to legitimate their authority so that they may lobby and negotiate for changes in market access for distant producers, are plainly in evidence, if not referred to directly.

As is commonplace, however, the mediating role performed by NGOs is reported in the study as a two-sided affair, a purported exchange between the 'local' and the 'global', when perhaps it is better understood as part of a single continuous space 'bound up' with itself. What is all too easily understood as a 'local' exercise in mobilizing support for Fairtrade concerns so that 'global' trade injustices can be confronted where, as the authors put it, 'local networks of global feeling' are mobilized, is arguably more akin to a Möbius-style stretching and twisting of the spaces involved. The mediated and indirect nature of the relationships involved can be said to draw within reach of one another both a mobilized 'public' in Bristol *and* a set of trade practices elsewhere; whether that be coffee producers in Costa Rica and Honduras, tea planters in Kenya and Malawi, cocoa farmers in Ghana and the Ivory Coast, or cotton producers in India and Kyrgyzstan. There is, after all, nothing particularly 'global' about Kyrgyzstan, or any of the other places mentioned for that matter, only the fact that they are part of a topological arrangement composed by NGOs exercising their power *through* Bristol and a series of producer locations.

Barnett and colleagues seem to grasp this intuitively, if not explicitly, when they follow Massey in drawing attention to how part of what is 'outside' Bristol, the Fairtrade producers operating elsewhere, has been effectively brought within, in the hope that part of the 'inside' can be turned into a fair deal for those far-off producers in Kyrgyzstan or wherever. As mentioned before, however, the vocabulary of inside/outside, as a means of conveying the interpenetration of spaces, only takes us so far. It is perhaps best thought about as more a *composed* space that, in the context of Fairtrade practices, enables distant actors to have a presence in terms of influence, despite being physically absent, and indeed trade practices elsewhere to have an impact upon everyday drinking, eating and clothing habits in places such as Bristol. Colourful references to 'turning localism inside out through fairtrade' (Malpass et al., 2007) may help us to reimagine the geometry somewhat, but do little to enable us to grasp the equivalences established between distant injustices and the everyday practices of others elsewhere whose lifestyles are bound up with them.

As such, it makes it all the more difficult to grasp how NGOs and social movement activists have exercised their power topologically to exert an influence often way beyond their means. Righting 'wrongs' or improving living standards for others elsewhere has its enabling side, but not without activists and campaigners experimenting with all manner of ways to enhance both the scope and reach of their power.

Experiments with responsibility at-a-distance

In his astute observations on the nature of social movements and their ostensible constituencies, Tilly (2002) draws particular attention to their contingent and volatile character, as well as their use of trial-and-error tactics to hold a campaign together, or at least keep its different elements moving in the same direction. The sense of practical expediency (my word not his) with which activists and campaigners have to work is evident in his writings:

> The actual work of organizers consists recurrently of patching together provisional coalitions, negotiating which of the multiple agendas participants bring with them will find a public voice in their collective action, suppressing risky tactics, and above all hiding backstage struggle from public view.
>
> (Tilly, 2002, 89)

Such expediency, in this context, refers to the organizational demands of keeping a campaign on track, so to speak, but it is further complicated by the fact that the political world around them is also likely to be changing at the same time. It too can be volatile, as Sidney Tarrow (1998) stressed, with opportunities for change opening up and closing down, sometimes to exist only briefly before shifting in terms of the possible pathways for concerted action. Opportunism, seeking out what works best given the chance to make a difference, tailoring campaigns to suit the political moment, and being alert to possibilities as and when they should arise, all speak to the expediency of political intervention and action. Or rather, I should say political *inter*action, as NGOs and campaign groups do not set out their claims and demands in a political vacuum; they are directed at the unjust or harmful practices of others who, in turn, are likely to respond, even if only to defend themselves or to ward off change. Social movements have to factor this and every other element of a moving political equation into their strategy and tactics. They are, above all else, it would seem, creatures of pragmatism.

But that, as underlined before, does not make them creatures of luck or serendipity. Political openings may sometimes turn on chance and happenstance, but NGOs seek to exploit them in calculated and often innovative ways. To borrow from Tilly again, activists and campaigners, whether in the Fairtrade, environmental or labour movement, aim to adapt to the contingency of political events by turning openings into opportunities. That, however, is itself a challenge, insofar as there may be limited public feeling for a particular grievance when it becomes politically opportune to confront it, especially if the sufferings of those less fortunate are indistinct and far away. Grievances have to matter to those not present and out of harm's way, and for that to happen, NGOs have to find ways of making concerns far removed from their lives matter to people elsewhere.

In short, they have to find ways of making 'publics' present around issues such as trade injustice in parts of Africa and Central Asia, environmental destruction in South America, or sweatshop exploitation in overseas garment supply chains. And for that, somewhat counterintuitively, they experiment with ways of making people responsible for things that they have *not* done.

Iris Marion Young (2004, 2007) has done more than most to shed light on what is involved in constructing such responsibilities at-a-distance. Her interest is less to do with how NGOs have skilfully brought different registers of power into play to enact such responsibilities, and more to do with the obligations of justice that arise from heightened global interdependence. Taking her cue from O'Neill (2000), she points out that in a world of dense trade and communications, where economic and political events tie people together across borders, our actions increasingly assume and depend upon others elsewhere to perform certain roles. As such, we have obligations to those who condition and enable our actions, as indeed they do to us. But, she goes on to argue, there is a clear asymmetry to these obligations because the ties that bind do so in unequal ways. The relative privilege and disadvantage that people experience in different parts of the world implies that those who benefit most from this close-knit interdependence and are able to change things have a greater responsibility to do so.

On this view, if, say, well off consumers benefit from a supply chain set-up that reproduces exploitation elsewhere, then they bear some responsibility to do something about the intolerable conditions found in faraway sweatshops, or about the price procurement practices that impoverish small agricultural producers in poorer countries. Both the anti-sweatshop movement and the Fairtrade movement have experimented with this version of 'taking' responsibility, primarily by framing the issue as one where the privileged can be seen to enjoy their benefits at the expense of distant others. Activists have not been slow to point out that if affluent consumers choose to wear the cheap T-shirt or drink the low-priced coffee, through no fault of their own, they play a part in a 'system' that produces harm and injustice elsewhere. Once persuaded of the equivalence between privilege and disadvantage, the responsibility naturally follows, or rather it follows for as long as consumers remain fully persuaded.

As a register of power, it is often easier to persuade people of something than it is to fix them in that persuasion. People do not always take too kindly to being told that just by going about their normal, everyday business of buying clothes or consuming beverages, the lives of countless others are harmed by their actions. A rift can open up between how things are and how they are experienced, especially if there are too many supply-chain relationships between producer and consumer, making the responsibility difficult to grasp. For Young, activists and, more generally, social movements have attempted to bridge this rift by constructing the responsibility owed to others as one based not simply upon privilege or fairness, but upon a shared political responsibility. It is at this point that acts of persuasion can mutate into experiments with manipulation and co-option in order to get people to do things they might not otherwise have done.

There are parallels here with Nye's (2004) sense of co-option, where agendas are framed to ensure certain messages get across. Ironically, though, it is the instrumental use of Arendt's account of political association that comes closest to conveying the kind of power and influence involved in the co-option practised by NGOs and activists. To make her point, Young enlists Arendt's (2003) version of political responsibility, which draws a clear distinction between moral and legal responsibility on one hand, and political responsibility on the other. The relevance of the distinction plays on the idea that with the former type of responsibility, the individual is held liable for any wrongdoing; whereas with the latter type, the responsibility is shared, borne collectively by all involved. Shared responsibility arises from the fact that people together, not as a collection of individuals, produce the close-knit interdependencies that produce harm and exploitation elsewhere. Whereas guilt singles out individual blame, our innocence as part of a larger system of privilege makes us collectively responsible for things that we have not done. It is the price we pay for living in an interdependent world and one, moreover, from which it is not possible simply to walk away.

On this interpretation of responsibility, then, co-option works by attempts to make people feel responsible, but not to blame, for the harmful situations that they cannot opt out from: be it the unedifying spectacle of the exploitation behind the production of low-cost clothing, or the threat of global climate change that stems from industrialized carbon emissions worldwide. The environmental movement, perhaps more so than the labour movement, has been quick to stress the all-encompassing nature of interdependence that leaves little or no room to escape the consequences of being part of a global community. Simply to acknowledge membership of such a community seems to be enough to ground this form of political responsibility. But, as Young recognizes, not everyone shoulders the same degree of responsibility, for example in relation to the destruction of the rainforests or pollution and toxic harm. Responsibility is both situated and distributed; it depends upon the ties and connections that people have between themselves and particular harms and abuses.

It is an open question as to how far the notion that responsibility is both situated and distributed actually motivates action for change, but Barnett and colleagues clearly believe this to be the case. They were able to show how NGOs not only brokered different kinds of felt responsibility, in their case, in relation to a better deal for trade relationships, but also experimented with various means of bringing different groups and organizations to apply pressure for change where it would be the most effective. Turning political openings into opportunities, in that respect, requires knowing when and how to mobilize such strewn responsibilities to make best use of them in a more-or-less concerted fashion. The leverage of such diverse energies, when achieved on an ongoing basis, can directly enhance the scope of an NGO's or campaigning group's power, although only, I would argue, if it is accompanied by an ability to leverage their *reach* topologically.

Topological claims-making

It is one thing to get people to bear some responsibility for 'wrongs' committed by others because they have benefited from or contribute towards such 'wrongs', but quite another to make the spectacle of suffering actually matter if it is remote or distant from their lives. The practical experiments that enhance the scope of an NGO's ability to mobilize public concern around a particular claim do not automatically make people identify with the experience of distant suffering or injustices of one kind or another. It is a moot question, for instance, just how many of those who sign up to Fairtrade practices could pinpoint the location of, say, Kyrgyzstan on a world map. So how do social movements make their political claims matter to those so far removed from the actual suffering?

Luc Boltanski's work *Distant Suffering* (1999) goes some way towards answering this question by setting out what, in his view, is required for people to take up the cause of those suffering in faraway places. Like Young, he draws upon the writings of Hannah Arendt to support his argument which, in this instance, is based upon a distinction drawn between compassion and pity. Compassion, we are told, requires the close presence of suffering or harm if others more fortunate are to be aroused by it, whereas pity relies upon distance, a lack of physical presence, to evoke a broad sentimentality towards those less fortunate than themselves. Compassionate acts are distinguished from acts of pity by their local and practical character: where compassion moves people to identify with the immediacy of the horror that confronts them, pity detaches itself from particular cases of suffering in order to generalize concern for those who are not there in person. A politics of pity, Boltanski argues, cannot take hold and flourish unless there is sufficient distance between the fortunate and the less fortunate. If the distance between the two is lost and the less fortunate share the same space or want the same things as the more fortunate, a politics of pity is said to collapse.

Boltanski is well aware, however, that a politics of pity that rises above local 'wrongs' in order to generalize concern for distant harms may risk losing the very affective dimension that is critical to it. Pity, he notes, is not inspired by generalities; it requires a 'typical' or exemplary portrayal of suffering to be conveyed if those not present are to be moved to sentimentality and action. Moreover, he recognizes that this kind of appeal does not just happen, it has to be actively put in place by groups intent on mobilizing public support to bring an end to such suffering. Even then, the struggle is seen to be an uphill one, given the lack of proximity to the actual suffering and the uncertainty that attaches itself to situations where so much goes on between a public 'here' and a misfortune over 'there', some distance away. The further away those not there in person are from actual abuse or hardship, the harder he believes it is to incite an individual or collective response to them.

Such reservations, of course, are entirely valid, but only if distance itself is thought about solely in terms of extension and measurement, where conventional metrics spell out how far people are removed literally from the actual site of suffering. When distance is conceived relationally, however, not in metric terms – that is, as a set of relationships that *compose* the distances enacted to place misfortune within or beyond reach – such reservations lose much of their force. Indeed, what Boltanski's topography of suffering seems unable to grasp is that campaigning groups actively experiment with ways of making remote harms equivalent to the privileges enjoyed by others elsewhere.

In practice, they do so by using trial-and-error tactics to gauge the best way to make the plight of, say, cotton producers in Kyrgyzstan or cocoa farmers on the Ivory Coast matter directly to those more fortunate in affluent places like Bristol, to create a politics not so much of pity as of obligation. Similarly, in respect of the anti-sweatshop movement, as we shall see shortly, campaign groups have experimented with ways of establishing a direct tie-up between consumers and corporate exploitation on the far side of the globe, in the hope of obliging consumers to take responsibility for working lives elsewhere. In both cases, a common tactic has involved them in fixing upon the value of the labels or brands associated with a particular product and linking them directly, in the case of Fairtrade companies, to improved and sustainable livelihoods elsewhere; and in the case of anti-sweatshop campaigns, to the abuse of workers overseas. Where the former intervention can lead to an enhancement of the value of a product and a positive collective identity for all those supporting Fairtrade, the latter may involve the devaluation of a corporate brand and the denunciation of the exploitative conditions under which workers are made to suffer (Feher, 2007).

By focusing on labels and brands, whether in a positive or negative manner, social movements effectively hit upon one way of *folding* in directly the conditions under which people live and labour in far-off locations. Cafédirect and Eatfair, two Fairtrade brands, for instance, work as a kind of semiotic experiment: the brands offer an immediate political entry point into a world of distant trading practices and regulations that often appear harmful, while at the same time holding out the prospect of a better deal to correct such harms. Equally importantly, such benchmarked brands enable activists to sidestep much of the global market machinery that passes for economic interdependence and draw the far-off closer politically. In doing so, they have been able to establish an equivalence between improved livelihoods among the marginalized 'over there' and the purchase at a premium price of coffee or chocolate by consumers 'back home'. The power of the tie-up, in this instance, derives from the ability of activists to once again dissolve, not traverse, the gap between 'near' and 'far' by 'lifting out' trading hardships and re-embedding them among those affluent enough to choose Fairtrade labels over regular brands.

When understood topologically, such tie-ups have little to do with 'scaled-up' campaigns from the 'local' level up to the 'global', and more to do with how NGOs and activists have been successful in folding in directly the plight of marginalized producers trying to eke out a living in often out-of-the-way places. A potential politics of pity, in that respect, has been turned into one of obligation through the directness of the equivalences established; that is, through a topological politics that has brought within reach what was previously seen as far away and placed responsibility for the plight directly in the hands of an affluent consumer base. Reach, to press the point, contra Boltanski, is thus more about *presence* than distance, where suffering and remote harms can be made to feel proximate to consumers already disposed towards such political sentiments.

The other side of the topological exercise performed by NGOs, once their constituency of support is in place, you may recall, is to use such broad-based support as a platform for change, or, in the case of the Fairtrade movement, to leverage it as a means to exert influence in the way markets are organized and regulated. This has involved them in a calculation as to where best to apply pressure for change, so that governments and international agencies have come under scrutiny for the limits they can place upon what farmers and producers in relatively poor countries can do in the marketplace. But it has also involved the movement in having to reach directly into the commercial and market operations of traders and producers abroad. When, for instance, fairtrade organizations seek compliance from overseas traders involved in the marketing and distribution of certified products bearing their label, their presence is felt through embedded contract and monitoring procedures (Whatmore and Clark, 2008). The outcome, where successful, is to stabilize a pattern of control and influence at arm's length, by aligning 'fairness' at the point of production with the certified 'fairness' of the brand consumed in the UK and beyond.

In this topological 'take' on the politics of social movements, one can think about the reach of NGOs and political activists as something that enables them to make their presence felt in a variety of relational ways. It is one of the means by which distant harms and hardships can be made to matter to people far removed from them, and it is something that can be leveraged by a range of claims-making organizations to exert power and influence often way beyond their means. It is, of course, possible to understand reach in these terms as nothing more than an extensive means of overcoming the barriers of physical distance. But there is little point in doing so, unless it is also assumed that nearby harms and injustices matter more because of the lack of physical distance between them and a neighbouring public. O'Neill (2000) seems to suggest that the plight of those near at hand is obviously a matter of moral concern, whereas Boltanski believes that local suffering can never arouse anything more than an act of compassion. Neither seems to consider that physical distance itself may not be the critical factor here. Rather, facing up to responsibility for something, whether distant or closer to home, turns on which *claims* for injustice or fairness are registered politically. Being 'near' or 'far' is not the issue, because both can be leveraged topologically.

It may well be the case, for instance, that hardships right in front of us are the most difficult to see. But that is probably because no demand has been made by NGOs and other political actors to register their presence; no equivalence has been established between disadvantage and privilege. The unfortunates who matter are those for whom a concern has been mobilized and their suffering brought within reach of a 'public'. The hardships suffered by coffee producers in previously little-known, out-of-the way places are now evident to many a Starbucks customer, as are the poverty wages paid to those in far-flung sweatshops who sew and stitch the clothing sold by the big retail brands. They have become more familiar to many precisely because a link has been drawn between distant working lives and the benefit gained by, as mentioned before, those who drink the coffee and wear the clothes. No such equivalence may obtain in any strong political sense, however, between, say, the foodstuffs eaten and the exploitative working conditions experienced by those labouring on farms just down the road or in nearby food-processing plants. The agricultural farms and processing plants outside of many a city, for instance, are hardly remote, yet the plight of their often casualized workforce rarely seems to make an impression on the urban population that they serve.

That is perhaps odd. After all, it is not as if such exploitative conditions are entirely unknown. In the UK, as well as instances of bonded labour and the employment of child labour, evidence of forced overtime, intimidation, concealed subcontracting and illegal deductions from pay, as well as unpaid wages, have all been documented as part of the 'normal' business of agricultural gang labour in places not far from the big metropoles (Lawrence, 2013). Such abuse and breach of employment regulations is not a distant feature of some agricultural smallholdings or offshore factory, but a daily occurrence among the casual, mainly migrant labour who pick and process the perishable foods enjoyed by urban consumers. Yet the link between exploitation and consumer benefit is often barely registered politically. The foods provided by migrant casual labour are eaten in a way similar to the way clothes made by sweatshop labour are worn – close up and personal – yet the tie-up between producer and consumer, and hence the obligation to care, is rarely drawn. Quite simply, the lives of those labouring physically nearby are *not* made to matter; their suffering and hardship is not brought within reach of neighbouring city dwellers.

If no claim for justice is voiced by a political group, then no demand for others to take responsibility is registered. In the absence of political claims-making, nothing near or far is made to matter. In the world of topological politics, however, claims for justice or some such concern can be leveraged so that harms on the far side of the globe or even close by can be made equivalent to the privileges enjoyed by others. In order to show what kind of experimentation is involved, I want to turn to the dynamics of the anti-sweatshop movement to show how it has leveraged its power and reach, and the response by corporations that have tried to distance themselves from taking responsibility for hardship and exploitation elsewhere.

Distant proximities of power

As is the case with many a social movement, the anti-sweatshop movement invented itself as it went along (Tilly, 2002). The movement has its roots in the 1970s, principally in the US, where firms in the garment and footwear industries sought to generate higher profits by relocating their manufacturing and assembly operations elsewhere, much of it to East Asian destinations (Dicken, 2008). The growing fragmentation of industrial production, whereby parts of the manufacturing process could be relocated over vast distances, gave rise to something new: subcontracted factory outlets producing cheap goods not for sale in their own countries, but for re-export to more affluent markets on the other side of the

globe. In contrast to offshore finance, offshore manufacturing led to factory closures and job losses, together with a growing fear that a 'race to the bottom' in
terms of wages and workers' rights was under way. This, in turn, was met by
demands from the trade unions and community groups to boycott the cheap goods
flowing into places like the US from abroad, coupled with displays of collective
action to put the issue of overseas sweatshops on the public radar (Robinson, 2007).
All this is well known, but its significance rests upon the fact that, from the beginning,
a *claim* was made upon consumers and the public at large to hold the retail corporations to account for what goes on in faraway factories – and this is the intriguing
point – that the corporations themselves neither owned, nor felt any responsibility
towards.

Much of the subsequent intervention that has characterized the anti-sweatshop
movement more-or-less represents footnotes to this initial claim and how it has
been pressed. Although mobilized around a singular purpose, ostensibly to end
factory sweatshop exploitation, the movement's energies have focused upon where
their impact is most likely to be effective. With one eye on the political opportunities opening up for change and the other on the responses of corporations to its
actions, much of the movement's history falls under the heading of practised
expediency. The sheer difficulty of knowing what works best as situations mutate
and change, and the potential to misjudge what is and is not possible, has produced
a surprisingly varied range of experimental repertoires: anything from demonstrations, lobbying and auditing right through to staged tribunals, fashion colleges and
clean clothes communities.

In topological terms, this repertoire of actions has been directed primarily
towards getting the big buyer corporations to take responsibility for sweatshop
conditions elsewhere by drawing them *within reach* of those who actually buy and
wear the shirts, socks, vests and trainers. Expertise that gives remote sweatshops a
heightened sense of presence for distant consumers has largely been a matter of
finding a particular sort of hurt, abuse or hazard by which to construct an obligation to act that makes it difficult for the corporations to avoid responsibility of one
sort or another. Such interventions, in turn, have brought forth a series of responses
from the corporations targeted that, with varying degrees of success, aim to place
such responsibilities *beyond reach*. At the risk of generalization, as nimble as the anti-
sweatshop movement has been in making distant harms proximate, the big corporations have been equally resourceful in their efforts to displace responsibilities,
the most significant of which has been their ability to exercise what has become
known as the 'power to' exit.

The 'power to' exit, Zygmunt Bauman's (2000) term, is far from a spatial fiction
and represents a summation of the different ways in which corporations have attempted to avoid or escape potentially binding state regulation and territorial confinement. Chief among such means is the well documented one of firms continuously
shifting their low-cost assembly work from one country to the next to reduce
operating costs, as for example Nike and Gap Inc. have more or less done since the
1970s (Donaghu and Barff, 1990; Hale and Wills, 2005). But the 'power to' exit

has been used by such organizations in other, less obvious ways, prompting activists within the anti-sweatshop movement to explore the range of options available to them to confront the demands of changeable situations. The skilful adaptations involved have been, on the whole, directed towards getting corporations to comply with practices that they would otherwise not have chosen to accept. In more general terms, such adaptations are a key part of what is involved when NGOs and campaign groups reproduce their power by bringing different registers of power into play: they are the means best suited to given ends at any one moment in time.

Power as a means to an end

Although the anti-sweatshop movement has its roots in the US in the 1970s, its European counterpart branched out organizationally and practically in ways that both complemented and extended the North American grouping. On the European side of the Atlantic, the heart of the movement is the Clean Clothes Campaign, a coalition of groups that includes Labour Behind the Label, itself a platform for UK trade unions and NGOs, which press their claims alongside other charitable organizations such as War on Want and Oxfam. Formed in the early 1990s and based in the Netherlands, the Clean Clothes Campaign takes its name from the demand that the clothes sold in Western markets should be produced under 'spotless' working conditions, untainted by exploitative labour practices (Sluiter, 2009). And, like its opposite number in the US, it set out to achieve that goal by holding the big retail corporations to account for what went on in their sub-contracted operations overseas through a series of actions. As boycotts, rallies and street demonstrations gave way to targeting the buying power of public authorities and institutions to promote 'no-sweat' communities, the growing pressure placed upon retail corporations to take responsibility for distant factories led to a shift from straightforward denial to qualified acceptance. In hindsight, however, such cumulative actions look more coherent and bounded than was actually the case. In practice, they often resemble a more hit-or-miss affair.

Labour Behind the Label, the platform for the Clean Clothes Campaign in the UK, and its annual 'Let's Clean Up Fashion' reports are a fair illustration of such practised expediency (Labour Behind the Label, 2006, 2009, 2011, 2014). From 2006 up to the present day, the platform has monitored closely the progress made by the big retail brands on the UK high street towards meeting their publicly disclosed responsibilities. Some forty companies, including H&M, Gap, Primark and Inditex, Zara's parent company, as well as supermarkets Asda, Aldi, Lidl and Tesco, are now subject to the platform's scrutiny on an annual basis. While the central focus of the reporting campaign has been on the commitments made by the big retailers to pay a 'living wage' to those elsewhere who make the clothes, in practice the monitoring covers just about anything that could be construed as a barrier to the implementation of a 'living wage', from the right to freedom of association and collective bargaining through to abusive working conditions, misguided productivity programmes and pernicious purchasing practices.

In order to keep the 'living wage' campaign on track, such progressive demands for the most part have amounted to an expedient set of tactics taken in response to company reactions. Attempts by individual retailers to avoid such demands, for instance, have been met by alternative ways of benchmarking progress or monitoring commitments. Positive progress made by companies towards meeting the standards demanded has often resulted in the stakes being raised to limit further manoeuvre, for example by drawing them into multi-stakeholder initiatives such as the European Fair Wear Foundation and the Ethical Trading Initiative, or by binding them into obligatory frameworks, of which the latest is the UN's 2011 *Guiding Principles on Business and Human Rights*. Despite the fine-sounding title of the latter, the principles have been seized upon because they offer yet another means to hold companies to account, in this case for human rights all the way along their supply chains, including the rights of homeworkers.

The pattern for such a sequence of improvised reactions was set almost from the very moment that the big retailers gave up their stance of outright denial and accepted a degree of responsibility towards their offshore operations. In the first 'Let's Clean Up Fashion' report in 2006, for example, two big retailers, Inditex and Gap Inc., were singled out as good performers in terms of meeting their public commitments, especially Gap for its progressive auditing schemes. In the 2009 report, Gap was further praised for such schemes as well as for new plans to integrate trade unions into the process of delivering a 'living wage'. In the same report, however, Inditex's monitoring and auditing procedures were now found wanting. By the time of the platform's sixth report, in 2011, though, the profiles of the two companies had practically reversed. Gap was now damned, having reneged on its responsibilities and gone back to 'square one', while Inditex was commended for its efforts in addressing the right of workers to freely associate in its subcontracted factories. Gap's reversion to a position where its suppliers audit themselves was considered reprehensible, especially given the company's membership of the Ethical Trading Initiative which was thought to bind them in terms of their responsibilities.

Three years on, in Labour Behind the Label's 2014 report, both companies were pulled up for a further set of shortcomings. Inditex, despite its progressive stance on workers' rights, was criticised for its low wage benchmarks, pricing practices and reluctance to engage with the Asia Floor Wage campaign, launched in 2009 to establish a 'floor' wage throughout Asia. Gap, in turn, was censored for its lack of engagement with the Asia campaign, ticked off for its adoption of productivity programmes as a means to boost wages, and broadly admonished for avoiding its responsibilities and commitments to multi-stakeholder initiatives. The context of the 2014 report, in contrast to the first report in 2006, reflected the cumulative shifts in the history of the anti-sweatshop campaign, away from simple 'naming and shaming' tactics and auditing schemes towards more binding frameworks and business-led initiatives that establish responsibilities. The switch in tactics over time, however, offers an insight into the strain of matching means to ends as anticipated responses fail to materialize and unexpected obstacles arise.

Another way to conceive of these messy dynamics, however, is to simply view them as Dewey-type *experiments* with power. Cumulative as the actions of the Clean Clothes Campaign may be, it still has to gauge public feeling towards its tactics and calculate how best to hold corporations to account. As peculiar as it may sound, chief among the registers of power drawn upon by anti-sweatshop campaigners is that of coercion. Not, I hasten to add, coercion as the threatened use of blunt force, but its quieter counterpart, that of the implicit threat of exposure and potential consequent loss of consumer confidence in a particular brand. Many of the experimental tactics adopted by Labour Behind the Label, for instance, rest upon an implied threat that retail corporations will be exposed for their failings over, say, lack of workers' rights or poverty wages. If followed through, the force of such threats may lead, among other things, to a loss of public support and market share. Such threats are rarely made explicit, however; rather they are hinted at as the price to be paid should corporations avoid their responsibilities. Social movements lack the ability to negotiate or bargain with the big retailers in the way that Susan Strange spelt out, so they have learnt to communicate their demands in ways that appear far from threatening.

Often this expertise revolves around anti-sweatshop campaigners probing the big retailers, along the lines of the 'Let's Clean Up Fashion' reports, to identify their vulnerabilities, that is, the sort of exposure that leaves them most open to consumer rejection and potential loss of sales in the marketplace. The 'living wage' campaign, for instance, strikes an obvious chord that requires little in the way of elaboration for consumers and enables activists to tie such a demand to other practices, such as collective bargaining rights and 'ethical' brands. The mere suggestion, for example, of the use of child labour in a contractor's supply chain is usually sufficient to extract compliance from retailers over a range of working conditions that they would not otherwise concede. Such 'pinch points' are hardly the stuff of strong-arm tactics, but they do carry a certain whiff of intimidation, backed up by the knowledge that retailers' profit margins may be put at risk. The credibility of exposure threats, however, tends to lessen over time with use and may even lose the capacity to shock. For that reason, it is perhaps unsurprising that platforms such as Labour Behind the Label continually probe retail organizations for suitable 'pinch points' that may overcome potential public exhaustion or indifference.

When vested threats no longer meet their purpose or prove inept, the Clean Clothes Campaign has been known to change tack, pointing out not the threat of loss, but the promise of gain to retailers who meet their commitments and responsibilities (Sluiter, 2009). The moment when the possibility of gaining sales through compliance, rather than losing them through public exposure, is recognized by corporations as the point at which the power exercised by activists mutates from coercion to that of inducement. The benefits, for example, of engaging with multi-stakeholder initiatives, such as the Ethical Trading Initiative are extolled not for the sake of collaboration, but for the potential advantages they can confer to organizations that sign up to them. The enhancement of a corporate brand, rather than its devaluation, offers a positive identity to all retailers who take part in the initiative, or at best, that is the promise that is held out. As stressed before, such adaptation is the hallmark of many a power-play. It is also evident, as we have seen, in the direct translation of 'labour rights' into 'human rights' by anti-sweatshop campaigners who have calculated the significance of human rights moving up the global political agenda.

Adaptation and mutation, in that respect, are just another way of talking about how a coalition such as the Clean Clothes Campaign experiments with possible ways of exercising its power, given its limited material resources. To be taken seriously by the big corporations, however, it first had to drape itself in some form of legitimate authority, in this case, the authority that derives from having already co-opted people into believing that they can 'make a difference' to sweatshop abuse overseas. Central to that has been the movement's ability to make sweatshop exploitation matter to people far removed from such abuses, that is, by equating such harms with the privileges enjoyed by those elsewhere who actually buy the clothes.

Drawing distant harms closer politically

While it seems possible to buy decent coffee or chocolate, sustainably produced, under the Fairtrade label, purchasing clothes 'cleansed' of economic harm and labour abuse has proved more of a challenge for the anti-sweatshop movement. 'Sweat-free' brands, it seems, cannot be guaranteed to be wholly sweat-free, given the long, subcontract supply chains that characterize the garment industry. The Clean Clothes Campaign, for that reason, has tended to shy away from endorsing such labels. Its approach has focused more upon the 'dirty' side of the industry, so to speak, where it has tried to hold the big companies to account more for what they have *not* done than for what they have done. Negative campaigning of this nature can take a variety of forms, one of which amounts to pursuing a politics of pity where individual consumers are exhorted to care, often by way of an emotional appeal, for those suffering abuse elsewhere. For the Clean Clothes Campaign, though, the obligation sought is not so much one of care for workers' individual suffering as it is of consumers taking shared responsibility for distant harms that, in true Iris Marion Young style, strictly speaking are not their fault.

The challenge is a tricky one politically, given the co-opted exercise of power involved. But it is a challenge that has been met in topological fashion.

The most obvious form of leverage is the tactic, shared with the Fairtrade movement, of using brands and logos to establish an *equivalence* between those who suffer 'behind the label' in faraway places and those who benefit from that suffering closer to home. The Clean Clothes Campaign was an early adopter of the strategy of fixing directly upon company logos – the likes of Nike, Adidas, Puma and Reebok have all figured in its campaigns, as have the supermarkets Asda and Tesco – and linking the actions of branded retailers directly to abuse overseas. In a number of staged events and street actions, logo artwork and branded slogans were often subverted in their meaning to portray the exact opposite of the positive messages that the big retailers wished to convey. The twisted meanings, playful in style, nonetheless performed a more serious exercise; that of reminding a 'public' that they were the ones who benefited from a system that reproduced harm and injustice elsewhere (Allen, 2008b).

In topological terms, targeting the most visible icons of the global garment trade enabled the anti-sweatshop movement to *fold in* directly its claims for justice and fairness. The logo artwork and subverted slogans were skilfully adapted as a kind of proximate shorthand, and made to stand in for anything from the use of forced or child labour through to intolerable and unsafe working conditions 'behind the label'. At a stroke, campaign groups were able effectively to erase from view the majority of the supply chain connections that separate factory worker from consumer, that is, the plethora of buyers and suppliers, trading companies and sourcing agents, as well as the subcontractors, subassembly firms and households involved (see Hale and Wills, 2005). By collapsing the economic distance between consumer and producer, and thereby removing from sight practically everything in between, activists were able to make present to those who buy and wear the clothes the exploitative conditions under which they had been produced.

Moreover, such folded arrangements, mediated through events, campaigns and social media, are often experienced *intensively*, where the force of the claim is undiminished by physical distance. By directly linking what goes on in places such as Dhaka in Bangladesh or Phnom Penh in Cambodia to the actions of branded retailers, exploitation distant in space, but not in time, was drawn closer politically to an audience open to persuasion and receptive to co-option. It is not that the hardships that take place in such locations are in any way experienced at first hand, but rather that the political equivalence of that exploitation is felt in an immediate and focused manner, undiluted by the extensive subcontractual chains that actually form the fragmented economic backdrop. Once the gap between 'near' and 'far' had been dissolved in this way, it became just that much easier, politically, for the likes of the Clean Clothes Campaign to place responsibility for what was previously seen as faraway back in the hands of North American and European corporate boardrooms.

Such direct leverage, however, is not the only topological means used by the anti-sweatshop movement to remind consumers of the harms and injustices meted out in their name on faraway factory floors. Taking a leaf out of Young's book, the Clean Clothes Campaign, and others such as War on Want and Oxfam, have gone out of their way at one time or another to frame overseas sweatshop exploitation as a shared responsibility, one that involves us all and that our collective actions indirectly bring about. On this view, disseminated through their campaign materials, publications and appeals, it is how individuals, groups and communities are tied into a market system that reproduces exploitation elsewhere that matters – and that draws them closer to the lives of distant others. In an attempt to align and channel interests, the 'normal' business of buying clothes at an affordable price is projected as a practice which, despite its innocuous overtones, sets up a chain reaction that leads to workers elsewhere being prevented from earning a 'living wage'. Because consumers, broadly speaking, set the price at which they are willing to purchase goods, their actions presuppose and depend upon others elsewhere to make them at a cost that simply fails to deliver a 'living wage' (Clean Clothes Campaign, 2006; War on Want, 2006, 2008, 2011).

Topologically speaking, through this means, the anti-sweatshop movement was able to *stretch* the ties of responsibility from those who shop for cheap clothes to those who stitch and sew them. Consumers, activists point out, merely buy and wear the clothes; they neither hire, nor fire, nor threaten workers on the factory floor, nor cause buildings that house sweatshops to collapse through the addition of illegal extensions. Yet the demand for clothes at low cost sets up a series of pressures that are transmitted through to the factory floor and that indirectly produce such harms and, on occasion, lead to disaster and tragedy. Factory fires and collapsed buildings in the Bangladesh garment industry are not uncommon, with tens and hundreds of workers killed in separate incidents going as far back as the 1980s, but they were really *made* to matter politically when the eight-storey Rana Plaza building in Dhaka collapsed in 2013, with the loss of over 1100 lives and many more injured.

There have been less spectacular disasters among Dhaka's 2000 or so sweatshops, with the loss of life rarely leading to any meaningful steps to prevent such tragedies (Seabrook, 2015). The Rana Plaza disaster changed that. The sheer scale of the disaster made it stand out, but that fact alone did not place demands upon consumers several thousands of miles away. That happened arguably for two principal reasons. One, because the three garment factories housed in the Rana Plaza building were revealed to have contracts to produce clothing for at least twenty-seven high-profile retail brands including Benetton, Primark, Matalan, Zara and Walmart. That connection enabled the Clean Clothes Campaign and others to hold a number of the big retail corporations directly to account. For that to be effective as a threat, however, the responsibility for such misfortune had to be placed within reach of remote consumers whose actions, although they did not cause the disaster, ostensibly made it possible. In practice, the responsibility for Rana Plaza stretched through a set of relationships which placed consumers at the 'normal' business end of an economic system that allowed such tragedies to occur.

Anti-sweatshop activists frame such responsibility as one of being caught up in a 'system' of exploitation, but the system in this case is perhaps best thought about as a political arrangement; one composed of co-opted 'publics' in Europe and North America *and* a series of harmful practices which stretch as far as factory sweatshops in Bangladesh, Cambodia, China and beyond. Campaign groups fill out the space of such arrangements relationally, drawing disasters such as Rana Plaza into a political arrangement for which distance, measured in miles or kilometres, has little if anything to do with it. It makes no real difference to the exercises in equivalence experimented with by the Clean Clothes Campaign whether the sweatshop calamities or misfortunes occur in Central Asia or East Asia, or on Asia's European fringe, in Turkey for example; only that the political claims made in relation to them are somehow *made* proximate.

But, as I have stressed all along, what can be made proximate can also be made distant in relational terms. Responsibility for distant harms can be placed out of reach as well as drawn within reach; displaced by resourceful corporations when they see an opportunity to evade the political responsibilities placed upon them by the anti-sweatshop movement.

Placing responsibilities beyond reach

One of the significant achievements of the anti-sweatshop movement, following the Rana Plaza disaster, was to oblige over 150 brands and retailers to sign up to a legally binding, five-year accord to address building and fire safety in garment factories in Bangladesh. It is the first collective multi-buyer agreement of its kind in the garment industry and reflects the leverage skills of the Clean Clothes Campaign and other European groups. The roll call of companies supporting the Bangladesh Safety Accord includes Benetton, H&M, Inditex, Next, Primark, PVH (the owners of Calvin Klein and Tommy Hilfiger), as well as the supermarkets Tesco, Sainsburys, Aldi and Lidl. Absent from the list, however, is the single largest buyer of clothing and attire from Bangladesh, the world's biggest retailer, the US giant Walmart. Along with another major US retailer, Gap Inc., it refused to sign up to the Accord, opting instead to set up its own alternative safety plan, one without binding legal agreement or the involvement of trade unions.

Such a move represents an opportunity for Walmart to evade a more constraining set of legal responsibilities, having made the calculation that the benefits outweigh the costs of non-compliance. In many respects, the alternative plan is a form of displacement, one that 'lifts out' the pressures placed upon them by the likes of the Clean Clothes Campaign and embeds them in a voluntary deal that places the company outside of the regulatory authority of the Bangladeshi government and trade unions, as well as the oversight of bodies such as the International Labour Organization and IndustriALL, a global federation of unions that covers the garment sector. In topological terms, the response amounts to a *folding out* of the political demands made upon Walmart, a displacement that shifts responsibility to a corporate framework where the company is not accountable to a range of authorities operating at different 'scales'.

This kind of displacement, however, is not the most common or significant practice used by the retail corporations to place their responsibilities to overseas sweatshop workers beyond reach: that can be traced to their resourcefulness in *stretching out* the subcontract relationships that separate them from factory sweatshops. The global subcontracting arrangements operated by the big brands, as campaign activists know only too well, are extensive and intricate. The clothing that sells in European and US retail stores will have passed through dozens of hands, factories and agents, across any number of international borders, before it reaches the consumer. From sourcing the raw materials to ending up in a retail outlet, as Hurley and Miller (2005) have shown, each stage of the process can be performed by different economic players dispersed across a range of countries: the yarn may be sourced in one country, woven and dyed in another, the zippers and buttons sourced from a third, and the whole garment put together in a string of factories wherever the cheapest labour and production costs prevail. Even the logistics of co-ordinating the process may well be conducted by trading companies and sourcing agents from yet another location.

When the buyer-driven retailers neither own any of the factories nor control the workforces, these kinds of supply relationship can be stretched and lengthened almost at will, enabling companies to distance themselves from what goes on in the protracted contract negotiations. Intriguingly, the same economic exchanges that the anti-sweatshop movement strives to erase by collapsing the distance between producer and consumer, the big corporates attempt to construct at arm's length in a more circuitous, fragmented manner. In doing so, the retail corporates are not only able to outsource their production, they are also able to contract out their legal and political responsibilities. The distances created, however, are the result not of a lengthening of physical distances, but of a multiplication of the exchanges between economic actors so that responsibility is placed out of reach. The distances stretched are *relational,* not physical, the outcome of the dispersal and fragmentation of the supply chain. Such intensive arrangements are often masked, however, when supply chain extensions are drawn as lines on a map, with little appreciation for the kinds of displacement involved.

A relatively recent adaptation to such outsourcing arrangements, largely in response to the noted achievements of the anti-sweatshop movement, has been for the big retailers to 'shorten' their own supply chains by placing responsibility for their requirements solely in the hands of one contractor or agent. That contractor, in turn, is then held accountable for all the supply chain interactions, from sourcing materials and orchestrating production right through to delivery times and distribution (ILO, 2000; Hurley and Miller, 2005). Such improvisation effectively makes it just that more difficult for the Clean Clothes Campaign and others to expose the retailers for falling down on their commitments, especially when the contractors themselves have a far lower public profile than the branded retailers purchasing their services. The 'pinch points', if possible to identify, lack any real traction, and threats of exposure tend to ring hollow. But as a reaction to the acknowledged successes of the anti-sweatshop movement, a single 'act' of outsourcing does offer the big brands another means to distance themselves from the demands placed upon them by activists. Which is ironic, perhaps, as it has meant them adopting their own form of economic erasure.

Despite the noted achievements of the anti-sweatshop movement, however, the buyer-driven corporations retain a significant practical tool, the 'power to' exit arrangements should opportunities to reduce their operating costs present themselves, or should the threat of exposure to a particular injustice prove too great a risk. More often than not, such a tool is interpreted as the threat of relocation, which itself can make it harder to hold the big corporations to account. The threat of shifting low-cost production to another country, say from Bangladesh to Burma or from India to Ethiopia, is a practice that has been opportunistically used in the past by corporations, and still retains credibility. At a time when branded retailers no longer simply deny any responsibility for their offshore operations, however, the importance of such a tool should be neither overstated, nor interpreted simplistically.

The retail companies do not switch their operating arrangements at the slightest hint of a possible economic gain or at the first sign of exposure. Other factors, such as political stability, labour laws, state regulation on wages and the relative strength of trade unions, all come into play when contemplating the 'power to' exit. Besides which, the big brands already operate in a number of countries, with the likes of Gap and Nike declaring supply relationships with contractors in over forty separate countries. Indeed, the numbers may be even greater once the trend towards using fewer contractors for a greater range of dispersed suppliers is taken into account. Switching suppliers, in that sense, is probably something that happens more routinely under the corporate radar than can be logged by anti-sweatshop campaigners such as Labour Behind the Label. On that basis, the 'power to' exit may be best interpreted as a more adaptable tool, one that is used by corporations to adjust their spatial tactics in line with both the relative economic situation and the latest demands placed upon them by groups such as the Clean Clothes Campaign.

Interpreted more broadly, the 'power to' exit encompasses the variety of ways in which the big retail firms can avoid, sidestep or, better still, displace their responsibilities. In a topological set-up, they use their organizational and financial resources to displace the claims made upon them by distancing themselves from such pressures in relational, not physical, terms. The almost continual fragmentation and dispersal of supply-chain relationships, in that sense, represents an expedient means for companies to place a whole host of responsibilities, economic as well as political, out of reach, not only of the anti-sweatshop movement and its campaigning antennae, but also of their customers 'back home'. With the result that the latter may remain largely indifferent to, or untouched by, the changing conditions under which the clothes they wear are produced. To that end, the outsourcing of their responsibilities amounts to a powerful topological tactic for the big retail brands.

Topological politics

Much of this chapter, the latter half in particular, represents an attempt to capture what is best described as an interplay of forces where NGOs, campaign groups and corporations, as well as governments, respond to the actions of the other, anticipating opportunities and adjusting reactions accordingly. Claims-making organizations and groups may skilfully draw distant harms and hardships within reach of people far removed from them, folding in demands for responsibility to be taken for events elsewhere, but equally corporations and other private authorities invariably seek new ways of avoiding or displacing such demands as a means to block or resist change. The ability of all parties involved to engage in such spatial twists and turns in response to the contingency of what confronts them is, as I hope is evident, largely down to a set of topological manoeuvres that enables them to transcend a landscape of fixed distances and well defined proximities.

Making things matter to those *not* present, experimenting with ways of making injustice equivalent to the benefits enjoyed by more privileged 'publics' elsewhere in the world, is something that social movements have learnt to achieve. Such topological practices, to my mind, are the means by which NGOs and campaign groups have been able to co-opt citizens and consumers alike into presuming that they have the 'power to' make a difference. Once mobilized and enrolled, such 'publics', in turn, have provided social movements with an organizational resource that can be used to legitimize their claims-making, whether that be for trade or labour justice, or equal and civil rights more generally. That practical resource reflects the scope and reach of a movement's powers and it is what, on the whole, has enabled them to 'punch above their weight'. More specifically, it has enabled NGOs and campaign groups to bring different registers of power into play to get other, more 'weighty' institutions and bodies to do what they would otherwise not have done.

John Dewey, I think, would have recognized the expedient, experimental side to such achievements, if not the topological leverage that underpins them (see Barnes, 2008). He would also have been aware of the anti-foundational nature of such power plays, grounded as they are in the shared experience of them as a dynamic set of exchanges and interactions. Far from assuming that size is all that matters, and the 'weightier' the resources the greater the power, Dewey would, I suspect, have drawn attention to the way in which social movements *use* resources to produce the tenuous effect that is power. That does not mean to say that they are not placed at a disadvantage by those with a greater amount of financial and institutional resources, merely that the practical tool that is power can, in the hands of NGOs and campaign groups, press claims in a more adaptive manner than those threatened by them and who have most to lose. Indeed, it is through such means that they have been able to reproduce their 'power to' make a difference in distinctly novel and diverse ways.

7

A DISTORTED STATE

Reproducing the power of borders differently

State borders, and the distorted shapes that they have taken in recent times, are no strangers to topology. Unlike the study of non-governmental politics and its global scope, or the analysis of disembedded financial money markets, the sense in which topological spatialities may have something to do with the transformation and intensification of border relationships has surfaced in the field of geopolitics. The particular case of the distorted territories of Palestine was mentioned in Chapter 4, but it was perhaps Etienne Balibar's observations that state borders, in particular those of the European Union, are no longer at the border, transposed, as it were, into 'the space of the political itself' (Balibar, 2002, 92), which prompted a surge of interest in the increasingly distorted nature of political borders. The sense in which borders are no longer simply at the edges of the territorial state, that they have been pushed outwards and pulled inwards, in concertina fashion, has fuelled topological speculation (Coleman, 2012; Giaccaria and Minca, 2011; Mezzadra and Neilson, 2012; Mountz, 2011b; Parker and Vaughan-Williams, 2009).

Of course, there are still high walls and barbed-wire fences that violently represent the exclusionary nature of sovereign borders in hard geometric lines, but the possibility of more distorted topological borders that exclude and include in more differentiated ways has struck a chord. Much, although by no means all, of the speculation over what bordering on topology amounts to revolves around an awareness that processes of exclusion and inclusion no longer discreetly map onto the separation between what is 'inside' and 'outside' a state border. Life on the inside, so to speak, is far from inclusive for migrants denied equal access to legal and social rights, for example. Equally, on the outside, those seeking entry may find themselves excluded well before reaching a border crossing by a state acting far beyond its sovereign territory. It is this so-called blurring of the distinction between the internal and external spaces of a political community, where the 'inside' and 'outside' of a sovereign state no longer appear mutually exclusive, that appears to have prompted a topological redescription.

Interestingly, the porosity of state borders is not so much the issue here as their continuous nature, despite their spatial and temporal distortion. Control over the movement and circulation of people now stretches from within states, as enforcement practices shift to the interior of places like the US and EU, to well beyond their outer territorial edges, offshored and outsourced to privately run agencies in often obscure, somewhat isolated locations. The idea floated by some of the border as a security continuum, one extended simultaneously overseas and inwards across a territory, conveys the continuous nature of dispersed controls (see Vaughan-Williams, 2010), but its topological expression has perhaps best been captured by the paradoxical figure of the Möbius strip and, relatedly, that of the Klein bottle. Didier Bigo (2000, 2001), in particular, has done much to draw attention to border security controls as part of a one-sided process of continuous exchange, making it difficult to know where the inside ends and the outside begins. It is this continuity of border relationships under transformation on which I want to focus in this chapter – not, I hasten to add, to highlight any particular blurring, but rather to show their topological equivalence.

As I see it, what remains related despite the deformation of state borders is a system of exclusion and inclusion that *reproduces itself differently*: not only within different spatial arrangements, but also with varying degrees of intensity and presence.

Perhaps one of the more intriguing aspects about the stretched or distorted nature of contemporary border relationships has been the efforts by states to be more-or-less consistently present wherever border controls take effect. If anything, the intensive exercise of power, the nature and degree of scrutiny involved, has become more, not less, focused as border controls have shifted away from conventional points of entry. The authoritative structures of control and regulation that serve to block, as well as facilitate, the movement of a population, if simply devolved bureaucratically, would be hard pressed to achieve such an outcome. When grasped topologically, however, authoritative power in the new spatial arrangements of borders is something mediated through technologies and practices that enable it to be stretched or folded without, it seems, undue loss of focus or dilution of presence.

Much of the first part of this chapter is an attempt to show how this demonstration of authority to exclude and include reproduces itself through such topological processes, often in a different register. In the second half, the focus switches to the displacement of borders, where access to a given territory for a migrant population is placed out of reach by authorities distancing themselves from the demands for access and entry. Particular attention is drawn to the fact that such intentional acts of exclusion can be seen to represent a series of spatial and temporal experiments with border controls; that is, practical improvisations in the ongoing exercise of state sovereignty.

Powers of exclusion and inclusion

The idea of political borders more-or-less constantly changing shape, dispersed throughout society and often remote from the very territory from which they draw their legitimacy, can be somewhat disorientating. The sense in which borders, if not everywhere, are certainly 'elsewhere' feeds off the impression that controls on movement no longer bear much of a relation to the familiar territorial moorings of the state. Borders still function at the border, so to speak, at traditional sites such as ports and airports, and now also offshore in processing and detention centres at one remove from such sites. But it has probably been the growth and sophistication of border security technologies, biometrics and pre-screening through data mining in particular, designed to sort out the 'safe' from the more 'risky' population, that has helped to anchor the idea that border controls and checks are now pervasive throughout society (Amoore, 2006). When largely faceless risk-management technologies can be deployed to screen, profile and filter the movements of a population, often without their knowledge, the question as to how such border-monitoring practices actually relate to any given territory is a pertinent one.

To my mind, however, the combination of such diffuse border practices, together with the distortion and displacement of state borders, does raise a more pressing concern: namely, how does the sovereign authority of the state play out across such a vacillation and multiplication of borders, to draw upon Balibar's description of events? How do states attempt to make their authority and presence felt across such a diverse range of settings without seeming loss of focus?

The beginnings of an answer can perhaps be found in the work of Mathew Coleman. Rather than a tidy sovereign territoriality of power, Coleman (2007), with US border statecraft in mind, has spoken about a 'proxy geography' of enforcement practices whereby Washington and US immigration authorities have gone out of their way to join up the dispersed surrogates of authority at, and away from, the Mexico–US border. Drawing upon the work of Ferguson and Gupta (2002), outlined in Chapter 3, he argues that US statecraft in relation to its diffuse borders resembles not so much a state exercising authority over its borders 'from above' as one able to establish arm's-length reach into new spaces of enforcement. On this view, US border statecraft works equally through the mutation and displacement of borders as it does by building and combining them.

The arm's-length reach that I have in mind here, however, as pointed out in Chapter 3, has little to do with the idea of an extended state effortlessly reaching out from 'on high'. Rather, when understood topologically, it involves an *intensive* exercise of power and authority, either folded in directly to a border setting, or stretched indirectly as part of an interplay between the practitioners of statecraft and those present at the points of enforcement. Coleman, I think, would be sympathetic to that interpretation of topological reach, if not to the precise vocabulary, then at least in spirit. It speaks to the sovereignty of the state and its authority not as something that has simply been devolved in a more roundabout manner or extended in extraterritorial fashion, but to its heightened presence at and away from the border.

In Coleman's case, the border in question is the Mexico–US border, but the topological framing of sovereignty is not restricted to it and chimes, I would have thought, with any number of EU border practices as well as those of other states and supernational bodies. It is one thing, however, to be able to apprehend such changes and distortions, but quite another to comprehend them. The habits of spatial geometry, in that respect, seem particularly hard to shake off.

Borders and territory

Sassen (2006), as noted in Chapter 2, is clearly aware that the relationship between territory and state sovereignty is no longer a simple mapping exercise, with legal and administrative forms of authority becoming detached from their conventional national moorings in the present moment. Elden (2009), too, recognizes that there is no tidy sovereign territoriality of power when states claim the right to render the sovereignty of other territories contingent should they not meet particular norms and standards of behaviour. Neither, however, picks up on the fact that the increasingly distorted spatiality of political borders may point to something more than a series of contingent or overlapping powers. The 'debordering' spoken about by Sassen, for instance, is not so much a superimposition of authority as a topological remaking of sovereignty, one that reaches into and beyond a given territory and enables the state to make its presence felt in a detached or stretched fashion. One can, of course, talk about the deterritorialization and reterritorialization of authority, but to my mind a more accurate depiction would be to foreground the state's ability to reproduce its power and presence topologically.

When understood from that angle, the distortion of the state and its borders, the creation of 'buffer zones', for instance, can be perceived in an altogether different light. Set up as a space between the given external borders of a territory and the territories from which others seek to gain entry, the policing of migrants before they travel is usually portrayed as a 'thickening' of security arrangements against unwanted migration. The EU has its version of a buffer zone between its southern borders and North Africa, deterring migrants from reaching Europe's borders. The US has a similar defensive arrangement between itself and Mexico, Central America and the Caribbean. Both arrangements can be seen as a straightforward outward extension of border controls, a way to keep unwanted migration at bay, but they can also be seen as a more recent form of state making at-a-distance (Bialasiewicz, 2012; Walters, 2010).

Rather than an uncomplicated spatial bulwark against the threat of undocumented migration, a simple shoring-up exercise, buffer zones represent one means by which states have attempted to *reach into* neighbouring countries to influence their political behaviour and seek compliance. If borders today are now firmly part of 'the space of the political', not merely lines on the ground that demarcate the limits of sovereignty, then they are better understood as a practical tool that serves the purpose of stretching the authority of a state or folding in its presence directly. In the context of US border arrangements with Mexico, for instance, Coleman (2007) has shown how immigration enforcement crept slowly southwards into Mexico and beyond. Operation Global Reach, for example, launched in the late 1990s, was an early forerunner of such creeping enforcement, with policing efforts established in a number of transit countries, most notably in Mexico City, which, as Coleman points out, effectively established a more-or-less permanent US enforcement presence throughout Mexico and Central America. Rather than think about the arrangement as a contemporary form of 'remote control' over immigration, however, topologically it amounts to a detached form of authority 'lifted out' and folded into the political interplay between Mexican and US immigration enforcement, with the latter having a direct say in its direction and outcome. They are literally 'on hand' as an authority, embedded regionally to secure an alignment of interests which dovetails with those of the US.

This, then, is not a mere physical projection outwards of a state border; it represents a form of co-option, an attempt by one state to frame the interests of another so that it is consistent with its own. The purpose looks to be one of instrumental compliance, but the means varies from authority and constraint through to incentivization and straightforward financial inducement. Indeed, much the same can be said for the European Union's border agency Frontex, which was established in 2005 to secure and integrate member states, ostensibly through their co-operation and partnership (Vaughan-Williams, 2012). The incorporation of member states into shared surveillance and information-gathering activities, as well as joint training exercises and border checks, may appear as an extension of routine migration management practices, but it can also be seen as a means of drawing neighbouring countries into the EU's orbit of influence, co-opting them into EU norms and standards that embody particular forms of statehood (Bialasiewicz, 2012). Again, a proximate form of authority and compliance is sought more or less through a form of detached presence on the outer limits of EU territory.

Where a less direct presence is sought, in part to play down the overt nature of the intervention, states may draw upon agencies such as the International Organization for Migration (IOM) to do the mediating work of statehood for them (Andrijasevic and Walters, 2010). The IOM, a self-declared 'migration agency', appears to exercise a more indirect reach, 'organizing in' countries in the Western Balkans for example, such as Serbia and Croatia, into the practices of regulation upheld by the EU. Not, it would appear, by simply imposing their contractual authority, but through the various kinds of emulation and attraction mentioned in Chapter 4, where the receiving country willingly adopts such practices in part because it seeks to be at one with the values and norms of the European Union. In this manner, the indirect presence of a central authority is mediated through a contract agency whose brief in this case includes:

> a whole set of norms and best practices concerning the appropriate organization of borders; the imperative and best methods for identifying and distinguishing between the citizen and the noncitizen, and the resident and the illegal; the most effective way of removing noncitizen and unwanted populations from a state's territory; and much else besides.
>
> (*Andrijasevic and Walters, 2010, 984*)

To all intents and purposes, this represents a form of mediated statecraft, one carried out by a private agency, but directed at-a-distance by EU authorities so that the management of borders works through indirect influence and pressure, so that neighbouring states bring themselves into line by adopting best practice. The 'problem' of how to manage borders effectively is solved for them, shaped by organizations that set out a categorization of migrants and how best to differentiate exclusion and inclusion (see Ashutosh and Mountz, 2011).

This 'proxy geography' of EU enforcement does not end at that point, however, as it stretches well beyond such territorial limits, reaching into North Africa and further afield. Stretching, that is, in a topological fashion to secure Europe's borders by establishing an even more mediated offshore presence along the North African coast in places such as the Canary Islands and the Spanish enclaves in Morocco and Libya, as well as mobilizing joint boat patrols off the West African coast near Mauritania, Cape Verde and Senegal (Vaughan-Williams, 2008). The former are not the 'offshore' processing centres that the EU wishes to introduce in some of those places, as well as Egypt and Niger, to stem the movement of thousands of people landing on EU shores from across the Mediterranean, but they serve more or less the same pre-emptive purpose, which is to deter would-be migrants before they arrive at the shoreline. Such practices, though, as we shall see later, have little to do with actual state making at-a-distance, and more to do with placing access to EU territory wholly out of reach for a given population. They speak to a threshold of sorts where the ability of one state to reach into the territory of another can be twisted to deny others from reaching its borders.

There is, of course, nothing unusual about the use of pre-emption as a means of taking border controls to a population elsewhere. Consulates overseas have long issued entry visas prior to travel, and customs and immigration facilities away from the actual territorial border are not a recent feature (Popescu, 2012). The difference from the 'offshoring' of borders today is in both their targeted purpose within a 'buffer zone', and the greater intensification of border restrictions involved. If the past 'offshoring' of border checks represented a loose, devolved form of power, extended horizontally over long distances, its present-day counterpart represents a more focused exercise of control and constraint enabled by the ability to leverage topologically a more-or-less direct presence regardless of the distance span. While it does not follow that the mechanisms of blocking and filtering are always effective or unambiguously applied, given their mediated nature, the concentration of authority remains largely undiminished through their topological reach.

That observation, it seems to me, holds, whether the sovereign reach in question is one that is detached or stretched 'offshore' or distorted so that the focus of authority is directed inwards into a given territory and its people. The ability of a state to *reach into* the lives of its migrant communities in an intensive manner, to stretch its authority in order to detain and remove those already present, places the management of borders once again firmly in the middle of Balibar's 'political space'. In the US, for example, enforcement practices similar to those of exclusion have been 'lodged in the interior, with the Department of Homeland Security exercising arm's length reach into the policing of immigration at the local level, both through joint forms of enforcement and the authorization of non-federal agents at the municipal level' (Coleman, 2007). In what could almost be a mirror image of the external 'buffer zone' of the US, an equivalent internal zone of 100 miles in from its outer borders was announced by the homeland security department in 2006 as an area within which removal could be expedited and the appeal rights of non-citizens severely curtailed (Coleman, 2012).

None of these proxy-type geographies, however, amounts to a simple redrawing of border lines or, indeed, the construction of box-like territories within which enforcement now takes place away from the border proper. The new spatial arrangement of borders, where they are mediated and translated for specific political ends, in the case of the US, draws in federal, state and local authorities as well as a migrant population into a space of their own making, where the centralized authorities are more or less able to make their presence felt close-up at a distance with a degree of force that can only be described as intensive. That composed authority, however, does not stretch all by itself; it has to be leveraged topologically by centres of authority such as the Department of Homeland Security. It is through such leverage that states appear able to reach into their own territories in a heightened fashion, as well as to reach into the territories of others, both neighbouring and distant.

The sovereign powers of exclusion and inclusion, in that sense, play out across a diversity of settings and sites by virtue of such processes of topological distortion, often bearing little resemblance to a state's formal borders (Axelsson, 2012). As such, it has become puzzling at times to know where exactly the inside of a state's sovereignty ends and its outside begins. How such a spatial distortion of borders has been captured topologically, however, has often coalesced around a handful of acknowledged figures drawn from the immeasurable world of topology.

Bordering on topology

Ever since the publication in 1993 of Rob Walker's classic *Inside/Outside* text on the difficulty of making any semblance of a division between the 'inside' and 'outside' of a sovereign political community when faced with the spatial and temporal dislocations brought about by a globalizing world, the question of topology has arguably been waiting in the wings, off-stage, so to speak. The elegance of a bounded state sovereignty no longer convinced him; nor indeed the lines of power and authority that granted a simple 'here here and a there there' to the presence and absence of rule and order:

> Its grand motifs of straight lines retains a certain charm, and an enormously powerful grip on the contemporary political imagination, but we are no longer so easily fooled by the objectivity of the ruler, by the Euclidean

theorems and Cartesian coordinates that have allowed us to situate and naturalize a comfortable home for power and authority.

(Walker, 1993, 178)

If some were less fooled back then by this power-geometry, some two decades on, others besides Walker have become even less convinced of the value of the 'inside/outside' distinction as a means of grasping how sovereign power and authority works itself out in practice. There is more at stake here than Eyal Weizman's 'elasticity of territory' in relation to the constant distortion of Palestine's occupied territories, as significant as that is for disrupting the objectivity of metric pronouncements around power. Rather, it has been the movement centre stage of the topological figure of the Möbius strip that has encapsulated the continuous exchange between what happens internally and what takes place outside of a sovereign body. Indeed, given Walker's (2010) more recent writing on borders and sovereign authority, it is perhaps surprising that the rearticulation of political space and time that he foregrounds in his work has not, like others, drawn upon this evident topological figure.

Bigo (2000, 2001), for one, has spelt out the potential significance of the Möbius strip as a means of grasping how the lines of internal and external state security have today become blurred and hard to differentiate. For him, this topological figure represents a way of charting the continuous relationship between different forms of security and insecurity, with the functions of border security and policing merging in response to transnational threats that arise from the growing movement of people across all manner of borders. Indeed, Coleman's 'proxy geographies' of enforcement, where the state is able to exert a presence, both externally to secure its internal realm and internally to physically deport those it deems a risk, chimes with the type of convergence of practices that Bigo seems to have in mind. The merging of the inside and outside is taken by him as a continuum of sorts, one analogous to the Möbius strip, which, when stretched along its length, reveals through a process of twisting locations on opposite sides that are in fact part of the same relational arrangement. The paradoxical nature of the figure, as noted in Chapter 3, reveals itself through an inside and outside that are part of a single, continuous space, yet nonetheless can be identified as two sides at any one point or location.

Bigo likens the conventional figure of sovereign territoriality, with its clear separation between an 'open' inside and a 'closed' outside, to the opposing surfaces of a cylindrical ring, a distinct two-sided figure without the slightest hint of paradox. A cylindrical ring can be represented as a strip of paper joined at the ends to convey an inside protected from an outside by a thin edge or borderline that represents the territorial limits of sovereignty. State sovereignty, as customarily understood, is defined by its outer edges or borders. If, however, as outlined in Chapter 3, you take that strip of paper and give it a half twist before joining the two ends, sovereignty in its analogous form reveals itself as a single continuous surface; one that seemingly merges the inside and outside into a continuum of authority. Crucially, it is not so much that the border itself is continuous, as the fact that the sovereign authority of the border remains undivided. It is the state's power to exclude and include that is stretched relationally, in a more intensive than extensive fashion.

The idea of a 'blurred' inside and outside, in that respect, seems to miss the point somewhat, for it is how those powers remain related in the same way, despite the stretching and twisting of borders, that is of significance. It takes us back to the question of *equivalence* and how the state has been able to reproduce its authority to exclude and include in a series of different bordering arrangements. Convergence, or the merging of internal and external realms of security, is not really the issue; rather it is how a system of authority has reproduced itself differently by making its presence felt at and away from the border proper. A focus upon the continuity of border relationships under transformation is perhaps a better way of exploring how the figure of the sovereign cylinder has morphed into a Möbius-style sovereignty that enables the powers of exclusion and inclusion to be exercised in a more differentiated manner.

Such a focus, I think, is more in keeping with the topological analysis of borders set out by Sandro Mezzadra and Brett Neilson (2012, 2013), as well as in line with those such as Paolo Giaccaria and Claudio Minca (2011) who draw upon Giorgio Agamben's (1998, 2005) work on sovereignty and the 'space of exception' to show how processes of exclusion work through inclusion. One of the more general insights that they draw from Agamben is that there are political spaces, 'spaces of exception', that we live within, which include people through specific rules and practices that serve the purpose of excluding them. People are included in a political order, yet with a legal status that leaves them open to exclusion. Although the concerns of Giaccaria and Minca are with the sovereign topology of Auschwitz and the contemporary variants of such camps, they share with Mezzadra and Neilson an interest in subjects who are neither fully included, nor fully excluded, by border regimes. For the latter authors, the sense in which migrants can be simultaneously inside and outside the law, neither fully admitted in terms of rights and legal protections, nor fully proscribed from setting foot in a given territory, represents a transformation of the relationships of exclusion and inclusion; a transformation that, for them, nonetheless still bears all the hallmarks of the state's ongoing power and authority to control its borders.

Mezzadra and Neilson are insistent that border controls should be seen as devices of inclusion as much as exclusion, working to select, filter and channel people as well as to block their passage. Inclusion and exclusion, as noted before, turn out to be matters of degree where migrants may have a physical presence on, for example, US or European soil, yet find themselves outsiders in terms of the law and other forms of protection and benefit. Having gained entry and settled in the US, for instance, as Coleman (2012) has shown, non-citizens suffer legal exclusion and the threat of removal because, as he astutely points out, they 'are "here enough" to be arrested but not "here enough" to address their detention in the courts' (Coleman, 2012, 419). Equally, migrants detained before the border are subjected to processes of filtering and differential inclusion, to use Mezzadra and Neilson's term, that place them in a subordinate legal position, as well as suspending their right of movement. From the enclosed borders of the sovereign cylinder, then, the transformation of the state's powers to exclude and include now appears more like an interpenetration of spaces, where the inside and outside realms are bound up with one another, rather than part of a single, uninterrupted space with a discernible borderline.

If that is indeed the case, then the topological figure that this continuity of border relationships under transformation most closely resembles, as Bigo (2001) seems fully aware, is that of the Klein bottle. I outlined such a possibility in an earlier chapter, where the folding in and stretching out of border relationships belies any enclosed continuum of authority and control. With the figure of the Klein bottle as sovereign, the state's powers of exclusion and inclusion may be folded in directly to establish a direct presence or be stretched indirectly in a more coextensive fashion. The more direct the presence, detached or otherwise, the more likely it is to retain its intensity. Sovereign reach, in that respect, whether it be into the lives of migrant communities within the likes of the US or the European Union, or beyond them into the political affairs of neighbouring countries, does not necessarily have its intensity curbed over long drawn-out distances.

In a topological world of distorted borders, the sense in which they have been pushed outwards or pulled inwards has little to do with their extension from the border proper, and everything to do with the ability of states to make their presence felt in more-or-less authoritative ways that cut across proximity and distance. I say more-or-less authoritative because, up to this point, I have not really drawn attention to the fact that, whilst the state exercises its sovereign authority through its borders, authority is rarely the only register of power in play.

Borders in a different register

The use of the term 'the border proper' takes us back to the familiar topography of entry and departure points, at ports and airports and such. It reminds us that the authority to exclude and include may be consolidated through controls that both enable circulation as well as constrain it. That borders are not experienced in the same way by everyone is now well recognized, with the 'wanted' filtered out from the 'unwanted' population, some fast-tracked through the use of smart-border programmes whilst others are blocked at the point of entry or detained on arrival. Less appreciated, however, is that for exclusion and inclusion to work as part of the same instrumental arrangement, different registers of power are often called into play. What may start out as a straightforward act of formal authority, backed up by a tightly bound set of rules and regulations, may, for highly skilled migrants, for example, be overlain by the inducement of minimal entry requirements, whereas for those with fewer skills to offer, acts of authority may mutate into outright constraint, even rejection. In any such powerful arrangement, whether topographical or topological, a variety of modes of exclusion and inclusion may be exercised in combination to suit a particular purpose.

Consider, for instance, the use of the risk-management technology mentioned earlier, biometrics that records and identifies a person's bodily features so that when presented at a border checkpoint, a comparison is made against data already stored to confirm identity (Amoore, 2006). Or the use of pre-screening to evaluate the risk profile of passengers by comparing past behaviour against what is deemed 'safe' or 'proper', to gauge the extent of deviation (Amoore and DeGoede, 2005). Both forms of risk assessment disturb any simple view of what it means to gain or be denied access to a territory based on the authority of the sovereign cylinder. The use of risk profiling as a means of discriminating between 'right' or 'wrong' behaviours, and the modelling of behaviours for the express purpose of excluding those who deviate from the norm, are less acts of rule-based authority and more a form of manipulation taking place behind people's backs. The two registers, authority and manipulation, work in tandem: they play across one another so that the formal rules of exclusion and inclusion conceal the profiling of risk.

Although the deployment of such 'high-tech' forms of border control may occur at and away from territorial borders, I am not suggesting that by virtue of that they are especially topological. To press the point, the diffusion of border practices is not the same as the distortion of state borders. While the use of biometrics and pre-screening technologies may disrupt the temporal rhythm between past and future behaviours, they do not, as such, constitute intensive spatial arrangements that recast the relationship between 'near' and 'far'. One of the arguments of this chapter is that it is precisely the folding and stretching of relationships of authority that has enabled centralized institutions such as the US Department of Homeland Security to reproduce its powers differently. It is through such spatial processes of distortion, not diffusion, that powerful state actors have been able to interact directly or indirectly with others elsewhere at-a-distance. That development may appear to some as a multiplication of borders, but in practice it represents the transformed ability of such actors to make their presence felt through a variety of different, more focused modes of exclusion and inclusion.

That, of course, is not to say that relationships of formal authority cannot mutate into something more coercive or discriminating at the conventional border. Indeed, we have already seen that to be the case. What is different about the topological reworking of borders is the ability that it confers on centralized bodies to *reach into* their own political communities, as well as those of others beyond, to exclude and include in ways hitherto unimaginable. It is precisely through such leveraged reach, it seems to me, that governments are able to reproduce border relationships in a different guise without, that is, sacrificing intensity.

Coleman, as well as Mezzadra and Neilson, in their accounts of inclusive exclusion, suggest as much, even if not quite in those terms. As they point out, the kinds of controls 'lodged' within the interior of the US and EU, respectively, are not directed so much at stopping migration as at redefining the status of people who are already present. The imposition of authority through arm's-length reach may result in exclusion, but it is achieved by first having manipulated the rights of those who have gained entry so that they are rendered vulnerable to the threat of exclusion. The arbitrary nature of their legal status leaves them open to the ever-present threat of removal, despite the fact that they may be living and working alongside others who take such rights for granted. Coercive acts, on their own, possess a high visibility that may well attract noisy political attention, especially if resisted publicly, but when cloaked in an acceptable form of authority and made possible by a manipulative restriction of rights, the combination makes for a particularly pernicious arrangement.

It may seem that such an overlay of powers acting through different registers could surface through any multiplication of borders, but that would be to lose sight of how centralized authorities stretch or fold their reach through a given population. The mix of quieter with more strident registers of power is an adaptable one, part of the changing same of exclusion and inclusion that pervades border relationships. What, arguably, has enabled their transformation and intensification at locations far away from the border proper has been the ability to leverage a potent presence that by and large does not diminish the further away it is exercised.

The same adheres, I would have thought, to the Global Reach-type enforcement practices south of the Mexico–US border, or to those of Frontex, which stretches EU border controls into North Africa and beyond. Directed not at a population already present, but at one seeking to gain entry, the pre-emptive enforcement practices involve what appear to be a recomposed set of institutions and agencies acting through overlapping instrumental arrangements. Whether through a detached presence or one where absent authorities are interleaved with agencies present on the ground, the co-option of neighbouring countries to manage entry routes may mutate from a blend of incentivized authority through to more constraining acts that close down possibilities for entry. In that sense, the incorporation of neighbouring states, their absorption into a set of normative standards and practices as part of an 'offshore' package of migration controls, may all too easily work alongside other modes of exclusion that delay or deter movement, placing the border, as we shall see shortly, out of reach. There is no blueprint to such arrangements, only different combinations through which the power of border relationships may reproduce itself in diverse ways.

In that respect, it would be a mistake to equate the potency of the border with a more blanket-style policing arrangement of sovereign control. In practice, the displacement of sovereign authority, it turns out, can work just as well.

Displacing the border

In Chapter 6 I drew attention to the way that big corporate retailers attempt to distance themselves from taking responsibility for overseas sweatshop exploitation by effectively displacing it, pushing it further away in relational terms. States do much the same thing – European, North American and Australian in particular – to the claims of asylum seekers and irregular migrants. They have been known to distance themselves from demands for entry from would-be asylum seekers, for example, by stopping them from reaching the shores of sovereign territories or by using delay and deterrence tactics to avoid their responsibilities under international refugee law (Mountz, 2011a). The use of detention and confinement serves as a means of displacement, not only by denying access to the border proper, but also by denying refugees and migrants 'the right to have rights', as no doubt Hannah Arendt (1951) would have observed. On both counts, access to a sovereign territory and its rights and protections are placed *out of reach*.

I mentioned this earlier in the context of the European border being stretched to parts of North Africa to deter access to potential migrants. When detention and confinement enter into the picture, however, the distortion of the border takes a different shape; that of the temporary holding centre, the waiting zone or internment in the country of transit, as well as, more routinely, detainment in prison and detention centres. Whether offshore or onshore, on remote island locations (Mountz, 2011b) or in prison facilities close by (Martin, 2012), detainment serves to interrupt or suspend the rights of those claiming inclusion. Detainees held in offshore detention facilities, unable to reach their destination or return home, may find themselves stateless as a result, whilst those detained onshore find themselves liable to deportation, having been shorn of their legal right to remain. Much like the indiscernible space of the Klein bottle, detainees on the 'inside' are removed as if already part of the 'outside', whereas those held 'outside' are denied rights lawfully theirs if present on the 'inside'.

Topologically, what is of interest about such forms of detainment is that they work through relational exclusion where access is pushed further away, made distant as opposed to simply remote, as would be the case with out-of-the-way, offshore detention centres. Remoteness is an issue for would-be asylum seekers and irregular migrants, insofar as it exacerbates the difficulty of gaining access to legal representation and asylum itself, but the distances that matter most are relational, not physical. Detainees in facilities both onshore and offshore have been denied access to protective rights by immigration authorities pushing them further away, by outsourcing their responsibilities, mediating demands in a more circuitous manner and multiplying the possibilities for delay and disruption. Moreover, isolation and separation, regardless of the actual distances involved, both work to exclude detainees from the public realm and deny them access to the juridical process.

None of this, of course, has happened purely by chance. The displacement of borders, the outsourcing of responsibilities, the exclusion from the public realm, are all intentional acts, the product, it would seem, of experiment and adaptation on the part of central immigration authorities borrowing and learning from one another. The use of islands offshore, for instance, as 'an enforcement archipelago', to use Alison Mountz's apt description, represents a certain spatial inventiveness as regards the circumvention of legal rights, but also a temporal innovation in all manner of ways to delay, disrupt and broadly slow down the pace of 'unwanted' migration. In doing so, however, states have become adept at reproducing their powers of exclusion and inclusion through different registers: manipulating the timing and tempo of migratory movements, combining forced with induced removals, and closing down possibilities through disruption and exhaustion. Central to that, arguably, has been the topological displacement of the border itself.

Placing rights beyond reach

Arendt's experience of migration before and after the Second World War did not encompass such inventiveness around borders and exclusion, but it did involve displacement and what it meant to be rendered stateless. For her, the plight of refugees and stateless people was one of political destitution, a specific form of isolation and exclusion that placed them outside of the realm of political rights. The 'right to have rights', for Arendt, arose in much the same way as power comes into being; something that is exercised in concert with others, a product of people acting together in the public domain laying claim to what is rightfully theirs by virtue of their political association (Arendt, 1951). If power holds people together through mutual action, likewise civil and political rights are sustained through collective action and inclusion in the public sphere. Exclusion from that sphere, the denial of the rights and protections that it denotes, on her view, leaves refugees and migrants exposed to the arbitrary violence of the state and a life of destitution.

Violence, when understood as acts of isolation and confinement, or removal and physical deterrence, on this account, would result in the public realm being placed out of reach for the destitute. Violence and power are distinct acts for Arendt (1970), the former coming into play where the latter recedes from view. That there are different modalities of violence, as much as power, not all of them raw or unvarnished, was not something explored by Arendt, but exclusion from the public sphere through deterrence and confinement are likely candidates in the context of irregular migration today. The sense in which the public realm has been pushed further away through isolation and detention, both offshore and onshore, points towards a more contemporary form of political destitution. The denial of access to legal and social rights – that is, being placed on the 'outside' of public space – is something that I think she would recognize, although not, I suspect, the various ways in which that access is presently blocked and delayed.

The mention earlier of detention facilities on islands offshore is a case in point. The detainment of potential asylum seekers and irregular migrants on islands offshore has been a strategy developed by Canada, Australia and the European Union, among others, to singular effect. The archipelago of exclusion that Mountz (2011a) refers to, for example, includes the use of detainment offshore in places such as Vancouver Island close to British Columbia, Christmas Island and Naura off the coast of Australia, and Lampedusa, an island in the Mediterranean south of Italy, just north of Libya. In each case, the offshore island status is important, but less I would say because of the tangible physical distances that separate them from their respective mainlands and more because access to a public realm of rights and protections for those detained has been placed out of reach. Exclusion from that realm is the result of the relational distances stretched from island to mainland, where reach is mediated in a more indirect manner, multiplying the possibilities for delay, disruption and displacement.

On that basis, it would be wrong to suggest that the further the actual physical distance between island and mainland, the greater the denial of access. The longer or shorter span of distance is not the prime consideration here, but rather how the process of isolation and confinement remove detainees from the public sphere, leaving access to be mediated in the main through private contract agencies such as the IOM. The more fragmented its nature, the more difficult becomes the passage to a bundle of rights and protections. In topological terms, relational distance and reach are leveraged to fill out the space and time between 'here' and 'there'.

Contrast, for example, Mountz's account of the use of the Canadian base of Esquimalt on Vancouver Island to detain would-be asylum seekers with her outline of Australia's use of detention on the likes of Christmas Island and Naura. The former island is part of British Columbia, in close geographical proximity to the mainland, whereas Naura, for instance is an independent nation state, north of Australia and physically remote from the mainland. One is administered by the Canadian Immigration authorities, the other, when it was part of Australia's 'Pacific Solution' to its asylum 'problem', was contracted out to the IOM to run its detention facility on the island. Yet both sets of authorities managed to delay and interrupt the right of refugees to claim asylum and seek legal representation; both used isolation and confinement as a tool to further restrict or deny access to sovereign territory; and both attempted to stretch the distance between the detainees and the public realm. In short, despite the geographical and administrative differences, both sets of authorities were more or less able to place access beyond reach by leveraging it topologically.

The point here is not to imply that all island authorities are much the same when it comes down to distancing themselves from the demands for access and entry. The use of third-party organizations – non-state actors and private agencies among them – to manage and run detention facilities is itself a means of displacement that can multiply the possibilities for further constraint. The Australian and Canadian authorities appear to be different in that respect or at least in this instance. The relational distances involved in island offshore exclusions will depend, in part, not on the degree of remoteness but on the extent of mediation, its indirectness, in any spatial arrangement. And that, in turn, will depend upon the purpose behind an authority deciding to outsource its responsibilities for border management in the first place.

In the case of the 'holding centre' operated by the IOM on Lampedusa, Italy's southernmost island, that purpose seems to have been primarily to block the entry of irregular migrants coming from Libya and beyond (Andrijasevic and Walters, 2010). Rather than slow down the pace of 'unwanted' migration through the use of delay and protracted detention, migrants were known to have been deported *en masse* back to Libya without their claims acknowledged (Andrijasevic, 2010). Such a push-back and deportation arrangement clearly places the right of entry or asylum even further out of reach, but again arguably that has less to do with the greater physical distances involved and more to do with, in this instance, the Italian authorities not wishing to appear wholly complicit. Sovereign states, as we saw earlier, may decide to co-opt neighbouring states into a border-management programme, establishing a detached presence of sorts, or make their authority felt, as noted above, through the mediated presence of contract enforcement agencies. But they can distance themselves further from any binding responsibilities under international law by actually displacing their sovereign *authority*.

As Luiza Bialasiewicz (2012) and others have pointed out, there would appear little that is legitimate about Italy's push-back arrangement and Libya's then role in preventing irregular migrants from travelling further, where the exposure to arbitrary violence and physical deterrence has echoes of Arendt's original account of political destitution. Violence, for her, was inevitably justified through the ends sought, and removal from the European public realm of rights appears to present a justification in this instance, regardless of its questionable legitimacy. It is in that sense that an 'inside that lies beyond', to draw once again upon Massey's (2007) topological-style insight, has been used by Italian authorities to place Europe further out of reach for the politically destitute of North and West Africa (Andrijasevic, 2010). A sovereign authority, the Italian state, though physically absent from the Libyan detention camps that it financed, was able to exert an influence over the movement of others far beyond its borders. Indeed, it has been through such efforts that Italy, up until the collapse of the Libyan state, was able to displace its responsibilities for the deported migrants onto another government willing to collude in such manipulative statecraft. It represents a twist, as it were, in the contemporary form of political destitution.

It is perhaps not the only contemporary twist, however, for the politically destitute in Arendt's sense can find themselves excluded today even when already present on sovereign territory. If having a far-reaching influence beyond the border proper is one way in which the 'inside' is stretched continuously to block or deny access, Massey's 'outside that can be found within' represents another form of topological exclusion. While detention on offshore islands and further beyond has tended to hold the political imagination, the detention and confinement of noncitizens in Europe and the US has taken place primarily onshore, not offshore; that is, after arrival and entry. Even in the case of those detained on Lampedusa, the majority of irregular migrants and asylum seekers have been transferred to detention centres on the Italian mainland, mostly in the south of Italy, from where as a rule they are released after having been served with deportation orders (Andrijasevic, 2010). Release, however, renders them 'illegal' if they overstay, and thus liable to a further period of confinement and detention. As such, they remain 'outside' of the public realm and, as noted before, excluded from a country's rights and protections, leaving them vulnerable to removal.

In practice, the form of exclusion is not dissimilar to that experienced by those detained on islands offshore. The process of exclusion is itself relational, in that access to legal rights and representation is pushed further away, despite being in close proximity to the institutional and advocacy support which could defend their 'right to have rights'. Like offshore detention, its onshore counterpart is largely mediated through organizations and contract agencies which fill out the space and time required to gain access of any sort. It is just that different means are employed to deny smooth access. The isolating nature of confinement which separates detainees from the public sphere, as before, serves to delay and interrupt the right to claim inclusion, but the manner of circumvention varies (Martin, 2012). If offshore detention slows down the arrival of migrants through the regulation of movement *en route*, onshore detention often works through parallel forms of interdiction.

Chief among them seems to be the frequent transfer of irregular migrants and asylum seekers between detention centres, which has the destabilizing effect of making all ties transient and locations interim and transitory (Gill, 2009). In such a situation, engagement with the judicial decision-making process, or progress made in respect of appeals and release dates, can be hampered by the constant upheaval involved and the difficulty of tracing the shifting whereabouts of detainees. The disruption such frequent movement has upon the ability of detainees to access their community of support, friends and relatives, as well as legal assistance, can compound that sense of dislocation. Not being allowed to settle may seem a fairly insignificant means of interdiction, but its effect is to place further out of reach any likely resolution to a detainee's predicament. The constant deferral of claims, the frustration of waiting and the exhaustion of upheaval, may all work to push further away the likelihood of a timely outcome to an assessment of the 'right to stay' (Martin, 2012).

Displacing that assessment is much the same as displacing access to Arendt's public sphere of rights where, under international law, detention is meant to be a brief period of confinement undertaken while an assessment is made on a detainee's 'right to stay' in a country. Whether that detention is onshore or offshore, the veiled introduction of an arbitrary element of delay and disruption adds a further dimension to the contemporary form of political destitution. Exclusion from the public realm can take a variety of relational forms, mediated temporally and spatially to fill out the distance between detention and rights. For Arendt, the 'right to have rights' is the right to belong to some kind of political community, so in that sense the harder it is for migrants to press such a claim, the more their presence is removed from the public gaze. Isolation and confinement, delay and disruption, on the part of the institutional authorities serve to create such a displaced presence.

Experiments with borders

Attempts to raise the visibility of detention centres and bring them into the public gaze have not been without success. Campaigning NGOs such as Migreurop in Europe, Australia's Refugee Action Collective and the international organization Human Rights Watch, in a manner similar to that discussed in Chapter 6, have leveraged their energy and reach to inform the public of the existence of such camps (Rodier, 2007; Human Rights Watch, 2015). They have drawn public attention, for instance, to the kind of push-back and deportation arrangements mentioned earlier, as well as to the plight of migrants intercepted *en route* far from the border proper. That success, however, appears to have been matched by the equally inventive ability of certain states to displace their borders, borrowing and learning from one another to keep the public realm at bay. In that respect, adaption and experimentation, qualities previously spoken about as largely the prerogative of NGOs and social movements, seem to be just as much a characteristic of central immigration and state-making authorities.

Bialasiewicz (2009, 2012), for example, has spoken about the Mediterranean as having long been 'the premier laboratory for creative solutions' to the management and control of Europe's borders, a place where 'border-work' is put into practice to trial different ways of 'securing the external'; that is, different ways to influence and co-opt those on the periphery of the European Union. Likewise, Mountz (2011a, 2011b) in her work on offshore islands as an enforcement archipelago has drawn attention to the 'creative exercises in power' involved and the invention of new ways to deploy spatiality as a tool to deny or block migrants accessing their rights. Along with Mezzadra and Neilson (2012, 2013), she has also pointed to the innovative use of temporality to serve a similar purpose, where the pace of migration is slowed down by ever more resourceful tactics of delay and disruption. Each, in their own way, has highlighted the degree of experimentation with borders that has taken place in recent decades, where states appear to have deliberately explored and adapted different spatial and temporal practices to meet the demands of a situation changing year on year.

It is not just borders that have been subject to trial and experimentation, however; so too have the possibilities for exclusion and inclusion enabled by the changing shape of borders. We saw this earlier with the adaptable mix of force and co-option that informs the Global Reach-style enforcement practices, as well those of Frontex, and much the same can be seen with the different ways that exclusion has been explored through the use of distance, displacement and detention. The much copied use of offshore islands as detention centres, as outlined, represents a crucible for such exploration, providing a confined context to explore what best suits as a means of exclusion: what combination of authority and inducement, or manipulation and outright coercion, might work to achieve the purpose of displacement. Insofar as there are no guarantees as to which combination is the more effective, private contractors such as the IOM occupy a pivotal position in the roll-out of possibilities. Their centrality to the whole process of border displacement puts them in a unique position to conduct what can only be termed trials of power.

The contractual role of the IOM was noted earlier in relation to the indirect influence and pressure that it brought to bear on 'peripheral' states to manage their borders. The scope of the IOM also extends to the running of detention camps, however, and all that entails in terms of managing expulsions and deportations, as well as the actual time spent in confinement. From what Andrijasevic (2010) and others have said about how they go about closing down possibilities by leaving detainees with little choice but to conform, the practice seems to be hedged by the expedient use of different means to achieve the purpose of removal or reduction in the numbers claiming their rights. With the implicit threat of removal ever present, the IOM has explored, for example, the use of financial inducements to entice return migration, coupled with a range of other incentives to enhance the lure of resettlement. Less conspicuous as a means of removal, detainees whose claims-making prospects appear diminished or impeded are targeted directly through such quieter registers.

On that basis, it seems that the further out of reach the prospect of residency is placed, the less the need for authority to be imposed or excessive force to be used by private agencies such as the IOM. In other words, the more circuitous the forms by which access to rights is mediated, the more hurdles placed in the way of securing entry, the easier it would appear for such authorities to trial different means to effect exclusion.

One such pilot means of displacement, as we have already seen, has been the manipulation of the time spent by detainees in confinement which, on Mezzadra and Neilson's (2012) reckoning, represents a kind of 'temporal border'. Experiments with the use of time to delay or defer applications for asylum and the onward movement of detainees, to disrupt the claims-making process by impeding access to legal support or by constant transfer between detention facilities, add up to a less-than-subtle exercise in attrition. Experiments are by nature provisional exercises, where there is no guarantee that the means adopted will match the ends sought, but the trial manipulations of time in this instance do appear to have had the intended effect of helping to slow down the pace of 'unwanted' migration and regulating its movement. As a resourceful means of exclusion, one less obvious than violence or physical removal, they represent a quieter, less overt way in which governments and agencies reproduce the power of the border differently.

The kinds of displacement discussed here, however, especially those that arise from states outsourcing their responsibilities to privately run agencies on a contract basis, nonetheless take us back to a question posed earlier on in this chapter: how do states maintain their authority and presence in the face of such a distortion and displacement of borders? For much of the chapter, that question has been answered by the state's ability to reproduce its power and presence topologically, whether directly or indirectly. But when the state displaces its own sovereign authority, as would appear to be the case in much offshore detention, the topological reach and intensity of the arrangement is also called into question. In such instances, it could be argued that states have not so much stretched out their responsibilities under international law, as abandoned them by pushing them so far away as to erase all trace of their sovereign authority. Indeed, that may well be the case where collusion in malpractice is concerned, but it seems to me that a displaced sovereign authority does not automatically equate to no presence at all. Whilst a sovereign authority can be absent, its influence and direction may still be felt at-a-distance.

It comes down to the fact that states, despite being physically absent from many offshore locations, still retain a focused purpose and presence, which is to limit the numbers reaching their shores and place the public realm of rights beyond reach.

That purpose may be delivered by means other than those deemed entirely legitimate by states themselves, even twisted to suit the goals of third parties, but the concentration of focus appears to remain nonetheless. What seeps away is sovereign responsibility, as any direct authority is effaced in favour of a more mediated arrangement whereby states seek to influence the pace of migration at-a-distance. What may appear as a centre–periphery relationship in geometric terms is perhaps best understood as a form of *topological equivalence*, where what remains related despite the distortions of the border is an ongoing system of exclusion and inclusion. As with offshore finance in Chapter 5, so too with offshore detention, the powers of an institutional body are reproduced but in a different spatial arrangement. In practice, the reach of state sovereignty is leveraged topologically to have an impact despite, in this instance, its wilful physical absence.

Above all, what this example pointedly illustrates is that presence and absence, as with notions of inside and outside, or indeed exclusion and inclusion, have to be grasped differently when topology enters the frame.

Sovereign topologies

At the beginning of this chapter I noted that topological speculation has been fuelled by the fact that sovereign borders increasingly no longer map onto the 'inside' and 'outside' of state territory in any meaningful way. That speculation, perhaps encouraged by the diffusion of sophisticated border technologies, in particular biometrics and pre-screening, appears to have given rise to the general impression that borders can now be pretty much everywhere and nowhere. As I hope is evident, this is not a view I share, principally for two main reasons.

In the first place, it is unhelpful to portray the distorted nature of political borders in generalized terms, with little or no sense of the specific difference that topology has made to the particular shape border relationships have taken, whether in Europe, North America, Australia or any other part of the globe. Topology is about the particular folds and distinct deformations of border relationships; as a peculiarly intensive exercise of sovereign powers, not an indeterminate or extensive spatiality. Another reason for not sharing such a general impression, however, is that when it is conveyed in topological terms, it makes everything that has happened to state borders of late seem the result of topological distortion. That is simply not the case. Again, it is the specific difference of topology for the reshaping of borders and the internal and external spaces of a political community that is of interest, not the diffusion of border practices in general.

That specific difference manifests itself topologically in the way states have been able to reach into their own territories, as well as beyond them, drawing migrant populations within reach of their authority and control, or displacing responsibility for them by placing access to the public sphere out of reach. What may appear as a general blurring of the 'inside' and 'outside' of a sovereign territory, in effect, is a particular configuration of an outside shaping the lives of those within, and an inside influencing the lives of distant others beyond. Whatever distances are involved are bridged relationally, mediated directly or indirectly, to compose the spaces of interaction between centralized authorities, public as well as private border agencies, and migrant communities both within and without. Put another way, the relationships of exclusion and inclusion fill out the space so that the topological reach of the state is exercised through a variety of means to reconfigure the distance between 'near' and 'far'.

But, as may well be apparent, that is not the only difference that topology has made to the operation of political borders today. A focus on the processes of leveraged reach that have made it possible for states to fold and stretch their borders is significant but, as I have stressed throughout, only because it has enabled them to reproduce their powers of exclusion and inclusion in a different register. Political borders may have changed shape, transforming the means by which the movement of people and their access to rights is regulated, yet the state has been able to more-or-less maintain a continuous powerful presence. It is this continuity of border relationships under transformation, their equivalence established despite the figure of the sovereign border having been stretched and distorted out of shape, that makes a significant difference, a topological difference, to the workings of the contemporary political border. It is what allows us to grasp the changing same of exclusion and inclusion that pervades many a border relationship in the present day.

8

CONCLUSION

Power on the quiet

The anthropologist Clifford Geertz once referred to definitions of power which never go beyond 'coercion (as) its expression, violence its foundation, and domination its aim' (1980, 134) as 'the great simple', a rock to which most social and political theory clings. His point was not that such a definition was plainly wrong, but that it was partial, a selective interpretation based upon particular historical circumstances. Geertz's concerns were with the 'theatre state' in nineteenth-century Bali and its dramatized, symbolic practices of power, and thus could not be further removed from my own. Yet he put his finger on something that I think has timely, indeed enduring, relevance: namely, that if you regard power only as a loud and overtly constraining practice, you will miss much in the way that power actually gets people to do things they would not otherwise have done. What I take Geertz to be curious about are the powerful practices that do not appear as such, yet nonetheless secure instrumental advantage over others for those who exercise them.

The parallels today, to my mind, are with the practices that fall under the benign heading of the 'power to' make things happen, to facilitate progressive outcomes, yet often end up constraining more possibilities than they enable. As I have been trying to show throughout, whether it be investment bankers in New York and London seeking to facilitate positive-sum returns, or NGOs mobilizing and enrolling a 'public' to back a worthy 'global' campaign, or governments attempting to exercise their influence through local associations and private agencies, the 'power to' secure an outcome does not always play to the benefit of all involved and, in fact, may turn into the kind of power that is actually held *over* others. Through such supposedly facilitative means, the power exercised may effectively obscure the instrumental character of the relationships involved and draw people into arrangements that work against their interests. What such practices lack in drama and ritual, they perhaps make up for with dissemblance and dissimulation.

Dissemblance and dissimulation are two practices rarely discussed in the power literature, unless the name of Niccolò Machiavelli should pepper the conversation. Which is, perhaps, a pity, given that such practices owe more to the routine ability of holding something back, of not revealing all, than any conscious act of deception or bare cunning. Machiavelli knew the difference, even if that is not always acknowledged. Dissimulation entails a lack of disclosure as to one's actual motives and intentions, but not by disguising them or pretending to be motivated by interests that are consciously false. As a peculiarly distinctive arrangement of power, the manipulation of a political or economic situation may obscure any instrumental advantage secured to suit some but not all interests, or by the glare of inducements that appear rewarding when the reality is in fact otherwise. Such quieter means of power, as I have indicated, may be overlain by more overt means of control and constraint, but they may also be alternated with them to avoid revealing all that really is at stake.

The point, as I have stressed all along, is not that power on the quiet, including the suggestive ploys of seduction and persuasion, has somehow replaced those of a more clamorous nature, but rather that the topological reach afforded to such quieter registers today opens up just such a possibility. When the same ends can be achieved by different means, when manipulative reach may stand in for the lack of recognized authority, or those elsewhere can be folded in through enticement rather than compulsion, then such relational proximities are more likely to be leveraged. The more pliable their leverage in terms of reach and composition, the more supple their hold in keeping political alliances or economic arrangements together, the keener the edge such registers have over more conspicuous means of control and influence. That, after all, has been one of the central arguments of this book: that topological processes have subtly altered many of the ways in which contemporary power is exercised, enabling quieter, more impalpable means to come to the fore.

Given the often tenuous nature of power relationships and the potential for circumstances to open up in unforeseen ways, the scope for improvisation and adaptation is a key issue when working out what means work better than others to achieve a particular end. Hitting upon the right course of action may involve a certain experimentation with different powerful manoeuvres, as was evident in the case of NGOs seeking out the best way to exploit political opportunities, or states displacing their borders by exploring and adapting different spatial and temporal practices trialled elsewhere. In the case of the latter, it is more likely to be a question of which combination of manipulated rights and coercive threats, or dangled incentives and objectified authority, best suits as a means of exclusion when sovereign borders have been stretched or distorted out of shape. Such acts may not amount to a piece of drama, but the use of islands as offshore detention centres, for instance, or the US Global Reach-style enforcement practices, are certainly dramatic accomplishments of power nonetheless.

What all such instances speak to, however, is the ability of states, NGOs and other organizations to actively reproduce their power on less-than-blunt terms to establish a continuous presence of one kind or another. Significantly, what I have tried to capture in this book is precisely those power relationships that have been reproduced differently through the processes of distorted reach, and that exploration has been advanced both analytically and empirically at various points in the text.

In the first half of the book, my main concern was to spell out where topology parts company with topography, and takes us beyond territorial and networked approaches to power and spatiality. Topology's concern with continuous but transformed relations that survive the process of distortion provided me with a vocabulary to redescribe how relationships of power are reproduced through space and time, often in a different register. It also provided me with a check on certain well worn spatial assumptions that power may be simply extended over mappable distances or distributed through pre-existing connections, in favour of a more composed spatiality where proximity and distance play across one another to form new spatial arrangements of power. Such a parting of ways, where familiar words have been used in less familiar ways to help shift a conversation around proximity, distance and power, can now, hopefully, be seen for the exploratory promise that a topology of power holds.

The second half of the book, in that respect, is an attempt to realize some of that promise, albeit in a discerning fashion through the contrasting worlds of finance and investment banking, NGOs and social movements, and states and border controls. It may have been assumed that those fields were chosen precisely because they lent themselves to topological exploration, and that itself would not be wrong, given the mix of times and spaces that appear to forge the relationships, exchanges and interactions peculiar to them. Above all, though, topology just seems to work better at grasping the more subtle ways in which power is now exercised by bankers and investment managers to reproduce their financial advantage, by NGOs and campaigners to mobilize and leverage dispersed 'publics' around particular claims, and by states to distort their political borders. Topology works better because the kinds of spatial distortion that are so central to it, the folded and stretched relationships, are precisely the processes that enable financial, political and institutional actors to practice such subtle, powerful interventions. It is, as I hope is apparent, what gives them their powers of reach, as well as singular relational presence.

Power reproduced differently

In setting out a manifest topological stall, however, I was concerned that the act of borrowing a vocabulary from what often appears an arcane branch of mathematics should amount to more than simply an act of metaphorical appropriation; that the equivalence of power relations and the processes of distortion that enable such a correspondence are actually part of the social material of the world. There is no question of it being merely a sculpting of one domain onto another, although of course I have not been immune to some chiselling of my own, in part to avoid lifting wholesale a vocabulary that pays no heed to the variations in the 'stuff' that is common to both social and topological domains. That the two domains admit some resemblance is part of the claim that underpins this text, but the vocabulary borrowed still requires a translation of sorts, one that helps us to understand, perhaps for the first time, what we have been bumping up against all along.

In talking about power relations as topologically equivalent, I have drawn attention to the fact that in whatever ways power is stretched or folded by a political agency or economic institution, it is possible for the same instrumental arrangement to prevail. 'Equivalence', here, refers to the fact that despite the distorted reach leveraged by such agencies and institutions, their powers remain the same, continuously related, although transformed by reaching out from 'here' to 'there'. The twist is in the last line, where such processes of distortion reproduce the 'sameness' of power differently, from one register to another. Put another way, power relationships are transformed when stretched or folded; they are reproduced, yet mutate in diverse ways depending upon the relational arrangement of which they are a part. Or, more colloquially, it is the topological distortion of reach that makes it possible to contemplate the 'changing same' of power.

What I have also tried to convey is that the distorted reach leveraged by a range of different bodies and groups may owe little to their institutional size and organizational shape. This is perhaps a more controversial aspect of a topological redescription of power, and somewhat counter-intuitive, given that, when it comes to leverage, it is conventionally assumed that size matters and that the more resources at an organization's disposal, the greater its power. In Chapters 3 and 4, I outlined a more pragmatist account of power that brought into question such an assumption.

Dispositional views of power tend to gauge the effectiveness of an organization by the size and magnitude of the resources at their disposal, regardless of whether or not they are actually used. The weightier an organization, the heftier its latent capacity, the more powerful it is deemed to be. From a pragmatist viewpoint, however, it seems baffling to think why this should always be the case: resources and power are not the same thing and an abundance of the former does not predetermine what institutions and organizations are capable of bringing about. Resources, as well as abilities, may be misplaced, misused, miscalculated or applied to no real effect. In some cases, incompetence and hubris may even play a part, a spectacle not unknown in the contemporary world of financial affairs and big banks. All of which suggests that what matters most is how such resources are used, put into practice, rather than simply calculated and mistaken for power. When practised topologically, the distorted reach leveraged by a variety of actors may make far more of a difference to the way their power is reproduced than any capacity-in-waiting.

That is not to say that institutional size and organizational capacity make no difference, just that there are other ways of putting power into practice which call upon less quantifiable resources. The clearest example of that was given in Chapter 6, where claims-making organizations and campaign groups drew distant harms and injustices within reach of those not present as a means of reproducing their 'power to' make a difference, mobilizing against far 'weightier' bodies than themselves to take responsibility for events elsewhere. The mobilization of political and moral energies by social movements, in that respect, is the organizational resource in question, rather than anything more substantial or of greater weight. Even in the surprisingly 'weighty' sphere of banking and investment, as I set out to show in Chapter 5, financial intermediaries seek to reproduce their economic advantage by making themselves indispensable through the deployment of deft negotiating and bargaining skills. The size of a bank's deposits is not unimportant, but nor is the ability to exploit information asymmetries by folding in others directly through real-time negotiations or reaching out to them through a succession of enrolling practices. It is through such leverage that indispensability is often achieved and maintained, enabling quieter means of authority and persuasion to take hold.

In making the case for quieter registers of power having come to the fore through the distorted reach of financial and other types of actors, I do nonetheless want to avoid the impression that it is the only way in which power gets to be reproduced differently. Should it be necessary to say it, there is, as John Agnew observed, 'a whole lot of domination going on' (2013, 454) out there. It is not part of my argument to suggest otherwise, only to signal the fact that the development of other ways of closing down possibilities and eroding choice has opened up, as the reach of institutions and social groups has progressed intensively. When the same ends can be secured by a wider variety of means, some more subtle and unobtrusive than hitherto, such options may be increasingly drawn upon to meet the demands of malleable situations. By that, I do not just mean, as mentioned in passing earlier, that manipulative reach may stand in for the lack of recognized authority, but that authority itself may actually be exercised in more understated ways.

Authority and influence can be exercised in a calm, unassuming fashion, demands can be communicated in ways that appear far from threatening, and you can find yourself in situations where you have no choice but to fall into line without anyone actually imposing their will. Domination always involves some degree of imposition and constraint, but the means of subjection does not have to be loud and conspicuous. Power may be exercised on the quiet in such ways, together with the manipulation of outcomes, the lure of inducement, the art of persuasion or the inviting gestures of seduction, but as I have argued all along, such registers progressively appear to form part of instrumental arrangements of power nowadays, in part simply because of their enhanced topological reach. They are, as pointed out, rarely exercised in isolation, and some combination where, say, persuasion and veiled threats play across one another, or mutate into something more manipulative, for example, when threats lose their credibility, is par for the course. To be sure, the likes of coercive force and armed violence fall outside of what is under consideration here, but we do not have to cling to that expression of power to deny the significance of less hard-hitting exercises of powers.

Certainly Joseph Nye shares that view, as noted in Chapter 4, and he has repeated it whenever possible, most recently in the immodestly entitled *The Future of*

Power (2011). As acknowledged, his account of 'soft', as opposed to 'hard', power has usefully drawn attention to the fact that there is more to power these days than economic domination and military might, as important as they continue to be. There are echoes of Geertz's 'great simple' line of argument present in Nye's thinking, although without a real grasp of the instrumental mobilization of advantage that underpins attempts to shape the preferences of others through persuasion and attraction. The ability to frame issues in persuasive ways is a central aspect of the way in which 'soft power' works itself out for him, although the manipulation and incitement involved in making some choices less attractive than others tends to be glossed over in his analysis. In part, I suspect that is because he is wedded to the view that persuasion and attraction work best when understood 'in terms of (the) power to accomplish goals that involve power *with* others' (Nye, 2011, xvii, emphasis in original). This, to my mind, is 'soft power' gone soft.

When power is exercised to channel and limit the preferences of others so that they want what you want, there seems little that is 'soft' about such behaviour. When it is portrayed as the 'power to' accomplish goals, to facilitate outcomes, as cautioned earlier, we should perhaps be more wary as to whose interests are being served and whether or not dissimulation is at work. Holding something back, not revealing all that is at stake, can mask the fact that the 'power to' make things happen has morphed into a quite different arrangement where the 'power over' others has quietly taken shape. Nye makes a lot of the increased importance of networked connectedness in contemporary power arrangements, of people drawing their power from their position in social and political networks, but it never seems to cross his mind that the topological shifts in the mix of times and spaces embedded in much 'networked' interaction might actually give some actors greater leverage over marshalling the wants and preferences of others.

It comes down again to opening up a topological conversation around proximity, distance and reach that makes it possible to perceive how quieter means of control and influence have helped to reproduce the power of a wide variety of institutions and organizations in different, yet distinctive, ways.

Topological reach

The notion of topological reach developed in this book is my attempt to translate the processes of spatial distortion that enable powerful actors to interact directly or indirectly with others elsewhere. I could have chosen to fall back on the folding or stretching of a wide variety of topological figures and shapes, from rubber inner tubes to doughnut-shaped cylindrical rings, but as stated, I wanted to go beyond simple metaphorical appropriation. In particular, I was concerned that the terms borrowed would be construed in a topographical frame, where for instance geographical scales could be 'folded' into one another, or lines of authority 'stretched' in extensive fashion across a well mapped landscape. The senses in which reach can be folded or stretched may not entirely avoid such interpretations, but they do point towards two significant characteristics of reach when it is understood topologically: one, that it is something that has to be actively *leveraged* for a powerful presence to be registered; and two, that such leverage *composes* the distances enacted to place others within or beyond reach. If the former produces a distorted spacing and timing of power relationships, the latter reproduces such relationships in intensive, not extensive, fashion.

It is not, as emphasized before, that intensive reach is somehow more illuminating than anything extended outwards in linear style; merely that intensive and extensive reach assume different types of distance. Extensive arrangements of power take place *over* defined physical distances, whereas intensive arrangements work *through* relational distances, composing them in space and time: the effectiveness of the former can be measured on a metric scale in terms of range and extent, the latter by its undiminished presence of one kind or another. If the stress upon presence sounds a little ethereal, that is only because distance as measured in miles or kilometres does not hinder powerful bodies from establishing a more-or-less direct presence; relationships can be made proximate or distant by drawing things closer or pushing them further apart. There is no extensive mapping of the mediated exchanges involved, only a diagrammatic feel for the intensive reach and transformation of the relationships that fill out the spaces between 'here' and 'there'.

The offshore world of finance outlined in Chapter 5 is perhaps a striking example of how topological relationships constitute the spaces of financial interaction, rather than merely operate across them. The continuous exchange between two jurisdictional spaces, one 'offshore', the other 'onshore', where financial transactions are recorded as having taken place in a location different from the actual operation, involves a purely relational set of distances. The reaching back and forth from one to the other is an intensive, not extensive, exercise in sidestepping the regulatory oversight of banking authorities. The barriers of physical distance do not impinge upon such a relational displacement. Much the same can be said for the displacement of corporate responsibilities in the world of offshore sweatshop production sketched in Chapter 6 or the movement of borders offshore described in Chapter 7. Although the 'offshore' family resemblances are just that, the likeness of which glosses over substantive differences between them, each provides an illustration of distances composed relationally to gain an advantage of one sort or another.

The tag 'offshore' however, if taken to an extreme (see Urry, 2014), can give rise to a misleading impression of reach as a somewhat 'effortless' exercise. The sense in which financial corporations and economic multinationals are said to possess a 'global reach', or that states can pretty much place their borders wherever they like these days, is contrary to the more particular, leveraged accounts of reach explored in previous chapters. The idea of 'global reach' as a capability of certain economic or political actors tends to conjure up an image of a far-reaching, widespread presence. If not all-encompassing on a 'global scale', the representation of a world criss-crossed by lines of economic and political activity can produce an easy geometry of extensive powers. Such an overblown representation, as intimated in Chapter 2, can woefully exaggerate the extended reach of economic and political organizations, but more importantly for my argument it can mask what is at stake when power is exercised intensively.

The intensive reach of governments and corporations, as well as a range of other bodies, is signalled by the directness and continuity of their presence and, as such, can be misread as something more 'global' or extensive. The kind of presence, as well as degree, turns on qualitative changes in the way that power is exercised; on the mediated arrangements that enable, say, some states to exercise control over the lives of migrants physically distant from their territorial borders; or investment banks like the Australian firm Macquarie to broker the interests of others in their favour, despite the physical distances that separate the parties involved. Whether heightened or not, the type of presence established takes a particular, not a ubiquitous form. In disembedded money markets, real-time technologies may be used to establish a simultaneous co-presence between investors distant from one another, whereas a more detached, political presence may be established at arm's length to regulate the movement or slow down the pace of 'unwanted' migration. In each case, the specificity of the arrangement belies any general notion of far-reaching, extensive powers as an accompaniment to the latest wave of globalization. They may nonetheless be mistaken for such.

Indeed, much the same could be said about the process of 'hegemonic reach', although for quite different reasons. Hegemonic formations – the term is obviously taken from Antonio Gramsci's *Prison Notebooks* (1971) – cannot be mapped as an extensive arrangement of power, but rather work themselves out through a blend of coercive and consensual practices that avoids much of the 'hard', constraining edges of power from coming fully into view. Ideas that 'go without saying', that take for granted much of the existing set-up of society and its skewed privileges, are woven into the 'common sense' of everyday life, making it difficult to recognize the interests served by such accustomed formations, let alone challenge them (Johnson, 2007). The supposedly encompassing reach of hegemonic constructions, however, differentiates it from the more actively leveraged, particular forms of intensive reach that I have documented on these pages.

Both types of reach, hegemonic and topological, work through a relational as opposed to a metric account of distance, but the former tends to assume its effects rather than demonstrate them. Hegemonic power, in its Gramscian mould, is understood to touch people in ways that are hard to pin down and are thus difficult to rebut. By way of contrast, power when leveraged topologically is more modest in its claims, making it possible in most instances to name the specific brush with power experienced, rather than falling back upon any general nomenclature. Not all accounts of hegemony are so sweeping in terms of their expressed popular reach (see Mouffe, 2013), although all are dependent upon there being a widespread acceptance of and assent to the dominant values and practices of the day as a means of conformity, without, that is, the need for coercion and constraint.

Few exponents of hegemony, though, refer to power as taking a particular shape, or one that goes beyond a straightforward, territorial arrangement. John

Agnew, mentioned earlier, is an exception in that regard. In *Hegemony: The New Shape of Global Power* (2005b) his concern is with the most recent configuration of US hegemony as a networked formation that reaches well beyond the sovereign shores of North America. Eschewing the idea that US power is simply a continuation of military and political power exercised territorially, he draws attention to the spread of marketplace values and practices which, following Nye, are thought to convince and co-opt others elsewhere into wanting what the US wants. Assent to such values and practices, if not set out strictly in the 'taken-for-granted' version of hegemony, is believed to have produced a new, global 'common sense' around economic and political ways of doing things that make it difficult to choose otherwise. Hegemony, as such, is perhaps better understood as the global spread and influence of neoliberal market values, a broad encompassing web of ideas and practices, rather than anything more focused or distorted in terms of reach.

On this account, Agnew's new-found hegemonic shape contrasts with the more mediated techniques and practices of reach leveraged by actors in an attempt to make their presence felt, whether by placing possibilities within reach or beyond it. In terms of actual presence, the taken-for-granted practices performed by the state described in Chapter 3, which seek to permeate everyday life, are closer to what I have in mind. The instantiation of authority through a whole host of mundane institutional practices performed by the courts, police, registrars and swathes of government officials aim to give 'the state' a presence in the here and now of daily life. Not, that is, an all-encompassing one, but rather one of sufficient intensity that enables the government to reproduce its power and authority through more pro-saic means (Painter, 2006). Whether it is successful or not depends upon the specific practices engaged and the ability of officials to leverage a presence in the everyday of one kind or another. Much like Geertz's 'theatre state', the authorities may draw upon a range of symbolic resources to produce the effect of 'state power', including the rituals of spatial hierarchy and the illusion of encompassment.

Even when it comes to the widespread reach of marketplace values and practices, in topological terms, the take-up of neoliberalism as a routine sentiment would be dependent upon the successful editing and translation of such values for particular targeted audiences, rather than the result of some form of blanket assent. When leveraged directly or indirectly, the adoption of marketplace values is more likely to be the product of a combination of quiet means, such as inducement and persuasion, than any general admiration for unfettered markets. This is not to suggest that a case cannot be made for the hegemonic reach of neoliberal values today, where choice and competition have become the currency of much everyday life, merely that such an all-encompassing reach deviates from the more mediated take-up of neoliberal practices described in Chapter 4. More cautious in tone, such an adoption of practices represented a tenuous achievement, dependent on the interplay of forces involved and the ability of actors to reach out to audiences on a more focused basis. What is lost in such a nominalistic formulation, however, is made up for by the specificity of the reach leveraged and the type of presence established.

A question of topology

Topology, however, even in its nominalistic guise, is not the answer to every question about space and power. Despite my enthusiasm for it as a spatial frame through which many of the ways in which power is exercised today may be understood, it is only one amongst other frames. As stressed early on, it has never been my intention to dismiss territorial or networked approaches to power in favour of a topological interpretation. Rather, my line of argument has been that each spatial frame has a place in understanding contemporary arrangements of power, and which frame works best really depends upon the *questions* asked about power and its diverse registers. The limits of much territorial and networked thinking around power, in that respect, often turn on such frameworks addressing questions that themselves challenge the spatial assumptions upon which they are based, or frameworks that, in today's spatially ambiguous world, they are ill-suited to answer. Certain questions lend themselves to topological investigation, whilst others are best accommodated within a conventional topographical approach. It matters that we can tell the two apart.

I began this book with a statement about the reach of power as not being what it once was, that its more heightened, relational character cuts across proximity and distance in ways that disrupt conventional senses of what is near and what is far. Shifts in the spacing and timing of power relationships, where it no longer becomes possible to simply 'read-off' presence and proximity from the calibrations of physical distance, have prompted a rethink of more familiar territorial and scalar distributions of power and authority. Such prompts, however, do not detract from the ongoing relevance of such familiar distributions; rather, they raise a different set of questions about space and power that are not easily answered within the more defined frameworks of territory and scale, or the more extensive connections of pre-existing networks. Let me try spell out the difference by referring back to the example of border controls discussed in Chapter 7.

If I ask a question about the combination of layered fencing and high walls that marks stretches of the territorial boundary between Mexico and the US, and am curious about its placement and layout, where such defences have been bolstered of late and where they tail off into the desert, I can frame an answer in topo-graphical terms. The hard lines of exclusion and points of entry can be mapped along the edges of both states, and the internal and external spaces of the respective sovereign communities conventionally defined. It matters how and where states construct such physical barriers, not just materially but symbolically, to differentiate the 'inside' from the 'outside' of a sovereign political community. But you do not need to draw upon a topological framework to seek such answers. If, however, it is also apparent that the 'inside' and the 'outside' of a sovereign state no longer appears mutually exclusive, that there has been an interpenetration of the two spaces, then a topological frame of reference is more likely to deliver answers, as to not only what distorted border relationships have taken shape, but what is at stake politically. When a question is asked about border security controls such as where the inside ends and the outside begins, a territorial response that traces the contours of authority is not likely to be of much help.

What is perhaps also evident from this example is that it is not the topic or issue itself that makes a topological rather than a topographical approach more suitable, but the question asked of the subject matter. True, I did say earlier that the worlds of finance and investment banking, NGOs and social movements, and states and border controls lend themselves to topological exploration, but that was because in each case a changing mix of times and spaces had shifted the ability of financial, political and institutional actors to make their presence felt. Why such shifts had occurred, why distance itself seems less relevant to the ability of such actors to reproduce their financial advantage, their political edge or their institutional controls, is a question on which a focus on blocs of economic or political power is not likely to shed much insight.

Likewise, with the discussion of the anti-sweatshop movement in Chapter 6, I could have focused on the whereabouts of consumer boycotts and the role of the Clean Clothes Campaign across its European organizational network of eleven countries, but the expanding repertoire of the movement's interventions to make the spectacle of distant suffering matter to those far removed from it altered the nature of the question posed. How NGOs oblige people to take responsibility for events elsewhere is not a question that has a simple locational or networked answer, but rather hinges upon their ability to establish an equivalence between such events and the privileges of those who depend upon them. This, for me, places the concern directly in the frame of topological, not geometric-style, politics. The question arises from a changing subject matter, but it is not the topic of social movements itself that automatically brings the topological to the fore.

The topics of citizenship or multiculturalism, for example, or the issues of climate change and urban development, are shot through with questions of power, but not all the questions raised will be ones that speak to interactions that, say, take place simultaneously across a variety of locations, or involve those physically elsewhere having an equivalent presence in the here and now. The ability of far-flung actors to make their presence felt at close quarters, to reach into the affairs of distant others, alerts us to the potential significance of topological explanations, but other exchanges may have more relevance for territorial or networked frameworks. In knowing the difference, the latter approaches are less likely to be drawn upon to account for too much, or to be extended to explain things that clearly point beyond multi-scalar or flattened landscapes of power.

Relationships, however, which compose the distances through which distant proximities are leveraged by the powerful are only one clue as to their potential topological relevance. The other, as underscored throughout, is when such powerful relationships are reproduced differently through such processes of leveraged distortion. The two together comprise the topological frame and here draw attention to questions of power that address the growing reach of quieter means of control and influence. Such questions can be overlooked when only the possibility of relations of domination and subordination is admitted, or deflected by 'softer' versions of power that lose sight of the instrumental advantage that processes of topological reach afford them. Topological questions about space and power require relational answers, but those answers also have to acknowledge that relations of power may be transformed by reaching out from 'here' to 'there': the same, yet different in terms of the presence registered. As you may recall, this is where the book started: with the changing same of power as a colloquial means of expressing how power often gets reproduced through a variety of registers.

Phrased thus, the changing same of power may be hard to disagree with. Its familiar ring, though, much like our topographical bearings, can make it harder to break with the habits, not only of a spatial geometry, but also of a simplistic narrative of continuity and change. Topology drops the conjunction so that it is not both continuity *and* change, but the same relationship reproduced differently when distorted in terms of its reach, whether proximate or otherwise. This is where topology has something to offer: it allows us to stand aside from familiar spatial and temporal trappings and see reach as more about presence than distance, a presence in the case of power that is continuous yet transformed in ways that enable quieter, more muted registers to exercise us. With luck, a topological grasp of space and spatiality will help us understand what it feels like today to be on the receiving end of such dissembling powers.

BIBLIOGRAPHY

Adams, P. (1998) 'Network topologies and virtual place', *Annals of the Association of American Geographers*, 88(1): 88–106.

Agamben, G. (1998) *Homo Sacer: Sovereign, Power and Bare Life*, Stanford, CA: Stanford University Press.

Agamben, G. (2005) *State of Exception*, Chicago, IL: Chicago University Press.

Agnew, J.A. (1994) 'The territorial trap: The geographical assumptions of international relations theory', *Review of International Political Economy*, 1: 53–80.

Agnew, J.A. (1999) 'Mapping political power beyond state boundaries', *Millennium*, 28: 499–521.

Agnew, J.A. (2005a) 'Sovereignty regimes: Territoriality and state authority in contemporary world politics', *Annals of the Association of American Geographers*, 95(2): 437–461.

Agnew, J.A. (2005b) *Hegemony: The New Shape of Global Power*, Philadelphia, PA: Temple University Press.

Agnew, J.A. (2013) 'Hidden or lost geographies of power', *Progress in Human Geography*, 37(3): 452–460.

Allen, J. (2003a) *Lost Geographies of Power*, Oxford: Blackwell.

Allen, J. (2003b) 'Power', in Agnew, J., Mitchell, K. and Toal, G. (eds) *A Companion to Political Geography*, Oxford: Blackwell, pp. 95–108.

Allen, J. (2004) 'The whereabouts of power: Politics, government and space', *Geografiska Annaler*, 86B: 19–32.

Allen, J. (2006) 'Ambient power: Berlin's Potsdamer Platz and the seductive logic of public spaces', *Urban Studies*, 43(2): 441–455.

Allen, J. (2008a) 'Pragmatism and power, or the power to make a difference in a radically contingent world', *Geoforum*, 39(4): 1613–1624.

Allen, J. (2008b) 'Claiming connections: a distant world of sweatshops?', in Robinson, J., Rose, G. and Barnett, C. (eds) *Geographies of Globalization*, Los Angeles, CA, London, New Dehli and Singapore: Sage.

Allen, J. (2009) 'Powerful geographies: Spatial shifts in the architecture of globalization', in Clegg, S. and Haugaard, M. (eds) *The Sage Handbook of Power*, Los Angeles, CA, London, New Dehli, Singapore and Washington, DC: Sage.

Allen, J. (2010) 'Powerful city networks: More than connections, less than domination and control', *Urban Studies*, 47(13): 2895–2911.

Allen, J. (2011) 'Topological twists: Power's shifting geographies', *Dialogues in Human Geography*, 1(3): 283–298.

Allen, J. and Cochrane, A. (2007), 'Beyond the territorial fix: Regional assemblages, politics and power', *Regional Studies*, 41(9): 1161–1175.

Allen, J. and Cochrane, A. (2010) 'Assemblages of state power: Topological shifts in the organization of government and politics', *Antipode*, 43(1): 1071–1089.

Allen, J. and Cochrane, A. (2014) 'The urban unbound: London's politics and the 2012 Olympic Games', *International Journal of Urban and Regional Research*, 38(5): 1609–1624.

Allen, J. and Pryke, M. (2013) 'Financialising household water: Thames Water, MEIF and "ring-fenced politics"', *Cambridge Journal of Regions, Economy and Society*, 6: 419–439.

Amin, A. (2007) 'Rethinking the urban social', *City*, 11(1): 100–114.

Amin, A. and Thrift, N. (2002), *Cities: Reimagining the Urban*, Cambridge: Polity.

Amoore, L. (2006) 'Biometric borders: Governing mobilities in the war on terror', *Political Geography*, 25: 336–351.

Amoore, L. and DeGoede, M. (2005) 'Governance, risk and dataveillance in the war on terror', *Crime, Law and Social Change*, 43(2/3): 149–179.

Anderson, J. (1996) 'The shifting stage of politics: new medieval and postmodern territorialities?', *Environment and Planning D: Society and Space*, 14: 133–153.

Andrijasevic, R. (2010) 'From exception to excess: Detention and deportation across the Mediterranean space', in Genova, N. and Peutz, N. (eds) *The Deportation Regime: Sovereignty, Space and the Freedom of Movement*, Durham, NC: Duke University Press.

Andrijasevic, R. and Walters, W. (2010) 'The International Organization for Migration and the international government of borders', *Environment and Planning D: Society and Space*, 28: 977–999.

Arendt, H. (1951 [1979]) *The Origins of Totalitarianism*, New York: Harcourt Brace and Company.

Arendt, H. (1958) *The Human Condition*, Chicago, IL and London: University of Chicago Press.

Arendt, H. (1961) *Between Past and Future: Six Exercises in Political Thought*, London: Faber & Faber.

Arendt, H. (1970) *On Violence*, San Diego, CA: Harvest.

Arendt, H. (2003) *Responsibility and Judgement*, New York: Schocker

Armitage, S. (2012) 'Demands for dividends: The case of UK water companies', *Journal of Business Finance and Accounting*, 39: 464–499.

Ashutosh, I. and Mountz, A. (2011) 'Migration management for the benefit of whom? Interrogating the work of the International Organization for Migration', *Citizenship Studies* 15(1): 21–38.

Axelsson, L. (2012) *Making Borders: Engaging the Threat of Chinese Textiles in Ghana*, Stockholm: Stockholm University Press.

Bachrach, P. and Baratz, M.S. (1962) 'The two faces of power', *American Political Science Review*, 56: 941–952.

Balibar, E. (2002) *Politics and the Other Scene*, London: Verso.

Balibar, E. (2004) *We, the People of Europe? Reflections on Transnational Citizenship*, Princeton, NJ: Princeton University Press.

Barnes, T. (2008) 'Why pragmatism is not useful for walking through walls: A brief history of a misunderstood philosophy' *Geoforum* 39(4): 1542–1554.

Barnett, C. (2008) 'Convening publics: The parasitical spaces of public action', in Cox, K.R., Low, M. and Robinson, J. (eds) *The Handbook of Political Geography*, Los Angeles, CA, London, New Delhi and Singapore: Sage.

Barnett, C., Cloke, P., Clarke, N. and Malpass, A. (2011) *Globalising Responsibility: The Political Rationalities of Ethical Consumption*, Malden, MA and Oxford: Wiley-Blackwell.

Barr, S. (1964) *Experiments in Topology*, New York: Dover Publications.

Bauman, Z. (2000) *Liquid Modernity*, Cambridge: Polity.

Beck, U. (2005*) Power in the Global Age*, Cambridge: Polity.

Belcher, D., Martin, L., Secor, A., Simon, S. and Wilson, T. (2008) 'Everywhere and nowhere: The exception and the topological challenge to geography', *Antipode*, 40(4): 499–503.

Benhabib, S. (1996) *The Reluctant Modernism of Hannah Arendt*, London and Thousand Oaks, CA: Sage.

Bernstein, R.J. (ed.) (1960) *John Dewey: On Experience, Nature and Freedom*, New York: Liberal Arts Press.

Bernstein, R.J. (1966) *John Dewey*, New York: Washington Square Press.

Bialasiewicz, L. (2009) 'The new political geographies of the European "neighbourhood"', *Political Geography*, 28: 79–80.

Bialasiewicz, L. (2012) 'Off-shoring and out-sourcing the borders of Europe: Libya and EU border work in the Mediterranean', *Geopolitics*, 17: 843–866.

Bigo, D. (2000) 'When two becomes one: Internal and external securitisations in Europe', in Kelstrup, M. and Williams, M. (eds) *International Relations Theory and the Politics of European Integration: Power, Security and Community*, London: Routledge, pp. 171–205.

Bigo, D. (2001) 'The Möbius ribbon of internal and external security(ies)', in Albert, M., Jacobson, D. and Lapid, Y. (eds) *Identities, Borders, Orders: Rethinking International Relations Theory*, London and Minneapolis: University of Minnesota Press, pp. 91–116.

Blackburn, R. (2006) 'Finance and the fourth dimension', *New Left Review*, 39: 39–70.

Blackburn, R. (2008) 'The subprime crisis', *New Left Review*, 50: 63–106.

Blackett, D.W. (1962) *Elementary Topology: A Combinatorial and Algebraic Approach*, London: Academic Press.

Boltanski, L. (1999) *Distant Suffering: Morality, Media and Politics*, Cambridge: Cambridge University Press.

Brenner, N. (2001) 'The limits of scale: methodological reflections on scalar structuration', *Progress in Human Geography*, 25(4): 591–614.

Brenner, N. (2004) *New State Spaces: Urban Governance and the Rescaling of Statehood*, Oxford: Oxford University Press.

Bryan, D. and Rafferty, D. (2006) *Capitalism with Derivatives*, New York: Palgrave Macmillan.

Bulkeley, H. (2013) 'Governance and the geography of authority: Modalities of authorisation and the transnational governing of climate change', *Environment and Planning A*, 44(10): 2428–2444.

Burt, R.S. (1976) 'Positions in networks', *Social Forces*, 55: 93–122.

Burt, R.S. (1992) *Structural Holes: The Social Structure of Competition*, Burton, MA: Harvard University Press.

Callon, M. (1986) 'Some elements of a sociology of translation: Domestication of the scallops and the fisherman of St Brieuc Bay', in Law, J. (ed.) *Power, Action and Belief: A New Sociology of Knowledge*, London: Routledge and Kegan Paul.

Callon, M. (1992) 'Techno-economic networks and irreversibility', in Law, J. (ed.) *A Sociology of Monsters*, London: Routledge.

Callon, M. (ed.) (1998) *The Laws of the Markets*, Oxford: Blackwell.

Callon, M. and Law, J. (2004) 'Absence–presence, circulation, and encountering in complex space', *Environment and Planning D: Society and Space*, 22: 3–11.

Castells, M. (1996) *The Rise of Network Society*, Oxford: Blackwell.

Castells, M. (2007) 'Communication, power and counterpower in the network society', *International Journal of Communications*, 1(1): 238–266.

Castells, M. (2011) *Communication Power*, Oxford: Oxford University Press.

Cave, M. (2009) *Independent Review of Competition and Innovation in Water Markets: Final Report*, London: HM Government.

Cerny, P.G. (2009) 'Reconfiguring power in a globalizing world', in Clegg, S.R. and Haugaard, M. (eds) *The Sage Handbook of Power*, Los Angeles, CA, London, New Delhi, Singapore and Washington, DC: Sage.

Clark, G.L. and Monk, A.H.B. (2013) 'Financial institutions, information, and investing-at-a-distance', *Environment and Planning A*, 45: 1318–1336.

Clean Clothes Campaign (2006) 'CCC Solidarity Action: Making a difference for workers', www.cleanclothes.org.

Clegg, S.R. and Haugaard, M. (2009) *The Sage Handbook of Power*, Los Angeles, CA, London, New Delhi, Singapore and Washington, DC: Sage.

Coleman, M. (2007) 'A geopolitics of engagement: Neoliberalism, the war on terrorism, and the reconfiguration of US immigration enforcement', *Geopolitics*, 12: 607–634.

Coleman, M. (2012) 'Immigrant il-legality: Geopolitical and legal borders in the US, 1882–present', *Geopolitics*, 17: 402–422.

Collier, S.J. (2009) 'Topologies of power: Foucault's analysis of political government beyond governmentality', *Theory, Culture and Society*, 26(6): 78–108.

Cox, K., Low, M. and Robinson, J. (eds) (2008) *The Handbook of Political Geography*, Los Angeles, CA, London, New Dehli and Singapore: Sage.

Crang, M. (2007) 'Speed = distance/time: Chronotopographies of action', in Hassan, R. and Purser, R.E. (eds) *24/7: Time and Temporality in the Network Society*, Stanford, CA: Stanford University Press, pp. 62–88.

Dahl, R. (1961 [1974]) *Who Governs? Democracy and Power in an American City*, New Haven, CT and London: Yale University Press.

DeLanda, M. (2006) *A New Philosophy of Society: Assemblage Theory and Social Complexity*, London and New York: Continuum.

Della Porta, D. and Tarrow, S. (2005) *Transnational Protest and Global Activism*, Lanham, MD: Rowman & Littlefield.

Deleuze, G. (1988) *Foucault*, London: Athlone Press.

Deleuze, G. (1993) *The Fold: Leibniz and the Baroque*, Minneapolis: University of Minnesota Press.

Deleuze, G. (1994) *Difference and Repetition*, New York: Columbia University Press.

Deleuze, G. (1995) *Negotiations: 1972–1990*, New York: Columbia University Press.

Dewey, J. (1916) *Essays in Experimental Logic*, Chicago, IL: Dover Publications.

Dewey, J. (1927) *The Public and Its Problems*, London: George Allen & Unwin.

Dewey, J. (1930) *Individualism Old and New*, New York: Minton, Balach & Co.

Dewey, J. (1934) *Art as Experience*, New York: Minton, Balach & Co.

Dewey, J. (1935) *Liberalism and Social Action*, New York: Capricorn Books.

Diani, M. and McAdam, D. (2003) *Social Movements and Networks: Relational Approaches to Collective Action*, Oxford: Oxford University Press.

Dicken, P. (2008) *Global Shift: Mapping the Changing Contours of the World Economy*, London: Sage.

Dodd, N. (2011) '"Strange money": Risk, finance and socialised debt', *British Journal of Sociology*, 62(1): 175–194.

Donaghu, M.T. and Barff, R. (1990) 'Nike just did it: International subcontracting and flexibility in athletic footwear production', *Regional Studies*, 24(6): 537–552.

Eagleton, T. (2005) 'Review of Martin Jay's 'Songs of Experience', *London Review of Books*, 23 June: 23–24

Elden, S. (2009) *Terror and Territory: The Spatial Extent of Sovereignty*, Minneapolis: University of Minnesota Press.

Elden, S. (2013) *The Birth of Territory*, Chicago, IL and London: University of Chicago Press.

Epstein, G. and Jayadev, A. (2005) 'The rise of rentier incomes in the OECD countries', in Epstein, G. (ed.) *Financialization and the World Economy*, Cheltenham: Edward Elgar, pp. 46–75.

Eturk, I., Froud, J., Sukhev, J., Leaver, A. and Williams, K. (eds) (2008) *Financialisation at Work: Key Texts and Commentary*, London: Routledge.

Feher, M., (2007) 'The governed in politics', in Feher, M., Krikorian, G. and McKee, Y. (eds) *Nongovernmental Politics*, New York: Zone Books.

Feher, M., Krikorian, G. and McKee, Y. (eds) (2007) *Nongovernmental Politics*, New York: Zone Books.

Fein, M.L. (2013) 'The shadow banking charade', *Social Science Research Network*, http://ssrn.com/abstract=2218812.

Ferguson, J. (2004) 'Power topographies: Beyond "the state" and "civil society" in the study of African politics', in Nugent, D. and Vincent, J. (eds) *A Companion to the Anthropology of Politics*, Malden, MA and Oxford: Blackwell.

Ferguson, J. and Gupta, A. (2002) 'Spatializing states: Towards an ethnography of neoliberal governmentality', *American Ethologist*, 29(4): 981–1001.

Folkman, P., Froud, J., Johal, S. and Williams, K. (2007) 'Working for themselves? Capital market intermediaries and present day capitalism', *Business History*, 49(4): 552–572.

Ford, J. (2008) 'Something big in the City', *Financial Times*, 15/16 November: 25–30 (Weekend Magazine Supplement).

Fraser, N. (2008) *Scales of Justice: Reimagining Political Space in a Globalising World*, Cambridge: Polity.

Gay, D. (2007) *Explorations in Topology: Map Colouring, Surfaces, and Knots*, Burlington, MA: Elsevier Academic Press.

Geertz, C. (1980) *Negara: The Theatre State in Nineteenth-Century Bali*, Princeton, NJ: Princeton University Press.

Giaccaria, P. and Minca, C. (2011) 'Topographies/topologies of the camp: Auschwitz as a spatial threshold', *Political Geography*, 30: 3–12.

Giddens, A. (1977) *Studies in Social and Political Theory*, London: Hutchinson.

Giddens, A. (1981) *A Contemporary Critique of Historical Materialism, Vol. 1, Power, Property and the State*, London and Basingstoke: Macmillan.

Giddens, A. (1984) *The Constitution of Society: Outline of a Theory of Structuration*, Cambridge: Polity.

Giddens, A. (1985) *The Nation State and Violence*, Cambridge: Polity.

Giddens, A. (1990) *The Consequences of Modernity*, Cambridge: Polity.

Gill, N. (2009) 'Governmental mobility: The power effects of the movement of detained asylum seekers around Britain's detention estate', *Political Geography*, 28: 186–196.

Gramsci, A. (1971) *Selections from the Prison Notebooks of Antonio Gramsci*, (trans.) Hoare, Q. and Nowell Smith, G., London: Lawrence & Wishart.

Gregory, D. (2003) 'Defiled cities', *Singapore Journal of Tropical Geography*, 24(3): 307–326.

Gregory, D. (2004) *The Colonial Present*, Oxford: Blackwell.

Gregory, D. (2014) 'Drone geographies', *Radical Philosophy*, 183: 7–20.

Habermas, J. (1977) 'Hannah Arendt's communication concept of power', *Social Research*, Spring, 3–24.

Hacking, I. (2014) *Why is There Philosophy of Mathematics At All?*, Cambridge: Cambridge University Press.

Haldane, A.G. (2009) 'Rethinking the financial network', speech delivered at the Financial Student Association, Amsterdam, April.

Hale, R. and Wills, J. (2005) *Threads of Labour: Garment Industry Supply Claims from the Workers Perspective*, Oxford: Blackwell.

Harvey, D. (1969) *Explanation in Geography*, London: Edward Arnold.

Harvey, D. (1989) *The Condition of Postmodernity*, Oxford: Blackwell.

Harvey, D. (2006) *Spaces of Global Capitalism: Towards a Theory of Uneven Geographical Development*, London and New York: Verso.

Haughton, G., Allmendinger, P. and Oosterlynch, S. (2013) 'Spaces of neoliberal experimentation: Soft spaces, postpolitics, and neoliberal governmentality', *Environment and Planning A*, 45: 217–234.

Hetherington, K. (1997) 'Museum topology and the will to connect', *Journal of Material Culture* 2(2): 199–218.

Hetherington, K. and Law, J. (2000) 'After networks', *Environment and Planning D: Society and Space*, 18: 127–132.

Human Rights Watch (2015) *The Mediterranean Migration Crisis: Why People Flee, What the EU Should Do*, www.hrw.org/report/2015/06/19/mediterranean-migration-crisis/why-people-flee-what-eu-should-do.

Hurley, J. and Miller, D. (2005) 'The changing face of the global garment industry', in Hurley, A. and Wills, J. (eds) *Threads of Labour: Garment Industry Supply Chains from the Workers' Perspective*, Malden, MA and Oxford: Blackwell, pp. 16–39.

ILO (2000) *Labour Practices in the Footwear, Leather, Textiles and Clothing Industries*, Geneva: International Labour Organization.

Jay, M. (2005) *Songs of Experience: Modern American and European Variations on a Universal Theme*, Berkeley, Los Angeles, CA and London: University of California Press.

Jefferis, C. and Stilwell, F. (2006) 'Private finance for public infrastructure: The case of Macquarie Bank', *Journal of Australian Political Economy*, 58: 44–61.

Jessop, B. (2005) 'The political economy of scale and European governance', *Tijdschrift voor Economische en Social Geographie*, 96(2): 225–230.

Jessop, B. (2007) *State Power*, Cambridge: Polity.

Jessop, B. (2009) 'The state and power', in Clegg, S.R. and Haugaard, M. (eds) *The Sage Handbook of Power*, Los Angeles, CA, London, New Dehli, Singapore and Washington, DC: Sage, pp. 367–382.

Johnson, R. (2007) 'Post-hegemony? I don't think so', *Theory, Culture and Society*, 24(3): 95–110.

Jones, A. (2002) 'The "global city" misconceived: The myth of "global management" in transnational service firms', *Geoforum*, 33: 335–350.

Jones, A. (2008) 'The rise of global work', *Transactions of the Institute of British Geographers*, 33: 12–26.

Jones, A. and Search, P. (2009) 'Proximity and power within investment relationships: The case of the UK private equity industry', *Geoforum*, 40: 809–819.

Kern, S. (1983) *The Culture of Time and Space 1880–1918*, Cambridge, MA: Harvard University Press.

Konings, M. (2010) 'The pragmatic sources of modern power', *European Journal of Sociology*, 51(1): 55–91.

Labour Behind the Label (2006, 2009, 2011) *Let's Clean Up Fashion: The State of Pay Behind the UK High Street*, Bristol: Labour Behind the Label.

Labour Behind the Label (2014) *Tailored Wages UK: Are the Big Brands Paying the People Who Make Our Clothes Enough to Live On?*, Bristol: Labour Behind the Label.

Latham, A. (2002) 'Retheorizing the scale of globalization: Topologies, actor–networks, and cosmopolitanism', in Herod, A. and Wright, M.W. (eds) *Geographies of Power: Placing Scale*, Oxford: Blackwell.

Latour, B. (1987) *Science in Action*, Washington, DC: Howard University Press.

Latour, B. (1999a) *Pandora's Hope: Essay on the Reality of Science Studies*, Cambridge, MA: Harvard University Press.

Latour, B. (1999b) 'On recalling ANT', in Law, J. and Hassard, J. (eds) *Actor Network Theory and After*, Oxford: Blackwell.

Latour, B. (2005) *Reassembling the Social*, Oxford: Oxford University Press.

Law, J. (1999) 'After ANT: complexity, naming and topology', in Law, J. and Hassard, J. (eds) *Actor Network Theory and After*, Oxford: Blackwell.

Law, J. and Mol, A. (2001) 'Situating technoscience: An inquiry into spatialities', *Environmental Planning D: Society and Space*, 19: 609–621.

Lawrence, F. (2013) *Not on the Label*, London: Penguin.

Leach, E.R. (1961) *Rethinking Anthropology*, London: Athlone Press.

Lukes, S. (1974) *Power: A Radical View*, London and Basingstoke: Macmillan.

Lury, C., Parisi, L. and Terranova, T. (2012) 'Introduction: The becoming topological of culture', *Theory, Culture and Society*, 29(4/5): 3–35.

Malpass, A., Cloke, P., Barnett, C. and Clarke, N. (2007) 'Fairtrade urbanism: The politics of place beyond place in the Bristol Fairtrade City Campaign', *International Journal of Urban and Regional Research* 31(3): 633–643.

Mann, M. (1986) *The Sources of Social Power, Vol. 1: A History of Power from the Beginning to AD 1760*, Cambridge: Cambridge University Press.

Mann, M. (1993) *The Sources of Social Power, Vol. 2: The Rise of Classes and National States, 1760–1914*, Cambridge: Cambridge University Press.

Mann, M. (2003) *Incoherent Empire*, London and New York: Verso.

Mann, M. (2011) *Power in the 21st Century: Conversations with John A. Hall*, Cambridge: Polity.

Mann, M. (2012) *The Sources of Social Power, Vol. 3: Global Empires and Revolution, 1890–1945*, Cambridge: Cambridge University Press.

Mann, M. (2013) *The Sources of Social Power, Vol. 4: Globalizations, 1995–2011*, Cambridge: Cambridge University Press.

Martin, L.L. (2012) '"Catch and remove": Detention, deterrence and discipline in the UK noncitizen family detention practice', *Geopolitics*, 17: 312–334.

Martin, L. and Secor, A.J. (2013) 'Towards a post-mathematical topology', *Progress in Human Geography*, 23 October, doi: 10.1177/0309132513508209

Massey, D. (1993) 'Power-geometry and a progressive sense of place', in Bird, J., Curtis, B., Putnam, T., Robertson, G. and Tickner, L. (eds) *Mapping the Futures: Local Cultures, Global Change*, London: Routledge.

Massey, D. (2005) *For Space*, London, Thousand Oaks, CA and New Dehli: Sage.

Massey, D. (2007) *World City*, Cambridge: Polity.

Massey, D. (2011) 'A counterhegemonic relationality of place', in McCann, E. and Ward, K. (eds) *Mobile Urbanism: Cities and Policymaking in the Global Age*, Minneapolis: University of Minnesota Press.

McCann, E. and Ward, K. (eds) (2011) *Mobile Urbanism: Cities and Policymaking in the Global Age*, Minneapolis: University of Minnesota Press.

McDonald, K. (2006) *Global Movements: Action and Culture*, Oxford: Blackwell.

Meek, J. (2014) *Private Island: Why Britain Now Belongs to Someone Else*, London: Verso.

Melucci, A. (1996) *Challenging Codes: Collective Action in the Information Age*, Cambridge: Cambridge University Press.

Mezzadra, S. and Neilson, B. (2012) 'Between inclusion and exclusion: On the topology of global space and borders', *Theory, Culture and Society*, 29(4/5): 58–75.

Mezzadra, S. and Neilson, B. (2013) *Border as Method or, the Multiplication of Labour*, Durham, NC and London: Duke University Press.

Mitchell, T. (1991) 'The limits of the state: Beyond statist approaches and their critics', *American Political Science Review*, 85(1): 77–96.

Mol, A. and Law, J. (1994) 'Regions, networks and fluids: Anaemia and social topology', *Social Studies of Science* 24: 641–671.

Montgomerie, J. and Williams, K. (2009) 'Financialised capitalism: After the crisis and beyond neoliberalism', *Competition and Change*, 3: 99–106.

Mouffe, C. (2013) 'Space, hegemony and radical critique', in Painter, J. and Featherstone, D. (eds) *Spatial Politics: Essays forDoreen Massey*, Malden and Oxford: Wiley-Blackwell, pp. 21–31.

Mountz, A. (2011a) 'The enforcement archipelago: Detention, haunting, and asylum on islands', *Political Geography*, 30: 118–128.

Mountz, A. (2011b) 'Where asylum-seekers wait: Feminist counter-topographies of sites between states', *Gender, Place and Culture*, 18(3): 381–399.

Murdoch, J. (1998) 'The spaces of actor–network theory', *Geoforum*, 29: 357–374.

Murdoch, J. (2006) *Post-Structuralist Geography*, London, Thousand Oaks, CA and New Dehli: Sage.

Nicholls, W. (2009) 'Place, networks, space: Theorising the geographies of social movements', *Transactions of the Institute of British Geographers*, 34: 78–93.

Nye, J.S. (2002) *The Paradox of American Power*, Oxford: Oxford University Press.

Nye, J.S. (2004) *Soft Power: The Means to Success in World Politics*, New York: Public Affairs.

Nye, J.S. (2011) *The Future of Power*, New York: Public Affairs.

O'Connell, J. (1993) 'Metrology: The creation of universality by the circulation of particulars', *Social Studies of Science*, 23: 129–173.

O'Neill, O. (2000) *Bounds of Justice*, Cambridge: Cambridge University Press.

O'Neill, P. (2009) 'Infrastructure investment and the management of risk', in Clark, G.L., Dixon, A.D. and Monk, A.H.B. (eds) *Managing Financial Risks*, Oxford: Oxford University Press, pp. 163–168.

Paasi, A. (2003) 'Boundaries in a globalizing world', in Anderson, K., Domosh, M., Pile, S. and Thrift, N. (eds) *Handbook of Cultural Geography*, London: Sage.

Paasi, A. (2009) 'Bounded spaces in a "borderless world": Border studies, power and the anatomy of territory', *Journal of Power*, 2(2): 213–234.

Paasi, A. (2011) 'Geography, space and the re-emergence of topological thinking', *Dialogues in Human Geography*, 1(3): 299–303.

Painter, J. (2006) 'Prosaic geographies of stateness', *Political Geography*, 25(7): 752–774.

Painter, J. (2008) 'Geographies of space and power', in Cox, K.R., Low, M. and Robinson, J. (eds) *The Handbook of Political Geography*, Los Angeles, CA, London, New Delhi and Singapore: Sage.

Palan, R. (2003) *The Offshore World: Sovereign Markets, Virtual Places, and Nomad Millionaires*, Ithaca, NY and London: Cornell University Press.

Palan, R. and Nesvetailova, A. (2014) 'Elsewhere, ideally nowhere: Shadow banking and offshore finance', *Politik*, 16(4): 26–34.

Parker, N. and Vaughan-Williams, N. (2009) 'Lines in the sand? Towards an agenda for critical border studies', *Geopolitics*, 14: 582–587.

Peet, R. (2007) *Geography of Power: The Making of Global Economic Policy*, London and New York: Zed Books.

Peterson, I. (1988) *The Mathematical Tourist: Snapshots of Modern Mathematics*, New York: W. H. Freeman & Co.

Picciotto, S. (1999) 'Offshore: The state as legal fiction', in Hampton, M. and Abbott, J.P. (eds) *Offshore Finance Centres and Tax Havens: The Rise of Global Capital*, London and Basingstoke: Macmillan, pp. 43–79.

Pike, A. and Pollard, J. (2010) 'Economic geographies of financialisation', *Economic Geography*, 86: 29–51.

Popescu, G. (2012) *Bordering and Ordering the Twenty-first Century: Understanding Borders*, Lanham, MD: Rowman & Littlefield.

Pozsar, Z., Adrian, T., Ashcroft, A. and Boesky, H. (2010) *Shadow Banking*, Staff Report 458, July, New York: Federal Reserve Bank of New York.

Roberts, S. (1994) 'Fictitious capital, fictitious spaces: The geography of offshore financial flows', in Corbridge, S., Martin, R. and Thrift, N. (eds) *Money, Power and Space*, Oxford: Blackwell, pp. 91–115.

Robinson, I. (2007) 'The consumer dimension of stakeholder activism: The antisweatshop movement in the United States', in Feher, M., Krikorian, G. and McKee, Y. (eds) *Nongovernmental Politics*, New York: Zone Books, pp. 200–221.

Robinson, J. (2011a) 'The spaces of circulating knowledge: City strategies and global urban governmentality', in McCann, E. and Ward, K. (eds) *Mobile Urbanism: Cities and Policymaking in the Global Age*, Minneapolis: University of Minnesota Press.

Robinson, J. (2011b) 'Cities in a world of cities: The comparative gesture', *International Journal of Urban and Regional Research*, 35(1): 1–23.

Rodier, C. (2007) 'The Migreurop network and Europe's foreigner camps', in Feher, M., Krikorian, G. and McKee, Y. (eds) *Nongovernmental Politics*, New York: Zone Books, pp. 446–467.

Rorty, R. (1982) *Consequences of Pragmatism*, Brighton: Harvester Press.

Rorty, R. (1989) *Contingency, Irony and Solidarity*, Cambridge: Cambridge University Press.

Rorty, R. (1991) *Objectivity, Relativism, and Truth: Philosophical Papers Vol.1*, Cambridge: Cambridge University Press.

Rorty, R. (1998) *Achieving Our Country*, Cambridge, MA: Harvard University Press.

Rorty, R. (1999) *Philosophy and Social Hope*, London: Penguin.

Rosen, S.M. (1997) 'Wholeness as the body of paradox', *Journal of Mind and Behaviour*, 18(4): 391–423.

Rosen, S.M. (2006) *Topologies of the Flesh: A Multidimensional Exploration of the Lifeworld*, Athens, OH: Ohio University Press.

Runciman, D. (2008) *Political Hypocrisy: The Mask of Power, from Hobbes to Orwell and Beyond*, Princeton, NJ and Oxford: Princeton University Press.

Ryan, A. (1995) *John Dewey And The High Tide of American Liberalism*, New York and London: W.W. Norton & Co.

Sack, R.D. (1980) *Conceptions of Space in Social Thought*, London and Basingstoke: Macmillan.

Said, E. (1994) *Culture and Imperialism*, London: Vintage.

Sassen, S. (1991) *The Global City: New York, London and Tokyo*, Princeton, NJ: Princeton University Press.

Sassen, S. (1995) 'On concentration and centrality in the global city', in Knox, P.L. and Taylor, P.J. (eds) *World Cities in a World System*, Cambridge: Cambridge University Press.

Sassen, S. (2000) 'Territory and territoriality in the global economy', *International Sociology*, 15(2): 372–393.

Sassen, S. (2006) *Territory, Authority, Rights: From Medieval to Global Assemblages*, Princeton, NJ and Oxford: Princeton University Press.

Sassen, S. (2013) 'When territory deborders territoriality', *Territory, Politics, Governance*, 1(1) 21–45.

Sayer, A. (2015) *Why We Can't Afford the Rich*, Bristol: Policy Press.

Seabrook, J. (2015) *The Song of the Shirt: Cheap Clothes across Continents and Centuries*, London: Fernwood.

Secor, A. (2013) '2012 Urban Geography Plenary Lecture: Topological city', *Urban Geography*, 34(4): 430–444.

Serres, M. with Latour, B. (1995) *Conversations on Science, Culture and Time*, Ann Arbor: University of Michigan Press.

Shields, R. (2012) 'Cultural topology: The seven bridges of Könisburg, 1736', *Theory, Culture and Society*, 29(4/5): 43–57.

Shields, R. (2013) *Spatial Questions: Cultural Topologies and Social Spatialisations*, London: Sage.

Sklar, L. (1974) *Space, Time and Spacetime*, Berkeley, Los Angeles and London: University of California Press.

Sluiter, L. (2009) *Clean Clothes: A Global Movement to End Sweatshops*. London: Pluto Press.

Smith, N. (2004) 'Scale bending and the fate of the national', in Sheppard, E. and McMaster, R. (eds) *Scale and Geographic Inquiry*, Oxford: Blackwell.

Soderström, O. (2014) *Cities in Relations: Trajectories of Urban Development in Hanoi and Ouagadougou*, Malden, MA and Oxford: Wiley-Blackwell.

Standard and Poor's (2008) *Thames Water Utilities Cayman Finance Limited*, www.thameswater. co.uk/tw/common/downloads/aboutus-financial/bonds-report-twucfl-poors-sep-2008.pdf.

Standard and Poor's (2011) *Thames Water Utilities Cayman Finance Limited*, Global Credit Portal.

Stiglitz, J. (2010) *Freefall: Free Markets and the Sinking of the Global Economy*, London: Allen Lane.

Strange, S. (1974) 'What is economic power, and who has it?', *International Journal*, 30: 207–224.

Strange, S. (1994) 'Rethinking structural change in the international political economy: states, firms and diplomacy', in Stubbs, R. and Underhill, G.R.D. (eds) *Political Economy and the Changing Global Order*, London and Basingstoke: Macmillan.

Strange, S. (1998) *Mad Money: When Markets Outgrow Governments*, Ann Arbor: University of Michigan Press.

Swyngedouw, E. (2000) 'Authoritarian governance, power and the politics of rescaling', *Environment and Planning D: Society and Space*, 3(4): 383–401

Tarrow, S. (1998) *Power in Movement: Social Movements, Collective Action and Revolution in the Modern World*, Cambridge: Cambridge University Press.

Tett, G. (2010) *Fool's Gold: How Unrestrained Greed Corrupted a Dream, Shattered Global Markets and Unleashed a Catastrophe*, London: Abacus.

Thompson, G.F. (2003) *Between Hierarchies and Markets: The Logic and Limits of Networked Forms of Organizations*, Oxford: Oxford University Press.

Tilly, C. (2002) *Stories, Identities and Political Change*, Lanham, MD, Boulder, CO, New York and Oxford: Rowman & Littlefield.

Tilly, C. (2008) *Contentious Performances*, New York: Cambridge University Press.

Urry, J. (2014) *Offshoring*, Cambridge: Polity.

Vaughan-Williams, N. (2008) 'Borderwork beyond inside/outside? Frontex, the citizen-detective and the War on Terror', *Space and Polity*, 12(1): 63–79.

Vaughan-Williams, N. (2010) 'The UK border security continuum: Virtual biopolitics and the simulation of the sovereign ban', *Environment and Planning D: Society and Space*, 28: 1071–1083.

Vaughan-Williams, N. (2012) *Border Politics: The Limits of Sovereign Power*, Edinburgh: Edinburgh University Press.

Walker, R.B.J. (1993) *Inside/Outside: International Relations as Political Theory*, Cambridge: Cambridge University Press.

Walker, R.B.J. (2010) *After the Globe, Before the World*, New York: Routledge.

Walters, W. (2010) 'Imagined migration world: The European Union's anti-illegal immigration discourse', in Geiger, M. and Pecoud, A. (eds) *The Politics of International Migration Management*, Basingstoke: Palgrave Macmillan.

War on Want (2006) *Fashion Victims: The True Cost of Cheap Clothes at Primark, Asda and Tesco*, London: War on Want.

War on Want (2008) *Fashion Victims II: How UK Clothing Retailers are Keeping Workers in Poverty*, London: War on Want.

War on Want (2011) *Stitched Up: Women Workers in the Bangladeshi Garment Industry*, London: War on Want.

Weber, M. (1978) *Economy and Society*, Vols 1 and 2, Roth, G. and Wittich, C. (eds), New York: Bedminster Press.

Weizman, E. (2007) *Hollow Land: Israel's Architecture of Occupation*, London: Verso.

Whatmore, S. and Clark, N. (2008) 'Good food: Ethical consumption and global change', in Clark, N., Massey, D. and Sarre, P. (eds) *Material Geographies: A World in the Making*, London: Sage.

Wojcik, D. (2011) 'Securitization and its footprint: The rise of the US securities industry centres 1998–2007', *Journal of Economic Geography*, 11: 925–947.

Wojcik, D. (2012a) 'Where governance fails: Advanced business services and the offshore world', *Progress in Human Geography*, 37(3): 330–347.

Wojcik, D. (2012b) 'The end of investment bank capitalism? An economic geography of financial jobs and power', *Economic Geography*, 88(4): 345–368.

Wolf, M. (2014) *The Shifts and the Shocks: What We've Learned – and Have Still to Learn – from the Financial Crisis*, London: Allen Lane.

Wrong, D.H. (1979 [1997]) *Power: Its Forms, Bases, and its Uses*, New Brunswick, NJ and London: Transaction.

Young, I.M. (2003) 'From guilt to solidarity: Sweatshops and political responsibility', *Dissent*, Spring: 39–44.

Young, I.M. (2004) 'Responsibility and global labor justice', *Journal of Political Philosophy*, 12(4): 365–388.

Young, I.M. (2007) *Global Challenges: War, Self-Determination and Responsibility for Justice*, Cambridge: Polity.

Young-Bruehl, E. (2006) *Why Arendt Matters*, New Haven, CT and London: Yale University Press.

INDEX